SILVER SECRETS

STÉPHAN DAIGLE

✳ Stéphan Daigle is a Canadian artist who uses patterns and symbols to create tapestry-like scenes. In this illustration, the rising moon casts a silver glow across the landscape. It's the artist's imagination that brings to light the hidden world of nature.

✳ What does Stéphan Daigle like about being an artist? He says, "The best part is reaching people, especially the young." Mr. Daigle has won numerous awards for his artwork. His home is in Montreal, Canada.

Acknowledgments appear on pages 542–544, which constitute an extension of this copyright page.

© 1993 Silver Burdett Ginn Inc.
Cover art © 1993 by Stéphan Daigle.

ISBN 0–663–54658–3

4 5 6 7 8 9 10 RRD 98 97 96 95 94

New Dimensions
IN THE
WORLD OF READING

SILVER SECRETS

P R O G R A M   A U T H O R S

James F. Baumann	Roselmina Indrisano	P. David Pearson
Theodore Clymer	Dale D. Johnson	Taffy E. Raphael
Carl Grant	Connie Juel	Marian Davies Toth
Elfrieda H. Hiebert	Jeanne R. Paratore	Richard L. Venezky

SILVER BURDETT GINN

NEEDHAM, MA   MORRISTOWN, NJ

ATLANTA, GA   DALLAS, TX   DEERFIELD, IL   MENLO PARK, CA

Unit 1 Theme

IMAGINE THAT!

4

Unit 2 Theme

Hidden WORLDS

6

Unit 3 Theme

Words, Words, Words

8

Unit 4 Theme
MAKE IT HAPPEN

IMAGINE THAT!

Imaginative stories delight us.

How can using your imagination make stories more fun to read?

THE GIANT, *oil on canvas, h: 72", w: 60", signed lower left: N. C. Wyeth, 1923. © 1990, Westtown School, Westtown, Pennsylvania, 1939. Photograph courtesy of Brandywine River Museum, Chadds Ford, Pennsylvania.*

Theme Books for
Imagine That!

*I*s your mind drooping from your everyday routine? Then treat your imagination to a vacation!

❖ When Arthur Bobowicz is sent to get a Thanksgiving turkey, all he can find is a very large chicken. At 266 pounds, the chicken is enough to panic the whole town in *The Hoboken Chicken Emergency* by Daniel Manus Pinkwater.

❖ What would you do if you found yourself in the Middle Ages, wearing knight's armor and fighting a duel on horseback? That's what happens to Steve when he and Max become time travelers in *Max and Me and the Time Machine* by Gery Greer and Bob Ruddick.

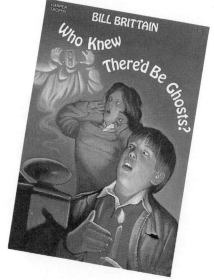

❖   Tommy and his friends feel desperate when they learn the old Parnell House is to be destroyed. Find out how two special ghosts come to the rescue in *Who Knew There'd Be Ghosts?* by Bill Brittain.

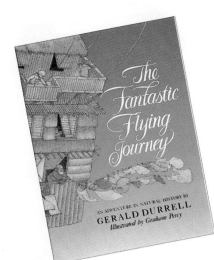

❖   Picture yourself far above the earth in a hot air balloon. *The Fantastic Flying Journey* by Gerald Durrell will take you on an imaginary voyage around the world. Get ready to meet the animals of the Sahara, Australia, the Arctic, and other fascinating places.

More Books to Enjoy

Bunnicula: A Rabbit-Tale of Mystery by Deborah and James Howe

My Father's Dragon by Ruth Stiles Gannett

Tuck Everlasting by Natalie Babbitt

Fat Men from Space by Daniel Manus Pinkwater

TEENY, TINY, TINNY Visitors

by Fonda Crews Bell

It all happened last June, but it's only now that I can finally talk about it.

I'm a normal kid. I have to tell you that right away. I'm ten, my name is Dawn, I've got black hair, and I'm tall for my age. I like to play softball and I like boys when they're clean. My friend Diondrea was with me, and she's even more normal than I am. She has brown hair and likes boys even when they haven't washed in a month. What I'm saying is that you can trust Diondrea and me. So listen to this. . . .

It was my birthday, and I was feeling bad because my father forgot about it. He lives twenty miles away from Mom and me and forgets a lot of things. Anyway, I got a sleeping bag like Diondrea's for my birthday, and it was a really nice night, so Diondrea and I slept out in my backyard. About 400 trillion stars were shining, and it was warm outside—a really nice night.

Now, listen, because this is the part you won't believe. I was lying in my new sleeping bag, when I heard a sound—a cricket-like sound next to my ear. I turned my head, and there it was—a tiny, metal, human-shaped creature about as tall as a paper clip. I thought I was having some kind of nightmare, so I did what I do when I'm having a bad dream: I tried to open my eyes—only they were open already. So I just lay there and waited for developments.

The little human-shaped robot thing was shaking all over, and tiny blue lights were blinking on his head. I sure didn't need to be scared of him because he was so scared of me, he was about to choke. He pulled a metal box that looked like a miniature calculator out of his backpack. He made trembly cricket sounds into it, and then the calculator thing said, "Hello, Earth people."

Diondrea jumped out of her sleeping bag. "What was *that*?" she yelled. The little robot man quaked. I was really impressed with his courage, though. He shook so hard he rattled and creaked, but he didn't run away.

"Don't move, Diondrea," I whispered, and she didn't. I lay there, she sat next to me, and the little man rattled. "Don't be scared, we won't hurt you," I said. The tiny calculator machine turned what I said into cricket talk, and the little robot creature stopped shaking so much.

"We knew you'd be big," the little man said through his talking machine, "but we had no idea you'd be *this* big."

Just then a series of weird little hot-dog-shaped machines walked toward us on thin metal legs. The machines opened their hatches, *munch crunch*, and about twenty little robots, some shiny silver and some the color of my mom's copper tea kettle, hopped out. They started rushing around, firing glittering pink lights out of little sticks. The little lights showered over Diondrea's jeans like tiny fireworks.

I sat up, a flurry of pink fireworks glittering around me. The tiny sparks were soothing, somehow, and I smiled. Diondrea was smiling, too.

The leader robot made some more cricket sounds, and his friends blinked and clicked as they climbed back up on their machines and sat in neat little rows.

The tiny leader spoke cricket into his talk converter and out came something like this: "Earth people, we pay tribute to you with our light display. We have not come to hurt you. Our asteroid has disintegrated, and we need to live on your planet. We have researched your American culture and now we ask only for permission from your great president before we colonize."

"But we're kids," I said. "You know—children. We can't—I mean . . . Diondrea, shouldn't we call the White House or something?"

Diondrea looked at me as if I were stupid. "Dawn," she said, "if I went in your house right now and asked your mom if I could use the phone so I could call the president to ask if some inch-tall robots could colonize your backyard, what do you think—?"

"Never mind," I said. I turned back to our visitor. He was standing very straight and still, blinking blue, and waiting. "There are people here even bigger than us," I explained. "Maybe twice bigger."

When the tiny talk converter converted that, I thought the poor little guy would rattle himself to pieces.

"We were trying to get to your White House in Washington," he said. "But we miscalculated. And we cannot go any farther. We have no more fuel and no means to make any. We are stranded here. Our families need rest and body work. Please talk to your great president and tell us his decision. If you deny us residence, we will submit to your decision and melt ourselves down. We do not want to live in a hostile world."

I thought for a minute. "Excuse us," I said to him. "We're going to go inside now and call the president." I looked at Diondrea. She was staring at me again. We got up slowly and walked toward the back porch. Diondrea opened the screen door and, for once, closed it without slamming the hinges off.

"Mom," I said, "can I call the president to ask if some little robots can settle in our yard?"

My mom looked up from her new self-help book and gave me one of those "what an imagination" looks. She smiled. "Be my guest, you little nut," she said.

Diondrea and I went into the kitchen and got out the phone book. We had to do some hunting, but we finally found the number for the White House under *United States Government*. I dialed. Diondrea paced.

"White House," a woman's voice said.

"Hi," I said. "May I please speak to the president?"

"What is the nature of your business?" the lady said.

"I want to ask him if some little aliens can settle in my yard."

"I'm sorry," the lady said. "You have the wrong number. You want the Immigration and Naturalization Service."

"But . . . you don't understand," I said. "I *have* to speak to the president!"

"I'm sorry," she said. "The president does not handle this sort of thing. Please call 555-2000 in the morning. Thank you for calling the White House."

She hung up, and I wrote down the number. "Diondrea, this isn't going to be as easy as I thought. The president doesn't handle aliens. And we have to wait till morning to call this other number. What are we going to do?"

"We're going to wait till morning," said Diondrea.

"But if I go out there and tell them the president won't even talk to me, they might melt themselves down!" I said. "We have to do something *now*."

I've never liked waiting. And if my own mother didn't believe us, I didn't think the president would.

If it were morning, we could take pictures with my instant camera, but tonight . . . .

We hurried back outside. The little robot people were waiting there, blinking out their feelings in pink and green. I looked at Diondrea. She looked at me. Sometimes responsibility is thrust upon you, my father says. So I accepted it. I got down on my knees and leaned close to the leader robot. He started blinking even harder, and the whole crew of his friends lifted their smile-making sticks in a salute.

"Welcome to 2525 Persimmon Drive, Arlington, Virginia, United States, Earth," I said. "You have permission to colonize my yard." When that was translated, a chorus of cricket cheers went up, and a stream of tiny sparks hit my leg. I looked at Diondrea. Her mouth was hanging open. I shrugged my shoulders again. "Well," I whispered, "it's my yard."

The little robot got into his space machine. He turned around and watched us quietly as the hatch closed. The machine tottered away into the shrubbery. All the other machines closed up, *munch crunch*, and tottered off behind it. We got up to follow them, but then the leader robot's voice came from his machine. "Please leave us alone now," it said. "We will make our settlement, then we will contact you again."

We didn't sleep much that night. We crawled back into our sleeping bags and lay there, looking at the stars and talking about what had happened. At dawn we got up and tiptoed over to the shrubbery. They were gone, and we've never seen them since. Don't think we haven't looked; we've looked everywhere. I don't know what happened.

Of course, nobody believes us. But strange things happen in this world, and that's the way it was. Anyway, I bet I never stop looking for those little robot people.

I don't know if I did the right thing. What would you have done?

Reader's Response 〜 If you had been Dawn, how would you have reacted to the visitors?

MANNY THE
Robot

Manny the robot is so lifelike, he sweats. He also walks, sits, bends, and crawls.

It's Manny's job to help scientists test protective clothing for special jobs. For example, firefighters need clothing that will protect them from the heat of fire. If the clothes protect Manny the robot, then they will also protect firefighters.

The scientists who designed Manny wanted him to be able to copy human movement very closely. So, they watched videos of people exercising. Then they programmed Manny to do the same kinds of movements.

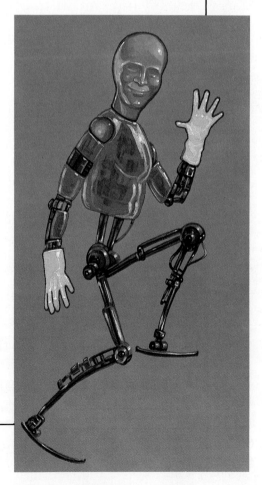

The more Manny does, the more Manny "sweats." For instance, if Manny walks up stairs, heaters warm Manny's "skin." Manny's "sweat" is actually water that is slowly pumped out of tiny tubes.

What does a robot do after a hard day of bending, squatting, climbing, and sweating? Absolutely nothing.

Young Night Thought

by Robert Louis Stevenson

All night long and every night,
When my mamma puts out the light,
I see the people marching by,
As plain as day, before my eye.

Armies and emperors and kings,
All carrying different kinds of things,
And marching in so grand a way,
You never saw the like by day.

So fine a show was never seen,
At the great circus on the green;
For every kind of beast and man
Is marching in that caravan.

At first they move a little slow,
But still the faster on they go,
And still beside them close I keep
Until we reach the town of Sleep.

THE MAD PUPPET

by Margaret Mahy

At the school concert Toby was dressed as a clown, and he danced and sang and pulled faces so that everybody in the audience laughed and cheered and clapped for him. His brother Alistair did not like it, though he was a year older and he could do everything already.

"You're not so great," he said to Toby afterwards. "It wasn't really you doing all that."

"It was!" cried Toby.

"No, it was me all the time. You're not really my brother. You're a puppet—a puppet from a Japanese robot firm."

"I am not a puppet," Toby said, amazed. "Look! I've got no strings or anything to make me work."

"That's because you work with electronics," Alistair explained. "I've got a special electronic controller in my pocket. I make you laugh and talk and sing and run and jump. Everything you do is because I'm making you do it."

"I *am* real," Toby insisted. He did not like the idea of being his brother's puppet. "If I get cut, I bleed. Puppets don't bleed."

"You call that blood?" Alistair said scornfully. "That isn't blood, it's just red oil. But it probably looks like blood to you."

"I can see myself in mirrors," Toby pointed out.

"Well, of course you can. It's vampires that can't see themselves in mirrors. You're a puppet, all right. So don't get any big ideas about yourself."

"I'm real! I'm realer than you!" Toby shouted, but Alistair just patted his pocket and smiled.

"I made you say that," he said. "I like to see you arguing, trying to pretend you're real when anyone can see you're not."

Toby knew he was real, but somehow the idea that he might be a puppet took hold of him. He stared at his hands, wriggling on the ends of his arms, and his feet, wriggling on the ends of his legs. Could electronics make fingers and toes work? The more he thought about being real, the more he began to feel like a puppet. And the next day, when he jumped and scrambled at school, he looked up and saw Alistair watching him with a meaningful smile.

"Old electronic Toby!" Alistair muttered as he pushed past, patting his pocket.

He's got to take it back, thought Toby. I've got to make him say I'm real or I'll go on thinking about it, and the more I think about being real the harder it is to believe it.

Then he thought, Maybe I'm doing it the wrong way round. Maybe I should start thinking I am a puppet and see how I feel.

What did it feel like to be a puppet? A bit stiff perhaps? Toby walked stiffly. How did a puppet sound? A bit crackly? Toby made his voice crackle.

"What's wrong with you?" Alistair asked the next day. "Are you getting a cold?"

"I need oil," creaked Toby.

Alistair gave him a funny look.

"I'm breaking down," Toby said, still creaking. "My gears are coming unmeshed."

"Don't be silly," Alistair cried. "I mean, you're in

perfect order. We got a warrant of fitness for you last
month. Your circuits are all functional."

"I'm breaking down," Toby said. "You're over-
working me."

"You've got years of operative life ahead of you,"
declared Alistair.

"BR..EA..K..ING DO..WN."

"Ha. Ha. Very funny," said Alistair.

Toby went on pretending he was an electronic
puppet. He imagined electricity running through his
veins, his hair flaring with lightning, his eyes shooting out
x-rays and alpha particles. Would an electronic puppet
wish to be free to move without its master?

That night, Toby woke up. In the middle of the room,
between his bed and Alistair's, was a square of
moonlight, white on the dark floor. He tried a phrase out
softly in the night.

"The mad puppet," he whispered. He liked the sound of it.

"The mad puppet!" He made his voice sound strange and echoing. Slowly, stiffly, he sat up in bed.

"I am the mad puppet," he wailed. His hair stood on end at the sound of his own voice. Alistair's eyes began to blink open. Very slowly, very stiffly, like a boy made of tappets and crankshafts, Toby stood up in the square of moonlight.

He looked down at Alistair.

"I am the mad puppet," he cried again, making his voice crackly, like static on the radio, or frying bacon.

"Hey, Toby," Alistair whispered, "Wake up, Toby!"

Toby held his arms out in front of him, his fingers spread wide. He made his eyes as round as he could.

The moonlight painted his face silver, but his eyes were like two black holes with no light in them.

"Tobe! Hey, Toby!" hissed Alistair. "Quiet down!" But Toby was too busy being a puppet to quiet down. Alistair sounded a little afraid, and Toby felt suddenly powerful— a boy of steel and wire, lighting up, thrilling with electricity.

"I am the mad puppet!" he screamed and flung himself on Alistair.

"You're real! You're real!" howled Alistair.

There were footsteps in the hall, and their mother came bursting in.

"What on earth's going on? Toby, what are you doing out of bed?"

"Alistair had a nightmare," Toby cried.

"Toby was walking in his sleep," yelled Alistair. "He looked all funny . . . he looked all silver and mad."

"You must be dreaming," said their mother. "Toby looks fine to me. Of course, you shouldn't let the moon shine in like that. No wonder you have nightmares." She tucked them both in and closed the curtains.

"Toby," said Alistair, after they had been lying in the dark for a moment, "I was making you do that." But he sounded uncertain.

"The mad puppet!" Toby replied in his mad puppet voice, and he felt the darkness shiver over by Alistair's bed.

Toby now knew for certain that Alistair couldn't make him do anything he didn't want to do. But he had walked with a puppet's legs and spoken with a puppet's voice. He had let a puppet come out of his mind and look through his eyes, mad and terrifying in the moonlight. Inside him, suddenly, a whole crowd of characters— kings, angels, horses, demons of the night, heroes, and the school concert clown—seethed and crowded, waiting to come alive. But he was their master.

"Go to sleep!" he told them, and after a moment they did.

Reader's Response ∽ What did you think of Toby's decision to go along with his brother and pretend to be a puppet?

IT'S NOT EASY BEIN'
GREEN

The most famous puppet in the world is a frog—to be exact, a Muppet puppet named Kermit. Kermit the Frog was one of the first of the Muppet puppets created by Jim Henson. Unlike traditional hand puppets, Muppets are a combination of a hand puppet and a marionette (a puppet moved by strings). Mr. Henson would put the Muppet on one hand and move it by wiggling his fingers. Then he used his other hand to operate the metal rods that make the Muppet puppet move in ways that other puppets cannot. Jim Henson made Kermit out of an old green coat that his mother gave him. Missing were the bulging eyes, which he created by cutting a ping pong ball in half. He named this Muppet *Kermit* after a grade school friend, Kermit Scott. . . . And the rest is history! Kermit talked and joked his way into the hearts of children and adults alike on "The Muppet Show." He played the banjo and sang the song that became his trademark—"It's Not Easy Bein' Green." Today he is the most famous, best loved puppet . . . Muppet . . . frog . . . in the world.

CALVIN and HOBBES

by Cartoonist Bill Watterson

How do *you* use your imagination? To have fun? To make your life more interesting? To solve problems?

In the story you just read, Toby used *his* imagination to picture how a puppet might behave. When Toby talked and acted like the puppet of his imagination, his brother stopped teasing him. By using his imagination, Toby had fun—and was able to solve his problem, too.

Calvin and Hobbes is a comic strip about a six-year-old boy named Calvin and his stuffed tiger. Calvin uses *his* imagination to turn his tiger into a playmate who can talk to him—and all kinds of funny things happen. Read the comic strips and watch how Hobbes changes when he and Calvin are alone together.

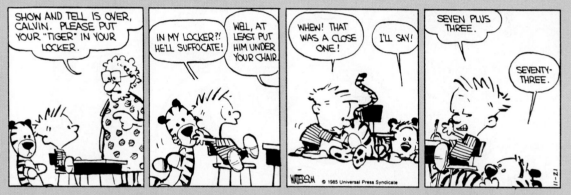

37

ELETELEPHONY

by Laura E. Richards

Once there was an elephant,
Who tried to use the telephant—
No! no! I mean an elephone
Who tried to use the telephone—
(Dear me! I am not certain quite
That even now I've got it right.)

Howe'er it was, he got his trunk
Entangled in the telephunk;
The more he tried to get it free,
The louder buzzed the telephee—
(I fear I'd better drop the song
Of elephop and telephong!)

The map labels, reading across the illustration: FRANCE, SPAIN, AFRICA, ATLANTIC, OCE[AN], MANHATTAN NEW YORK, HUDSON, RIVER, LIBERTY ISLA[ND], HOBOKEN, NEW JERSEY, PENNSYLVANIA

Arthur's Thanksgiving Emergency

from The Hoboken Chicken Emergency
by Daniel Manus Pinkwater

Nobody in Arthur Bobowicz's family really liked turkey.
Certainly, the kids didn't like it as much as chicken or
duck. They suspected that Momma and Poppa didn't like
it very much either. Still, they had a turkey every

Thanksgiving, like almost every family in Hoboken. "Thanksgiving is an important American holiday," Poppa would say. "You kids are Americans, and you ought to celebrate important American holidays. On Thanksgiving, you eat turkey. Would you want people to think you were ungrateful?" Poppa came from Poland, and he was very big on holidays, and being an American. There was no arguing with him. They had turkey every year.

Most of the kids in the neighborhood had the same scene at home. Some of them liked turkey, some of them didn't—but they all had it on Thanksgiving. They all had fathers like Arthur Bobowicz's father—they came from Italy, and the Ukraine, and Puerto Rico, and Hong Kong. The kids were all being raised to be Americans, and everyone's father knew that Americans eat turkey on Thanksgiving. Late in November, in the windows of the stores in Hoboken, where ducks had hung, and sausages, and legs of lamb—turkeys appeared. For the rest of the year, anyone who wanted a turkey would have had to go clear out of town. The turkeys appeared in Hoboken at Thanksgiving, no other time.

It was Arthur's job to go and get the family turkey. Poppa had reserved a turkey weeks in advance at Murphy's Meat Market. On Thanksgiving morning, Arthur was supposed to go to the market and bring back the turkey, a big one. The whole family was going to be there—uncles and aunts, and some cousins, Momma and Poppa, and Arthur's little brother and sister. Bringing back the turkey was an important job. Once it came into the house, all the cooking and rushing out for last-minute things from the store, and all the good smells would start.

It was a good holiday, and all the kids enjoyed it—but it would have been even better if they had a duck or a chicken.

Something had gone wrong at Murphy's Meat Market. Somehow Poppa's turkey reservation had gotten lost. Every turkey had some family's name on it—none of them had the name Bobowicz. Arthur ran down Garden Street and up the stairs of the apartment house. He told his mother about the mistake at the meat market. "Maybe you'd better go back and get two chickens and a duck," his mother said. She was almost smiling, "I'll explain it to your father." Arthur was sure she didn't like turkey either—why wouldn't she admit it?

Things had gone even more wrong than Arthur thought. When he got back to Murphy's Meat Market, there wasn't a single chicken in the place—no ducks either. All they had were turkeys, and every one of them

was reserved for somebody else. Arthur was bothered by this, but not terribly worried. There are lots of stores and markets in Hoboken—German and Italian butchers, Spanish groceries, supermarkets. You can get almost anything to eat in the world in Hoboken—except a turkey, a chicken, or a duck on Thanksgiving, as Arthur found out. He went to every store in town that might possibly have a bird. He went to a few stores that probably did not have birds—just in case. "This is a fish market! What makes you think we'd have turkeys or chickens, you silly kid?"

"No chickens in a vegetable store, you silly kid!"

"Silly kid! This is an Indian spice store. Curry powder, we've got; mango chutney, we've got; flash-frozen chapatis, we've got—birds we do not have."

Arthur was looking for turkeys, chickens, ducks, geese—he would have taken any kind of bird at all. There wasn't anything of the kind to be found in the whole town.

It was getting to be late in the morning, and it was snowing a little. Arthur was getting depressed. This was the first time he had the job of getting the Thanksgiving bird, and he had messed it up. He had tried everyplace; he had sixteen dollars in his pocket, and he hadn't found one single bird. He walked along River Street. He didn't want to go home and tell his mother the bad news. He felt tired, and the cold was going right through him. He noticed a card stuck in the window of an apartment house door:

PROFESSOR MAZZOCCHI
Inventor of the Chicken
System
By Appointment

Arthur rang the bell. What did he have to lose? The door-buzzer buzzed, and he pushed it open. He stood at the bottom of the stairs. A voice from above shouted, "You will not get me evicted! My brother owns this building! I am a scientist! If you people don't stop bothering me, I'll let the rooster loose again!"

"Do you have a chicken for sale?" Arthur shouted—he was desperate.

"What? You want to buy a chicken? Come right up!" the voice from above answered. Arthur climbed the stairs. At the head of the stairs was an old man. He was wearing an old bathrobe with dragons embroidered on it. "I have been waiting for years for someone to come to buy a

45

superchicken," the old man said. "The only people who ever come here are neighbors to complain about my chickens. They don't want me to keep them."

"You keep chickens in your apartment?" Arthur asked.

"A farm would be better," Professor Mazzocchi said, "but my brother lets me stay here without paying any rent. Also they are special chickens. I prefer to keep them under lock and key."

"We need one to cook for Thanksgiving," Arthur said.

"A large family?" Professor Mazzocchi asked.

"All my cousins are coming," Arthur said.

"And how much money did you bring?" the old man asked, "sixteen dollars? Good. Wait here." The old man went inside the apartment with Arthur's sixteen dollars. When he opened the door, Arthur heard a clucking sound, but not like any clucking he had ever heard—it was deeper, louder. Arthur had a feeling that this wasn't going to work out.

He was right. Professor Mazzocchi came out of the apartment a few minutes later. He was leading a chicken that was taller than he was. "This is the best poultry bargain on earth," he said, "a medium sized superchicken—six cents a pound—here's your two-hundred and sixty-six pound chicken, on the hoof. She'll be mighty good eating. Please don't forget to return the leash and collar," and Professor Mazzocchi closed the apartment door.

Arthur stood on the landing with the giant chicken for a while. The chicken looked bored. She shifted from foot to foot, and stared at nothing with her little red eyes. Arthur was trying to understand what had just happened.

He was trying to believe there was a two-hundred and sixty-six pound chicken standing in the hallway with him. Arthur was feeling numb.

Then Arthur found himself pounding on Professor Mazzocchi's door. "No refunds!" Professor Mazzocchi shouted, without opening the door.

"Don't you have anything smaller?" Arthur shouted.

"No refunds!" Professor Mazzocchi, Inventor of the Chicken System, shouted. Arthur could see that this was all he was going to get from Professor Mazzocchi. He picked up the end of the leash.

"She is a bargain, when you consider the price per pound," Arthur thought. The chicken tamely followed Arthur down the stairs.

Everybody noticed the chicken as Arthur led it home. Most people didn't want to get too close to it. Some people made a sort of moaning noise when they saw the chicken. Arthur and the chicken arrived at the apartment house where the Bobowicz family lived. Arthur led the chicken up the stairs and tied the leash to the bannister. Then he went in to prepare his mother. "That took a long time," she said, "did you get a bird?"

"I got a chicken," Arthur said.

"Well, where is it?" his mother asked.

"I left it in the hall," Arthur said, "It only cost six cents a pound."

"That's very cheap," his mother said, "Are you sure there's nothing wrong with it? Maybe it isn't fresh."

"It's fresh," Arthur said, "It's alive."

"You brought home a live chicken?" his mother was getting excited.

47

"It was the only one I could find," Arthur started to cry, "I went to all the stores, and nobody had any turkeys or chickens or ducks, and finally I bought this chicken from an old man who raises them in his apartment."

Arthur's mother was headed for the door, "Momma, it's a very big chicken!" Arthur shouted. She opened the door. The chicken was standing there, shifting from foot to foot, blinking.

"CLUCK," it said. Arthur's mother closed the door, and just stood staring at it. She didn't say anything for a long time.

Finally she said, "There's a two-hundred pound chicken in the hall," she was talking to the door.

"Two-hundred and sixty-six pounds," Arthur said; he was still sobbing.

"Two-hundred and sixty-six pounds of live chicken," his mother said, "It's wearing a dog collar."

"I'm supposed to return that," Arthur said. Arthur's mother opened the door and peeked out. Then she closed the door again. She looked at Arthur. She opened the door and looked at the chicken.

"She seems friendly, in a dumb way," she said.

"I thought we could call her Henrietta," Arthur said. "You were supposed to bring home an ordinary chicken to eat," Arthur's mother said, "Not a two-hundred and sixty-six pound chicken to keep as a pet."

"It was the only one I could find," Arthur said.

Arthur's little brother and sister had been watching all this from behind the kitchen door. "Please let us keep her," they shouted, "we'll help Arthur feed her, and walk her, and take care of her."

"She walks on the leash very nicely," Arthur said, "I
can train her, and she can cluck if burglars ever come.
She's a good chicken, PLEASE!"

"Put her in the kitchen, and we'll discuss it when your
father comes home," Arthur's mother said.

That night the family had meatloaf, and mashed pota-toes, and vegetables for Thanksgiving dinner. Everybody thought it was a good meal. Henrietta especially liked the mashed potatoes, although Poppa warned everybody not to feed her from the table. "I don't want this chicken to get into the habit of begging," he said, "and the first time the children forget to feed or walk her—out she goes."

Poppa had decided to let Arthur keep Henrietta. "Every boy should have a chicken," he said.

Reader's Response ∼ Tell how Arthur's Thanksgiving Day reminds you of a holiday that you will never forget.

Library Link ∼ *This story is an excerpt from the book* The Hoboken Chicken Emergency *by Daniel Manus Pinkwater. You might enjoy reading the entire book to find out what other adventures Arthur has.*

The Forty Minute Egg and Other Funny Food

The **ostrich** is the world's largest bird, so it's not surprising that it lays the world's largest eggs. One ostrich egg weighed over five pounds. If you want to eat an ostrich egg, boil it for forty minutes!

Pumpkins come in all sizes. The biggest pumpkin on record in 1990 weighed 816½ pounds. Imagine carving that pumpkin for Halloween!

What are the largest seeds in the world? If you guessed seeds of the **double coconut tree,** weighing more than forty-four pounds, you're right.

A forty-pound **lobster** was caught off the coast of Nova Scotia in 1977. That's twice as large as a big Thanksgiving turkey.

The largest **cucumber** was grown in England in 1992 and weighed over seventeen pounds. How much do you think an average cucumber weighs?

Lee Bennett Hopkins
INTERVIEWS

Daniel Manus Pinkwater

Daniel Manus Pinkwater is a very
funny man. How could he not be,
since he created such wild fantasies
as *Lizard Music, Fat Men from
Space,* and *I Was a Second Grade
Werewolf*?

Yet there is also a very serious side to Mr. Pinkwater. He is a writer who both entertains readers and likes them very, very much.

"I enjoy the fact that there are so many lively boys and girls around, that they are as bright as they are, and that they tend to choose me among their favorite writers," he said.

"The most rewarding type of letter from a reader says, 'I don't usually like to read, but I've read five of your books and I'm looking for more.' That gladdens my heart."

Mr. Pinkwater was born in Memphis, Tennessee, but grew up in Chicago, Illinois; Los Angeles, California; and parts of the East Coast. His brothers, sisters, and friends turned him on to reading.

"A kid next door had an older brother who told me about *The Three Musketeers*," he says. "I read it and continued to read adventure stories. I especially liked stories written by Mark Twain. I liked Mark Twain when I was seven years old, I like Mark Twain now, and I'll like Mark Twain until the day I die."

In college, Mr. Pinkwater learned about sculpture. "I ate, slept, and breathed sculpture for two years," he states. "My work as a sculptor makes me a good writer—strong and daring. When you carve wood or stone, the moment comes when you've got to actually go *into* the piece of material and start knocking hunks off it.

"I didn't decide to write children's books. I floated into it. I was at a party where a children's book editor said she was looking for examples of modern African art. Since I had just returned from Tanzania, in Africa, I showed her some of my artwork. She suggested that I try illustrating a story. I had to get a story first, however, and I did." His first book became *The Terrible Roar,* published in 1970, under the name Manus Pinkwater.

How does a writer such as Mr. Pinkwater begin a novel for young readers? How does he work? "When I'm beginning a new book," he states, "I am almost like an actor getting into character. I listen to music. I watch television, I talk to people. I turn up at a K-Mart store and go through all the motions of being an ordinary citizen.

"When I start a novel, all I'm really doing is waiting for the characters to show up. It's like the movie *Close Encounters of the Third Kind.* The people who have been 'selected' to be in this story show up. It is a very interesting experience."

He does not sit down and write every day. "It would be terrible if I had to work that way. I show up at my office every day in the event that something may want to happen, but if nothing happens, I don't feel that I have failed to perform. If something gets started, fair enough. If it doesn't, and I feel I've given it enough time, I go to K-Mart. I showed up, the story didn't! When I do work, I work every single day, and I usually get from four to twenty pages each session, which I consider good going.

"I love the story as it is being written. Sometimes it's as though it were happening without my doing it. I'll go to bed, excited about what's going to happen tomorrow. I know something's got to happen because I've only got 175 pages done and I've got to do more.

"To me, the beauty in writing is making the words come out as clear as a pane of glass. That I can do, and

I'm rather pleased because it took me years to learn how.

"Writing for girls and boys has helped me to remember my own childhood. And since I'm writing books for a specific reader, namely myself at different ages, I've gotten more and more expert at revisiting that person within me at different ages."

He sometimes uses a computer. "The computer allows me to think in a different way. It helps me to be a better, more daring writer. Using a computer was a breakthrough for me.

"But," he jokes, "if it makes the story come easier, I'll also try the typewriter—or a screwdriver or a chisel!"

After living for many years in Hoboken, New Jersey, Mr. Pinkwater and his writer/artist wife, Jill, moved north of New York City.

"I moved to the country because my wife wanted a garden. We bought a nice farmhouse that is almost two-hundred years old and fixed it up. It's only two hours from New York City by train. Jill likes horses very much. We now own three Icelandic horses. And believe me, three is enough!"

Mr. Pinkwater is a very busy man. In addition to writing and illustrating, he appears on the program *All Things Considered*. It is a talk show that is carried on more than 350 radio stations throughout the United States.

I asked Mr. Pinkwater if he has any advice for young writers. "My advice to those who want to write is this," he told me. "Write things that are fun to you. Do it for your own pleasure, just as I do. Have a good time when you are writing something."

The selection you have just read is a chapter from Mr. Pinkwater's book *The Hoboken Chicken Emergency*.

Reader's Response ∼ What do you think was Mr. Pinkwater's most interesting observation about being a writer? Why? What kinds of things are an inspiration for your own writing?

Mr. Pinkwater's Favorite

Mark Twain is the pen name for one of America's most popular authors, Samuel Langhorne Clemens. He was born in 1835 in Florida, Missouri, and grew up in the nearby town of Hannibal.

Before Samuel became a writer, he was a steamboat pilot on the Mississippi River, a printer, and a journalist. It was the people and events along the Mississippi River and his travels out West that gave him ideas for many of his stories.

One of Mark Twain's most famous books, *Life on the Mississippi*, is based on his steamboat days on the Mississippi. He even took his pen name from a term used by boatmen to tell how deep the water was. *Mark twain* was the term for two fathoms, or 12 feet, deep.

An early story of Mark Twain's, "Jim Smiley and the Jumping Frogs," was so funny that it was printed in newspapers and magazines across the country. Daniel Pinkwater still laughs when he thinks about the story.

You might enjoy reading it, too. Or check out the film version at your local video store.

The earliest picture of Mark Twain, age fifteen

LAUGHING GAS

from Mary Poppins
written by P. L. Travers
illustrated by Mary Shepard

Mary Poppins had come to the Banks's home to take care of Jane and Michael. The children were quite surprised when they first met Mary Poppins. She did things that no one else could do. Her magic made the unbelievable happen.

"Are you quite sure he will be at home?" said Jane, as they got off the Bus, she and Michael and Mary Poppins.

"Would my Uncle ask me to bring you to tea if he intended to go out, I'd like to know?" said Mary Poppins, who was evidently very offended by the question. She was wearing her blue coat with the silver buttons and the blue hat to match, and on the days when she wore these it was the easiest thing in the world to offend her.

All three of them were on the way to pay a visit to Mary Poppins's uncle, Mr. Wigg, and Jane and Michael had looked forward to the trip for so long that they were more than half afraid that Mr. Wigg might not be in, after all.

"Why is he called Mr. Wigg— does he wear one?" asked Michael, hurrying along beside Mary Poppins.

"He is called Mr. Wigg because Mr. Wigg is his name. And he doesn't wear one. He is bald," said Mary Poppins. "And if I have any more questions, we will just go Back Home." And she sniffed her usual sniff of displeasure.

Jane and Michael looked at each other and frowned. And the frown meant: "Don't let's ask her anything else or we'll never get there."

Mary Poppins put her hat straight at the Tobacconist's Shop at the corner. It had one of those curious windows where there seem to be three of you instead of one, so that if you look long enough at them you begin to feel you are not yourself but a whole crowd of somebody else. Mary Poppins sighed with pleasure, however, when she saw three of herself, each wearing a blue coat with silver buttons and a blue hat to match. She thought it was such a lovely sight that she wished there

had been a dozen of her or even thirty. The more Mary Poppins the better.

"Come along," she said sternly, as though they had kept *her* waiting. Then they turned the corner and pulled the bell of Number Three, Robertson Road. Jane and Michael could hear it faintly echoing from a long way away and they knew that in one minute, or two at the most, they would be having tea with Mary Poppins's uncle, Mr. Wigg, for the first time ever.

"If he's in, of course," Jane said to Michael in a whisper.

At that moment the door flew open and a thin, watery-looking lady appeared.

"Is he in?" said Michael quickly.

"I'll thank you," said Mary Poppins, giving him a terrible glance, "to let *me* do the talking."

"How do you do, Mrs. Wigg," said Jane politely.

"Mrs. Wigg!" said the thin lady, in a voice even thinner than herself. "How dare you call me Mrs. Wigg? No, thank you! I'm plain Miss Persimmon *and* proud of it. Mrs. Wigg indeed!" She seemed to be quite upset, and they thought Mr. Wigg must be a very odd person if

Miss Persimmon was so glad not to be Mrs. Wigg.

"Straight up and first door on the landing," said Miss Persimmon, and she went hurrying away down the passage saying: "Mrs. Wigg indeed!" to herself in a high, thin, outraged voice.

Jane and Michael followed Mary Poppins upstairs. Mary Poppins knocked at the door.

"Come in! Come in! And welcome!" called a loud, cheery voice from inside. Jane's heart was pitter-pattering with excitement.

"He *is* in!" she signalled to Michael with a look.

Mary Poppins opened the door and pushed them in front of her. A large cheerful room lay before them. At one end of it a fire was burning brightly and in the centre stood an enormous table laid for tea—four cups and saucers, piles of bread and butter, crumpets, coconut cakes and a large plum cake with pink icing.

"Well, this is indeed a Pleasure," a huge voice greeted them, and Jane and Michael looked round for its owner. He was nowhere to be seen. The room appeared to be quite empty. Then they heard Mary Poppins saying crossly:

"Oh, Uncle Albert—not *again?* It's not your birthday, is it?"

And as she spoke she looked up at the ceiling. Jane and Michael looked up too and to their surprise saw a round, fat, bald man who was hanging in the air without holding on to anything. Indeed, he appeared to be *sitting* on the air, for his legs were crossed and he had just put down the newspaper which he had been reading when they came in.

"My dear," said Mr. Wigg, smiling down at the children, and looking apologetically at Mary Poppins, "I'm very sorry, but I'm afraid it *is* my birthday."

"Tch, tch, tch!" said Mary Poppins.

"I only remembered last night and there was no time then to send you a postcard asking you to come another day. Very distressing, isn't it?" he said, looking down at Jane and Michael.

"I can see you're rather surprised," said Mr. Wigg. And, indeed, their mouths were so wide open with astonishment that Mr. Wigg, if he had been a little smaller, might almost have fallen into one of them.

"I'd better explain, I think," Mr. Wigg went on calmly. "You see, it's this way. I'm a cheerful sort of man and very disposed to laughter. You wouldn't believe, either of you, the number of things that strike me as being funny. I can laugh at pretty nearly everything, I can."

And with that Mr. Wigg began to bob up and down, shaking with laughter at the thought of his own cheerfulness.

"Uncle Albert!" said Mary Poppins, and Mr. Wigg stopped laughing with a jerk.

"Oh, beg pardon, my dear. Where was I? Oh, yes. Well, the funny thing about me is—all right, Mary, I won't laugh if I can help it!— that whenever my birthday falls on a Friday, well, it's all up with me. Absolutely U.P.," said Mr. Wigg.

"But why—?" began Jane.

"But how—?" began Michael.

"Well, you see, if I laugh on that particular day I become so filled with Laughing Gas that I simply can't keep on the ground. Even if I smile it happens. The first funny thought, and I'm up like a balloon. And until I can think of something serious I can't get down again." Mr. Wigg began to chuckle at that, but he caught sight of Mary Poppins's face and stopped the chuckle, and continued:

"It's awkward, of course, but not unpleasant. Never happens to either of you, I suppose?"

Jane and Michael shook their heads.

"No, I thought not. It seems to be my own special habit. Once, after I'd been to the Circus the night before, I laughed so much that— would you believe it?—I was up here for a whole twelve hours, and couldn't get down till the last stroke of midnight. Then, of course, I came down with a flop because it was Saturday and not my birthday anymore. It's rather odd, isn't it? Not to say funny?

"And now here it is Friday again and my birthday, and you two and Mary P. to visit me. Oh, Lordy, Lordy, don't make me laugh, I beg of you—" But although Jane and Michael had done nothing very amusing, except to stare at him in astonishment, Mr. Wigg began to laugh again loudly, and as he laughed he went bouncing and bobbing about in the air, with the newspaper rattling in his hand and his spectacles half on and half off his nose.

He looked so comic, floundering in the air like a great human bubble, clutching at the ceiling sometimes and sometimes at the gas bracket as he passed it, that Jane and Michael, though they were trying hard to be polite, just couldn't help doing what they did. They laughed. *And* they laughed. They shut their mouths tight to prevent the laughter escaping, but that didn't do any good. And presently they were rolling over and over on the floor, squealing and shrieking with laughter.

"Really!" said Mary Poppins. "Really, *such* behaviour!"

"I can't help it, I can't help it!" shrieked Michael as he rolled into the fender. "It's so terribly funny. Oh, Jane, *isn't* it funny?"

Jane did not reply, for a curious thing was happening to her. As she laughed she felt herself growing lighter and lighter, just as though she were being pumped full of air. It was a curious and delicious feeling and it made her want to laugh all the more. And then suddenly, with a bouncing bound, she felt herself jumping through the air. Michael, to his astonishment, saw her go soaring up through the room. With a little bump her head touched the ceiling and then she went bouncing along it till she reached Mr. Wigg.

"*Well!*" said Mr. Wigg, looking very surprised indeed. "Don't tell me it's *your* birthday, too?" Jane shook her head.

"It's not? Then this Laughing Gas must be catching! Hi—whoa there, look out for the mantelpiece!" This was to Michael, who had suddenly risen from the floor and was swooping through the air, roaring with laughter, and just grazing the china ornaments on the mantelpiece as he passed. He landed with a bounce right on Mr. Wigg's knee.

"How do you do," said Mr. Wigg, heartily shaking Michael by the hand. "I call this really friendly of you—bless my soul, I do! To come up to me since I couldn't come down to you—eh?" And then he and Michael looked at each other and flung back their heads and simply howled with laughter.

"I say," said Mr. Wigg to Jane, as he wiped his eyes. "You'll be thinking I have the worst manners in the world. You're standing and you ought to be sitting—a nice young lady like you. I'm afraid I can't offer you a chair up here, but I think you'll find the air quite comfortable to sit on. I do."

Jane tried it and found she could sit down quite comfortably on the air.

She took off her hat and laid it down beside her and it hung there in space without any support at all.

"That's right," said Mr. Wigg. Then he turned and looked down at Mary Poppins.

"Well, Mary, we're fixed. And now I can enquire about *you,* my dear. I must say, I am very glad to welcome you and my two young friends here today—why, Mary, you're frowning. I'm afraid you don't approve of—er—all this."

He waved his hand at Jane and Michael, and said hurriedly:

"I apologise, Mary, my dear. But you know how it is with me. Still, I must say I never thought my two young friends here would catch it, really I didn't, Mary! I suppose I should have asked them for another day or tried to think of something sad or something—"

"Well, I must say," said Mary Poppins primly, "that I have never in my life seen such a sight. And at your age, Uncle—"

"Mary Poppins, Mary Poppins, do come up!" interrupted Michael. "Think of something funny and you'll find it's quite easy."

"Ah, now do, Mary!" said Mr. Wigg persuasively.

"We're lonely up here without you!" said Jane, and held out her arms towards Mary Poppins. "*Do* think of something funny!"

"Ah, *she* doesn't need to," said Mr. Wigg sighing. "She can come up if she wants to, even without laughing—and she knows it." And he looked mysteriously and secretly at Mary Poppins as she stood down there on the hearth rug.

"Well," said Mary Poppins, "it's all very silly and undignified, but, since you're all up there and don't seem able to get down, I suppose I'd better come up, too."

With that, to the surprise of Jane and Michael, she put her hands down at her sides and without a laugh, without even the faintest glimmer of a smile, she shot up through the air and sat down beside Jane.

"How many times, I should like to know," she said snappily, "have I told you to take off your coat when you come into a hot room?" And she unbuttoned Jane's coat and laid it neatly on the air beside the hat.

"That's right, Mary, that's right," said Mr. Wigg contentedly, as he leant down and put his spectacles on the mantelpiece. "Now we're all comfortable—"

"There's comfort *and* comfort," sniffed Mary Poppins.

"And we can have tea," Mr. Wigg went on, apparently not noticing her remark. And then a startled look came over his face.

"My goodness!" he said. "How dreadful! I've just realised—that table's down there and we're up here. What *are* we going to do? We're here and it's there. It's an awful tragedy—awful! But oh, it's terribly comic!" And he hid his face in his handkerchief and laughed loudly into it. Jane and Michael, though they did not want to miss the crumpets and the cakes, couldn't help laughing too, because Mr. Wigg's mirth was so infectious.

Mr. Wigg dried his eyes.

"There's only one thing for it," he said. "We must think of something serious. Something sad, very sad. And then we shall be able to get down. Now—one, two, three! Something *very* sad, mind you!"

They thought and thought, with their chins on their hands.

Michael thought of school, and that one day he would have to go there. But even that seemed funny today and he had to laugh.

Jane thought: "I shall be grown up in another fourteen years!" But that didn't sound sad at all but quite nice and rather funny. She could not help smiling at the thought of herself grown up, with long skirts and a hand-bag.

"There was my poor old Aunt Emily," thought Mr. Wigg out loud. "She was run over by an omnibus. Sad. Very sad. Unbearably sad. Poor Aunt Emily. But they saved her umbrella. That was funny, wasn't it?"

And before he knew where he was, he was heaving and trembling and bursting with laughter at the thought of Aunt Emily's umbrella.

"It's no good," he said, blowing his nose. "I give it up. And my young friends here seem to be no better at sadness than I am. Mary, can't *you* do something? We want our tea."

To this day Jane and Michael cannot be sure of what happened then. All they know for certain is that, as soon as Mr. Wigg had appealed to Mary Poppins, the table below began to wriggle on its legs. Presently it was swaying dangerously, and then with a rattle of china and with cakes lurching off their plates onto the cloth, the table came soaring through the room, gave one graceful

turn, and landed beside them so that Mr. Wigg was at its head.

"Good girl!" said Mr. Wigg, smiling proudly upon her. "I knew you'd fix something. Now, will you take the foot of the table and pour out, Mary? And the guests on either side of me. That's the idea," he said, as Michael ran bobbing through the air and sat down on Mr. Wigg's right. Jane was at his left hand. There they were, all together, up in the air and the table between them. Not a single piece of bread-and-butter or a lump of sugar had been left behind.

Mr. Wigg smiled contentedly.

"It is usual, I think, to begin with bread-and-butter," he said to Jane and Michael, "but as it's my birthday we will begin the wrong way—which I always think is the *right* way—with the Cake!"

And he cut a large slice for everybody.

"More tea?" he said to Jane. But before she had time to reply there was a quick, sharp knock at the door.

"Come in!" called Mr. Wigg.

The door opened, and there stood Miss Persimmon with a jug of hot water on a tray.

"I thought, Mr. Wigg," she began, looking searchingly round the room, "you'd be wanting some more hot—Well, I never! I simply *never!*" she said, as she caught sight of them all seated on the air round the table. "Such goings-on I never did see. In all my born days I never saw such. I'm sure, Mr. Wigg, I always knew *you* were a bit odd. But I've closed my eyes to it—being as how you paid your rent regular. But such behaviour as this—having tea in the air with your guests—Mr. Wigg, sir, I'm astonished at you! It's that undignified, and for a gentleman of your age—I never did—"

"But perhaps you will, Miss Persimmon!" said Michael.

"Will what?" said Miss Persimmon haughtily.

"Catch the Laughing Gas, as we did," said Michael.

Miss Persimmon flung back her head scornfully.

"I hope, young man," she retorted, "I have more respect for myself than to go bouncing about in the air like a rubber ball on the end of a bat. I'll stay on my own feet, thank you, or my name's not Amy Persimmon, and—oh dear, oh *dear*, my goodness, oh *DEAR*—what *is* the matter? I can't walk, I'm going, I—oh, help, *HELP!*"

For Miss Persimmon, quite against her will, was off the ground and was stumbling through the air, rolling from side to side like a very thin barrel, balancing the tray in her hand. She was almost weeping with distress as she arrived at the table and put down her jug of hot water.

"Thank you," said Mary Poppins in a calm, very polite voice.

Then Miss Persimmon turned and went wafting down again, murmuring as she went: "So undignified—and me a well-behaved, steady-going woman. I must see a doctor—"

When she touched the floor she ran hurriedly out of the room, wringing her hands, and not giving a single glance backwards.

"So undignified!" they heard her moaning as she shut the door behind her.

"Her name can't be Amy Persimmon, because she *didn't* stay on her own feet!" whispered Jane to Michael.

But Mr. Wigg was looking at Mary Poppins—a curious look, half amused, half accusing.

"Mary, Mary, you shouldn't—bless my soul, you shouldn't, Mary.

The poor old body will never get over it. But, oh, my Goodness, didn't she look funny waddling through the air—my Gracious Goodness, but didn't she?"

And he and Jane and Michael were off again, rolling about the air, clutching their sides and gasping with laughter at the thought of how funny Miss Persimmon had looked.

"Oh dear!" said Michael. "Don't make me laugh any more. I can't stand it! I shall break!"

"Oh, oh, oh!" cried Jane, as she gasped for breath, with her hand over her heart.

"Oh, my Gracious, Glorious, Galumphing Goodness!" roared Mr. Wigg, dabbing his eyes with the tail of his coat because he couldn't find his handkerchief.

"IT IS TIME TO GO HOME." Mary Poppins's voice sounded above the roars of laughter like a trumpet.

And suddenly, with a rush, Jane and Michael and Mr. Wigg came down. They landed on the floor with a huge bump, all together. The thought that they would have to go home was the first sad thought of the afternoon, and the moment it was in their minds the Laughing Gas went out of them.

Jane and Michael sighed as they watched Mary Poppins come slowly down the air, carrying Jane's coat and hat.

Mr. Wigg sighed, too. A great, long, heavy sigh.

"Well, isn't that a pity?" he said soberly. "It's very sad that you've got to go home. I never enjoyed an afternoon so much—did you?"

"Never," said Michael sadly, feeling how dull it was to be down on the earth again with no Laughing Gas inside him.

"Never, never," said Jane, as she stood on tiptoe and kissed Mr. Wigg's withered-apple cheeks. "Never, never, never, never . . .!"

Reader's Response ∼ If Mary Poppins telephoned you and said, "What would you like to do when you visit Jane and Michael this afternoon?" what would you say?

Library Link ∼ *This story is from the book* Mary Poppins *by P. L. Travers. If you enjoyed the story, you might enjoy reading the entire book.*

THE REAL
MARY POPPINS?

Pamela Lyndon Travers says she did not really invent Mary Poppins—that Mary Poppins just came to her once when, as an adult, she was recovering from an illness. A good friend came to visit, read some of Pamela's stories, and convinced her that people would be interested in them.

When Pamela was growing up in Australia, she spent many hours reading and dreaming about fairy tales. She began writing poems and stories before she reached the age of seven. As a child, she always kept her writing to herself.

Pamela has said that books alone are the author's true biography. Do you think P. L. Travers could be the real Mary Poppins?

Special Effects in the Movies

by Robert Quackenbush

When you read about Mary Poppins flying through the air, you may have formed pictures in your mind as you read the words. The pictures were in your imagination. Your imagination lets you go anywhere and do anything. Your imagination makes anything possible—even flying—while you are sitting at home in your comfortable chair.

Movie makers use techniques called special effects to make it possible for you to see pictures like those in your imagination on a movie screen. Because of special effects, you can see Mary Poppins fly across the screen the way you pictured it when you read the story.

Georges Méliès Invents Special Effects

Special effects were invented quite by accident. In 1898, a French movie maker and former magician, Georges Méliès, was filming a street scene in Paris. As a bus was passing by, his camera suddenly jammed. He stopped the camera and fixed it. Then he went back to filming the same street scene. Of course, the bus had passed by, but a carriage was in the place the bus had been. When Méliès developed the film, much to his surprise he saw the bus had changed into a carriage!

From that day, Méliès became known as "the magician of the movies." He invented many other amazing techniques. His 1902 film, *A Trip to the Moon,* used many special effects that are still used today.

The projection technique was also used in the movie *E. T.* to make Elliot and E. T. look like they are flying.

Projections

The most common special effect is one Méliès invented, called projection. When a movie maker uses the projection technique, he or she projects a picture or a movie on a screen behind the actors. The actors act in front of the screen, and the camera films the actors and the picture or the movie shown on the projection at the same time. Projections make it possible for actors to look like they are in imaginary places. For example, a film of sky and moving clouds was shown on a screen behind Julie Andrews, who played Mary Poppins in the movie. This projection made it look as if she were truly flying.

Animation

Another special effect Méliès invented is called animation. He used it to make the moon look like it was crying when a rocket landed smack in its eye. Animation makes lifeless models or objects come to life when they are shown on the screen. To animate a scene, a model is filmed in one position. Then the model is moved a bit. Click! The camera films the scene. The model is moved a bit more. Click! The final result is one complete movement that takes many hours to shoot. This was how Willis O'Brien, another movie genius, created some of his special effects for *King Kong,* in 1933. His ideas are still used today.

Drawings and paintings can also be animated to make movies. Artists work directly on pieces of clear celluloid, called cels. For each tiny movement a character makes, the artist makes a new cel. Then a camera shoots one cel after another onto movie film. When the film is sped up, the artist's drawings and paintings seem to move across the screen. Each second of running film takes twenty-four of the artist's cels. Animated movies like *Bambi* and *Snow White and the Seven Dwarfs* were made this way. Thousands of cels were needed to make these movies.

These cels show the artist's drawings that will be used to make an animated cartoon of *King Kong*.

Matte Shots

One of the most widely used techniques in modern special effects is called the matte shot. It was used in 1915 by American cameraman, Billy Bitzer. He used the technique to shoot the early films of D. W. Griffith, producer and director of the world's first feature-length films.

Bitzer knew how to cover, or matte out, the part of a film that he did not want. Afterwards, he would film something else in the matted-out part. This way two or more actions could take place at the same time in one scene. For example, to show two people dreaming of a city of the future, he began by covering a small part of the moving picture camera lens. This kept a bit of the film from being photographed. Then he started the camera rolling. He filmed the two people. After he did that, he rewound the film in the camera so that the film was back at the beginning.

Next Bitzer covered the part of the lens that had been uncovered before and uncovered the part that had been covered. He started the camera rolling again. This time he photographed a painting of a city of the future on the unused part of the film. When done, Bitzer had filmed two different scenes on one roll of film. Movie audiences were amazed that they could see the city of the future that the two people on the screen were dreaming about.

The matte technique caught on quickly. Another way of making a matte shot was to paint a scene on glass and place the glass between camera and actors. The actors would keep their movements within the unpainted portion of the glass. The final effect made the actors appear to be wherever the scene placed them.

Today's perfected techniques use an invention called the optical printer to make most matte shots.

First, the background of a picture is matted out so that only the actors are filmed.

Next, the actors are matted out so that only the background is filmed.

When the film is rewound and played, the actors seem to be walking toward Emerald City.

The Optical Printer

The optical printer can put together a combination of two or more motion picture images in a single frame. Willis O'Brien was the first special effects director to make major use of this process. Modern movie makers depend on it. The optical printer was used for the special effects in *Mary Poppins*. Some scenes in the movie show the stars acting in a cartoon. This was done by filming their actions in front of a blank, blue screen. The film was then taken to a film lab where an optical printer replaced the blue background with a cartoon. The blue-screen shots could show the stars' movements while many different actions were going on around them at the same time. The stars could be seen dancing on rooftops or flying over busy London streets.

The optical printer makes our wildest dreams come to life on a movie screen. It can combine models of spaceships with action-filled backgrounds to show a thrilling space battle. The effects can be so real that you may feel like you are on one of the spaceships. You may forget that what you are really watching on the screen are the creations of special-effects teams using an optical printer.

In this scene from the film *Mary Poppins*, Mary and her friend appear to be carried across the water on the backs of turtles.

Computer-Age Special Effects

Today's special-effects teams use computers and high-power cameras that can shoot hundreds of frames of film in a second. Computers were used to plan each step of the enormous snow walkers in *The Empire Strikes Back*. High-power cameras were used to film the realistic explosions in *Star Wars*. The lovable *E.T.* was created with miniature models, computers, and high-power cameras. This modern technology allows us to go places and do things we never did before by making our imaginations come to life.

Special effects used in *Star Wars* and *The Empire Strikes Back* made the spaceships seem to soar through space.

Reader's Response ⌒ In your opinion, what are the best special effects you have ever seen in movies or on television?

Take a Bow

One hot August night twelve-year-old Steven Spielberg found his father's old movie camera in the garage. He pointed it into the air and pushed the button. Soon Steven began making movies of everything. His mother could not open a can of beans for dinner until he got his camera loaded. Even camping trips were an unusual experience for his family—when Steven was around, everyone became a movie star!

At age thirteen, Steven won his first filmmaking award—a Boy Scout merit badge—for a three-minute movie of his friends performing a story Steven wrote about stagecoach robbers. Three years later, he made his first feature-length film, called *Firelight*. And by the time he was 21, Steven had become the youngest director ever hired by a major film studio.

Today Steven Spielberg is one of Hollywood's most inventive directors. He is famous for the special effects he has created for

E. T.'s face is not a beautiful one. Steven wanted his real beauty to come from the inside.

movies like *Jaws, E. T.—The Extra Terrestrial*, and *Gremlins*.

E. T. is the most successful movie ever shown in America. It is also Steven Spielberg's favorite "because it is about kids." "I'm still a kid," he has said. "When people call me Mr. Spielberg, in my head I'll yell, 'Don't call me Mister. I'm not a grown-up yet!'"

A Spooky Sort

# of Shadow

by Jack Prelutsky

There's a spooky sort of shadow
dancing weirdly on the wall,
it's a creature that
I've never seen before,
it's creepy, and it's eerie,
and so positively tall,
that it stretches from
the ceiling to the floor.

Its mouth is full of needles,
and it has a giant eye,
and it's moving
in a hungry sort of way,
it surely could destroy me
if it only cared to try,
so I hope it's had enough
to eat today.

That shadow makes me nervous,
I don't dare to close my eyes,
I'm afraid I may be eaten,
head and all—
if I fall asleep tonight,
I'll be taken by surprise
by that shadow dancing
on my bedroom wall.

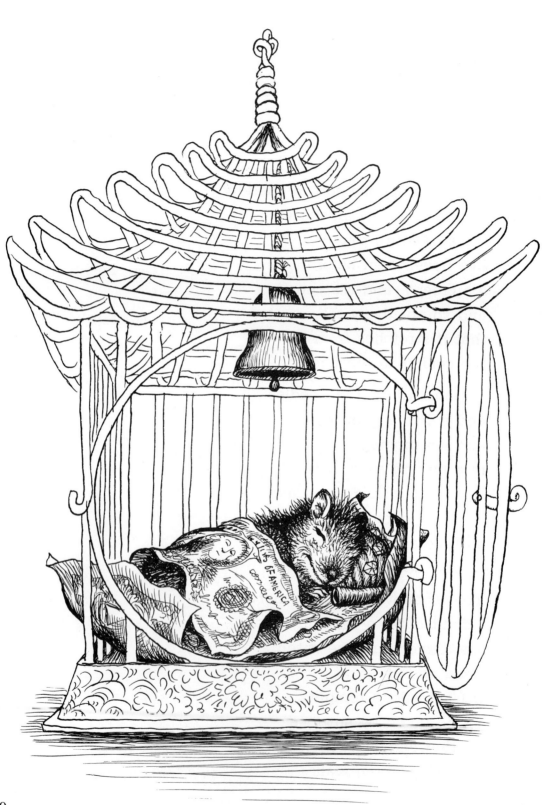

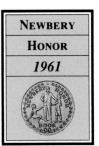

TUCKER'S LIFE SAVINGS

from *The Cricket in Times Square*
written by George Selden
illustrated by Garth Williams

Mama and Papa Bellini own a newsstand. The newsstand is underground in a subway station in New York City. One day their son Mario finds a cricket near the newsstand. Although Mama hates mice and insects, she agrees to let her son keep the cricket. Mario names the cricket Chester and makes a home for him in a Chinese cricket cage.

Chester's friends Tucker Mouse and Harry Cat also live in the subway station. When this story begins, Tucker talks Chester into letting him sleep in the cricket cage. Tucker uses dollar bills for blankets because they make him feel rich.

Chester Cricket was having a dream. In his dream he was sitting on top of his stump back in Connecticut, eating a leaf from the willow tree. He would bite off a piece of leaf, chew it up and swallow it, but for some reason it didn't taste as good as usual. There was something dry and papery about it, and it had a bitter flavor. Still Chester kept eating, hoping that it would begin to taste better.

A storm came up in his dream. The wind blew clouds of dust across the meadow. They swirled around his stump, and Chester began to sneeze because the dust got in his nose. But he still held onto the leaf. And then he sneezed such a big sneeze that it woke him up.

Chester looked around him. He had been walking in his sleep and he was sitting on the edge of the cash register. The storm had been a gust of air that blew into the newsstand when the shuttle pulled up to the station. He was still choking from the dirt that flew around him. Chester looked down at his two front legs, half expecting to find the willow leaf. But it was no leaf he was holding. It was a two dollar bill and he had already eaten half of it.

He dropped the bill and leaped over to the cricket cage, where Tucker Mouse was sleeping peacefully. Chester shook the silver bell furiously; it rang like a fire alarm. Tucker jumped out from under his blanket of dollar bills and ran around the cage shouting. "Help! Fire! Murder! Police!"

Then he realized where he was and sat down panting. "What is the matter with you, Chester?" he said. "I could have died from fright."

"I just ate half of a two dollar bill," said Chester.

Tucker stared at him with disbelief. "You did *what*?" he asked.

"Yes," said Chester, "look." He fetched the ruined two dollar bill from the cash register. " I dreamed it was a leaf and I ate it."

"Oh oh oh oh," moaned Tucker Mouse. "Not a one dollar bill—not even a one dollar bill and a fifty cent piece—*two dollars* you

had to eat! And from the Bellinis too—people who hardly make two dollars in two days.''

"What am I going to do?'' asked Chester.

"Pack your bags and go to California,'' said Tucker.

Chester shook his head. "I can't,'' he said. "They've been so good to me—I can't run away.''

Tucker Mouse shrugged his shoulders. "Then stay and take the rap,'' he said. He crept out of the cage and examined the remains of the money. "There's still half of it left. Maybe we could put scotch tape along the edge and pass it off as a one dollar bill.''

"No one would believe it,'' said Chester. He sat down, still forlornly holding the bill. "Oh dear— and things were going along so nicely.''

Tucker Mouse put his bed clothes back in the cash register drawer and came to sit beside Chester. "Buck up,'' he said. "We could still figure something out, maybe.''

They both concentrated for a minute. Then Tucker clapped his paws and squeaked, "I got it! Eat the rest of it and they'll never know what happened.''

"They'd accuse each other of losing it,'' said Chester. "I don't want to make any bad feeling between them.''

"Oh you're so honorable!'' said Tucker. "It's disgusting.''

"Besides, it tastes bad,'' added Chester.

"Then how about this,'' Tucker had a new idea. "We frame the janitor who cleans the station. I'll take the evidence over and plant it in his water closet. He whopped me with a mop last week. I would be glad to see him go to jail for a few days.''

"No, no,'' said Chester. "We can't get somebody else in trouble.''

"Then a stranger,'' said Tucker. "We tip over the Kleenex, break the glass in the alarm clock and throw all the small change on the floor. They'll think a thief came in the night. You could even put a bandage on and make out like a hero. I could see it all—''

"*No!*" Chester interrupted him. "The damage we'd do would cost even more than the two dollars."

Tucker had one more idea: he was going to volunteer to go over and swipe two dollars from the lunch counter. But before he could suggest that, the top of the stand was suddenly lifted off. They had forgotten what time it was. Mama Bellini, who was on duty in the morning, stood towering, frowning down on them. Tucker let out a squeak of fear and jumped to the floor.

"Catch the mouse!" shouted Mama. She picked up a *Fortune* magazine—very big and heavy— and heaved it after Tucker. It hit him on the left hind leg just as he vanished into the drain pipe.

Chester Cricket sat frozen to the spot. He was caught red handed, holding the chewed up two dollars in his front legs. Muttering with rage, Mama Bellini picked him up by his antennae, tossed him into the cricket cage and locked the gate behind him.

When she had put the newsstand in order, she pulled out her knitting and began to work furiously. But she was so angry she kept dropping stitches, and that made her angrier still.

Chester crouched in a far corner of the cage. Things had been going so well between Mama and him—but that was all ruined now. He half expected that she would pick him up, cage and all, and throw him onto the shuttle tracks.

At eight-thirty Mario and Papa arrived. Mario wanted to go to Coney Island for a swim today, but before he could even say "Good morning," Mama Bellini stretched out her hand and pointed sternly at Chester. There he was, with the evidence beside him.

A three-cornered conversation began. Mama denounced Chester as a money eater and said further that she suspected him of inviting mice and other unsavory characters into the newsstand at night. Papa said he didn't think Chester had eaten the two dollars on purpose, and what difference did it make if

a mouse or two came in? Mama said he had to go. Papa said he could stay, but he'd have to be kept in the cage. And Mario knew that Chester, like all people who were used to freedom, would rather die than live his life behind bars.

Finally it was decided that since the cricket was Mario's pet, the boy would have to replace the money. And when he had, Chester could come out again. Until then—the cage.

By working part time delivering groceries, when he wasn't taking care of the newsstand, Mario thought he could earn enough in a couple of weeks to get Chester out of jail. Of course that would mean no swimming at Coney Island, and no movies, and no nothing, but it was worth it. He fed the cricket his breakfast—left over asparagus tips and a piece of cabbage leaf. Chester had practically no appetite after what had happened. Then, when the cricket was finished, Mario said, "Good-bye," and told him not to worry, and went off to the grocery store to see about his job.

That night, after Papa had shut up the newsstand, Chester was hanging through the gilded bars of his cage. Earlier in the evening Mario had come back to feed him his supper, but then he had to leave right away to get in a few more hours of work. Most of the day Chester had spent inventing hopping games to try to keep himself entertained, but they didn't work, really. He was bored and lonely. The funny thing was that although he had been sleepy and kept wishing it were night, now that it was, he couldn't fall asleep.

Chester heard the soft padding of feet beneath him. Harry Cat sprang up and landed on the shelf. In a moment Tucker Mouse followed him from the stool, groaning with pain. He was still limping in his left hind leg where the *Fortune* magazine had hit him.

"How long is the sentence?" asked Harry.

"Until Mario can pay back the money," sighed Chester.

"Couldn't you get out on bail for the time being?" asked Tucker.

"No," said Chester. "And anyway, nobody has any bail. I'm surprised they let me off that easily."

Harry Cat folded his front paws over each other and rested his head on them. "Let me get this straight," he said. "Does Mario have to work for the money as punishment—or does he just have to get it somewhere?"

"He just has to get it," said Chester. "Why should he be punished? I'm the one who ate the money."

Harry looked at Tucker—a long look, as if he expected the mouse to say something. Tucker began to fidget. "Say Chester, you want to escape?" he asked. "We can open the cage. You could come and live in the drain pipe."

"No," Chester shook his head. "It wouldn't be fair to Mario. I'll just have to serve out the time."

Harry looked at Tucker again and began tapping one of his paws. "Well?" he said finally.

Tucker moaned and massaged his sore spot. "Oh my poor leg!

That Mama Bellini can sure heave a magazine. Feel the bump, Harry," he offered.

"I felt it already," said Harry. "Now enough of the stalling. You have money."

"Tucker has money?" said Chester Cricket.

Tucker looked nervously from one to the other. "I have my life's savings," he said in a pathetic voice.

"He's the richest mouse in New York," said Harry. "Old Money Bags Mouse, he's known as."

"Now wait a minute, Harry," said Tucker. "Let's not make too much from a few nickels and dimes."

"How did you get money?" asked Chester.

Tucker Mouse cleared his throat and began wringing his two front feet. When he spoke, his voice was all choked up with emotion. "Years ago," he said, "when yet a little mouse I was, tender in age and lacking in experience, I moved from the sweet scenes of my childhood—Tenth Avenue, that is—into

89

the Times Square subway station. And it was here that I learned the value of economicness—which means saving. Many and many an old mouse did I see, crawling away unwanted to a poor mouse's grave, because he had not saved. And I resolved that such a fate would never come to me."

"All of which means that you've got a pile of loot back there in the drain pipe," said Harry Cat.

"Just a minute, please, if you wouldn't mind," said Tucker. "I'll tell it in my own way." His voice became high and pitiful again. "So for all the long years of my youth, when I could have been gamboling—which means playing—with the other mousies, I saved. I saved paper, I saved food, I saved clothing—"

"Save time and get to the point," said Harry.

Tucker gave Harry a sour smile. "And I also saved money," he went on. "In the course of many years of scrounging, it was only natural I should find a certain amount of loose change. Often—oh, often,

my friends," Tucker put his hand over his heart, "would I sit in the opening of my drain pipe, watching the human beings and waiting. And whenever one of them dropped a coin—*however small!*—pennies I love—I would dash out, at great peril to life and limb, and bring it back to my house. Ah, when I think of the tramping shoes and the dangerous galoshes—! Many times have I had my toes stepped on and my whiskers torn off because of these labors. But it was worth it! Oh, it was worth it, my friends, on account of now I have two half dollars, five quarters, two dimes, six nickels and eighteen pennies tucked away in the drain pipe!"

"Which makes two dollars and ninety-three cents," said Harry Cat, after doing some quick addition.

"And proud I am of it!" said Tucker Mouse.

"If you've got all that, why did you want to sleep on the two dollar bills in the cricket cage?" asked Chester.

"No folding money yet," said Tucker. "It was a new sensation."

"You can get Chester out and still have ninety-three cents left," said Harry Cat.

"But I'll be ruined," whimpered Tucker. "I'll be wiped out. Who will take care of me in my old age?"

"I will!" said Harry. "Now stop acting like a skinflint and let's get the money."

Chester rang the silver bell to get their attention. "I don't think Tucker should have to give up his life savings," he said. "It's his money and he can do what he wants with it."

Tucker Mouse poked Harry in the ribs. "Listen to the cricket," he said. "Acting noble and making me look like a bum. Of course I'll give the money! Wherever mice are spoken of, never let it be said that Tucker Mouse was stingy with his worldly goods. Besides, I could think of it as rent I pay for sleeping in the cage."

In order that Tucker could keep at least one of each kind of coin, Harry Cat figured out that they should bring over one half

dollar, four quarters, one dime, five nickels and fifteen cents. That would leave the mouse with a half dollar, a quarter, a dime, a nickel and three cents.

"It's not a bad beginning," said Tucker. "I could make up the losses in a year, maybe."

The cat and the mouse had to make several trips back and forth between the drain pipe and the newsstand, carrying the money in their mouths. They passed the coins into the cage one by one, and Chester built them up into a column, starting with the half dollar on the bottom and ending with the dime, which was smallest, on top. It was morning by the time they were finished. They had just time enough to share half of a hot dog before Mama Bellini was due to open the stand.

Mario came with her. He wanted to feed Chester early and then work all morning until he took over the newsstand at noon. When they lifted off the cover, Mama almost dropped her end. There was Chester, sitting on top of the column of change, chirping merrily.

Mama's first suspicion was that the cricket had sneaked out and smuggled all the money from the cash register into the cage. But when she looked in the drawer, the money from the night before was still there.

Mario had the idea that Papa might have left it as a surprise. Mama shook her head. She would certainly have known if he had two dollars to leave anybody.

They asked Paul, the conductor, if he'd seen anyone around the newsstand. He said no. The only thing he'd noticed was that that big cat who sometimes prowled through the station had seemed to be busier than usual last night. And of course they knew that he couldn't have had anything to do with replacing the money.

But whoever left it, Mama Bellini was good to her word. Chester was allowed out of the cage, and no further questions were asked. Although she wouldn't have admitted it for the world, Mama felt the same way about money that Tucker Mouse did. When you had it, you had it—and you didn't bother too much about where it came from.

Reader's Response ∼ Chester Cricket, Tucker Mouse, and Harry Cat are three of the characters in "Tucker's Life Savings." Which one would you like to have as a companion or pet? Why?

Library Link ∼ *This story is an excerpt from the book* The Cricket in Times Square *by George Selden. If you enjoyed the story, you might enjoy reading the entire book to find out what other adventures Chester has.*

New York's Secret Subway

Did you know that over two billion people ride New York City's subway each year? Yet one hundred years ago, many people argued that a subway would be expensive and dangerous.

Alfred Ely Beach disagreed. He wanted to solve the city's traffic problem by building an underground train. He decided to build a subway without telling anyone! Working at night, he dug a tunnel and put in tracks, a rail car, and waiting room. When he opened his secret subway to the public, it was an instant success. Alfred Beach thought he had proved that a subway would be good for his city. But the government did not agree. Mr. Beach closed his subway and sealed it off.

After Boston, Massachusetts, opened the first subway in the United States, New Yorkers decided it was time to build their own. Twelve thousand people, many of them immigrants from Ireland, Poland, and Italy, helped build it. It opened in 1904.

The story of Mr. Beach's subway wasn't over. Can you guess what happened? In 1912, workers accidently broke into Beach's tunnel. They were surprised to find everything in good condition.

Today, Beach's tunnel is part of City Hall Station, where a plaque honors the creator of New York's secret subway.

New York's First Subway, (Pneumatic tube) Museum of the City of New York

McBroom Tells a Lie

by Sid Fleischman

It's true—I did tell a lie once.

I don't mean the summer nights we hung caged chickens in the farmhouse for lanterns. Those hens had eaten so many lightning bugs they glowed brighter'n kerosene lamps.

And I don't mean the cold snap that came along so sudden that blazing sunshine froze to the ground. We pickaxed chunks of it for the stove to cook on.

READING
CORNER

That's the genuine truth, sure and certain as my name's Josh McBroom.

The time I told a lie—well, I'd best start with the spring day the young'uns came home from school. They were lugging an old black stovepipe, which they put in the barn.

The next day they dragged home a broken buggy wheel. They put that in the barn, too.

95

Gracious! It wasn't long before that barn was filling up with empty coffee cans, scrap pieces of lumber, tin funnels, busted chairs, a rusted bicycle and all manner of throwaway stuff.

Then they began a-sawing and a-hammering and hardly came out of the barn to eat. They were building a hoopde-doodle of some sort. The scamps kept it covered with a sheet. I reckoned they'd tell us when they were ready.

"Will*jill*hester*chester*peter*polly*tim*tom*mary*larry*and little*clarinda!*" my dear wife Melissa called out every evening. "Supper!"

We had hardly sat down to eat one night when Jill asked, "Pa, would Mexican jumping beans grow on our farm?"

I hadn't seen anything yet that wouldn't grow on our wonderful one-acre farm. That trifling patch of earth was so amazing rich we could plant and harvest two-three crops a day—with time left over for a game of horseshoes. Why, just last month Little Clarinda dropped her silver baby fork and by time we found it the thing had grown into a silver pitchfork.

"Mexican jumping beans?" I answered. "I don't think they make good eating."

"We don't want them to eat," Will said.

"Will you let us grow a crop?" Polly asked. "We need bushels and bushels."

"For our invention," Tom put in.

"In that case," I said, "jump to it, my lambs."

They traded with a boy at school who owned a jar of the hopping beans. First thing Saturday morning they lit out the back door to plant their crop.

And along came our foxy-eyed neighbor, Heck Jones. You never saw such a spareribbed and rattleboned man.

Why, he was so skinny he could slip through a knothole without tipping his hat. He wore a diamond stickpin in his tie and was swinging a bamboo cane. Our dog, Zip, stood barking at him.

"Josh McBroom," he said, "I'm here to do some trading."

"Trade what?"

"My big farm for yours—even. You can keep the dog."

"No sir and nohow," I said. His farm was so worn out he had to plant his own weeds.

He leaned both hands heavily on his bamboo cane. *"Hee-haw!"* he snickered. "Reckon I'll get your land, neighbor—one way or t'other."

And off he ambled up the road, *hee-hawing* through his nose. He'd been visiting almighty often lately. I stomped over the hole his cane had left in the ground. I had to be careful not to let holes get a good start in our rich topsoil—the blamed things grow.

Meanwhile the young'uns had laid out the rows and began sowing the beans.

Well, that was a mistake. I should have known that our soil was too powerful strong for jumping beans. The seeds sprouted faster'n the twitch of a sheep's tail and those Mexican bushes shot up lickety-bang. As they quick-dried in the prairie sun the pods began to shake and rattle and Chester shouted: "Pa, look!"

Merciful powers! Those buzzing, jumping, wiggle-waggling pods jerked the roots clear out of the ground. And off those bushes went, leaping and hopping every which way.

"Willjillhesterchesterpeterpollytimtommarylarryand-littleclarinda!" I called out. "After them, my lambs!"

Didn't those plants lead us on a merry chase! A good many got clean away, hopping and bucking and rattling across the countryside. But we did manage to capture enough for the young'uns' invention.

They were shelling the beans when the dog reared up barking. Heck Jones was back with four scrawny hens and a bobtailed rooster out for a walk.

"Howdy, neighbor," he said. "I'm here to do some trading. My farm for yours and I'll throw in this flock of fat hens. My prize rooster, too. You can keep the dog."

I looked at those sorry fowl, scratching and pecking away in the dirt. "No sir and nohow," I said. "Our farm's not for trade, Heck Jones."

"*Hee-haw*, I'll get it one way or t'other," he said, tipping his hat toward the end of his nose. "Good day, neighbor."

It was the next morning, before breakfast, when the young'uns finished tinkering with their invention. They called my dear wife Melissa and me out to the barn and whipped off the sheet.

Glory be! There stood an odds and ends contraption on four wheels. A rain barrel was mounted in front with three tin funnels sticking out of the top. The scamps had fixed up their collection of broken chairs to seat all eleven of them.

"We're going to call it a Jumping Beanmobile," Jill said.

"If it runs we won't have to walk all that five miles to school and back," said Peter.

"My stars," Mama declared.

"Pile in, everybody," Will said, "and let's start 'er up."

The young'uns flocked to their seats. Will, Jill and Hester began pouring beans into the funnels.

Mercy! You never heard such a racket inside that rain barrel. The beans began to hop, jump and leap something fearful, bouncing against tin cans from the sound of things. I found out later the cans were fitted into stovepipe— looked something like the cylinders on my broken-down Franklin automobile. They had the things hooked up to the front wheels with bicycle chains.

"More fuel!" Will called out, and more jumping beans poured down the funnels.

I declare. The next moment the Jumping Beanmobile clanked forward—a full inch.

"More beans!" Polly shouted happily.

But tarnation! The barrel was already so hopping full that beans were leaping like fleas out of the tops of the funnels.

The young'uns sat there with the smiles dropping from their faces, one by one.

"A splendid invention, my lambs," I said. "Why, all you need is a stronger fuel."

"Hee-haw." Heck Jones had come up behind us and was helping himself to the water dipper. "That infernal machine'll never run, neighbors. Make good firewood, though."

The young'uns rolled their Jumping Beanmobile back into the barn. I was feeling mighty low for them, the way Heck Jones made fun of them. He was cackling so that he spilled most of the dipper of water on his shoes.

"McBroom, you drive a hard bargain. I'll trade you my farm, a flock of fat hens, my prize rooster and two plump hogs. You can keep your farm dog."

Plump? Those hogs of his were so puny they could hide behind a broomstick.

"No sir and nohow," I said.

"I'll get what I'm after one way or t'other," he *hee-hawed*, and ambled out of sight around the barn.

When the young'uns came in to breakfast they said they'd seen him scraping the mud off his shoes into an old flour sack.

"By thunder!" I exclaimed. "That's why the confounded rascal's been paying us so many visits."

The older young'uns were standing at the stove breaking fresh eggs into skillets. "Pa—there's something wrong with these breakfast eggs," said Will.

But I was hardly listening. "Why, Heck Jones doesn't intend to trade for our farm," I declared.

"Pa, come look," said Jill from the stove.

"Valuable as gold dust, our topsoil. And he's been stealing it! Yup, out of that hollow bamboo cane he pokes in the earth. And off his wet shoes. And out of the craws of the chickens he brings along to peck dirt!"

"Pa—come quick, but stand back!" my dear wife Melissa exclaimed.

I hopped to the stove as she broke another fresh egg into a skillet. Why, soon as it was fried on one side that egg jumped up in the air. It flipped over and landed on the other side to fry.

"Well, don't that beat all," I said. "The hens must have been eating your Mexican jumping beans. Yup, and they're laying eggs that *flip* themselves. An amazing invention, my lambs!"

But they wouldn't be cheered up by the flip-flopping eggs. A gloom was on them because they wouldn't be riding to school in their Beanmobile.

I scratched my head most of the day. It wouldn't do any good to fence the farm to keep Heck Jones off. You might as well put up a windbreak out of chicken wire.

The young'uns were still feeling almighty low and downsome at supper when my dear wife Melissa tried to jolly everybody up. "Let's pop some corn."

Well, a strange look came over all those sad faces. "Popcorn," Jill whispered.

"Popcorn!" said Hester, beginning to smile.

"POPCORN!" Will laughed. "Bet that'll run our machine!"

Didn't those kids light out for the barn in a hurry! In no time at all they were clanking and hammering to do over the Beanmobile into a Popcornmobile.

They were still at it the next day, after school, when Heck Jones came running with his shoes off. I reckoned he planned to steal pinches of our farm between his toes.

"I'll have the law on you, McBroom!"

Egg was dripping off his nose and chin. "Do tell," I said coldly.

"You grew them jumping beans, didn't you?"

"Best ever. Looks like your hens pecked 'em down and you didn't step back from the egg skillet fast enough."

"Hang them blasted eggs. Look there at my blue ribbon cow, Princess Prunella!"

My eyes near shot out of my head. There on the horizon that stupid, worthless cow of his was leaping and high-jumping and bucking.

"Kicked holes right through the barn roof!" Heck Jones snorted. "You allowed them dangerous bushes of yours to get loose and now Princess Prunella's stomachs are full of jumping beans—all four of 'em!"

"Didn't know she was royalty," I said. "Got her name changed kind of sudden."

"That cow's ruined. It would take ten men on ladders to try and milk her. Worth a fortune, Princess Prunella was, with all her blue ribbons."

I knew for a fact that dumb cow hadn't won a ribbon in her life—but she did eat several once at the county fair.

"Reckon I'll have to shoot her before she does any
more damage," he said, beginning to dab at his eyes.
"Poor creature."

Well, all that dabbing didn't fool me. Heck Jones
could peel an acre of onions without dropping a tear. But I
reckoned I was responsible for all the mischief, letting
those bushes get away from us.

"Sir," I said. "If you'll guarantee not to set foot on
this farm I'll pay for a barn roof. And I'll buy that ignorant
cow from you. I reckon when she settles down she'll give
churned butter for a month. Mighty valuable now,
Prunella is."

"She ain't for sale!" Heck Jones snapped. "Don't think you're going to slip out so light and easy. I intend to see you in jail, McBroom! Farming with intent to poison up my livestock with crazy-beans. Unless . . ."

"I'm listening, sir."

He cleared his throat. "Neighbor, I'm a kindly man. If you want to trade farms we'll call it fair and square."

"Well, no sir and nohow," I said. "And if I weren't a kindly man I'd have the sheriff after you for trying to steal our topsoil, trifle by trifle."

He caught his hat as a wind sprang up and flapped his coattails. "Slander, sir! I'll have the law on you double. Anyway, you can't prove it!"

"Why, the proof is right between your toes."

He looked down at his feet. "Dear, dear me," he grinned. "I declare if I wasn't in such a rush I forgot my shoes."

"And your hollow bamboo cane."

"Well now, neighbor, we ought to be able to settle things between ourselves." He lifted his thin nose into the wind—that man could sniff things miles off. "Why, you just grow me a crop of tomatoes to make up for my barn roof and we'll forget the rest."

"I'll deliver 'em before supper."

"No, neighbor. Can't use 'em yet. Gotta find a buyer at a good price." He whipped out a pencil and piece of paper. "I'll just write out the agreement. Best to do things honest and legal. You deliver the tomatoes when I say so— fresh off the vine, mind you—and I'll guarantee not to set foot on your farm again."

Glory be! We'd be rid of that petty scoundrel at last.

"But fair's fair, McBroom. I'm entitled to a guarantee too. I'll just put down that if you don't live up to the bargain—why, this useless, worn-out one-acre farm is mine. Sign here."

Useless? Worn-out? My pride rose up and arched like a cat's back. I could raise a crop of tomatoes in an hour. The *hee-haw* would be on him. I signed.

"And no more skulking around, sir," I said.

"A bargain's a bargain," he nodded solemnly. But as he ambled off I thought I heard him snicker through his nose.

It was about sunset when the young'uns rolled their Popcornmobile out of the barn. "It's finished, Pa," Will said.

They had attached black tin stovepipe underneath the floorboards with bailing wire. It made a mighty stout-looking exhaust pipe.

"And look, Pa," Larry said. "We got headlights, just like your broken-down Franklin."

Indeed they did! Two quart canning jars were fixed to the front. And the scamps had filled the jars with lightning bugs!

"Pa," Mary said. "Can we have a chunk of frozen sunlight out of the icehouse?"

"Not much left," I replied. "But help yourself."

By early candlelight they had dropped a clod of sunlight in the barrel together with a dozen ears of corn. They piled into the seats and waited for the sunshine to thaw and pop the corn and start the machinery clanking.

My dear wife Melissa hurried out to take the sheets off the line—the prairie wind was turning a mite gritty—and there stood Heck Jones.

"Evenin', neighbors," he said. There was a tricksy look in his eye and a piece of paper in his hand. "McBroom, you guaranteed a crop of tomatoes on demand. Well, I'm demanding 'em *now*."

My eyebrows jumped. "Drat it, you can see the sun's down!" I declared.

"There's nothing about the sun in the contract. You read it."

"And it's going to kick up a dust storm before long."

"Nothing in the contract about a dust storm. You signed it."

"Sir, you expect me to grow you a crop of tomatoes *at night in a dust storm?*"

"*Hee-haw,* neighbor. If you don't, this farm's mine. I'll give you till sunup. Not a moment later, McBroom!"

And off he went, chuckling and snickering and *hee-hawing* through his nose.

"Oh, Pa," my dear wife Melissa cried. Even the young'uns were getting a mite onion-eyed.

My heart had sunk somewhere down around my socks, only lower. "Tarnation!" I said. "That rascal's slippery as an eel dipped in lard."

Just then corn began popping like firecrackers inside the young'uns' rain barrel.

"Pa, we're moving!" Jill exclaimed.

Sure enough, the chunk of frozen sunlight had thawed out and the corn was exploding from the stored-up heat.

I tried to raise a smile. Will grabbed the steering wheel tight and began driving the young'uns around the barn. Popcorn shot out of the exhaust pipe, white as snow.

We didn't have enough of that frozen sunshine left
to grow a crop, worst luck! But when I saw those two
headlights coming around the barn my heart leaped back in
place. The jars full of fireflies lit up the way like it was
high noon!

"Willjillhesterchesterpeterpollytimtommarylarryand-
littleclarinda!" I shouted. "Fetch canning jars. Fill 'em up
with lightning bugs. Quick, my lambs. Not a moment to
waste."

The Popcornmobile sputtered to a stop, spitting out the
last corncobs from the tailpipe.

Chester said, "The critters have got kind of scarce around here, Pa."

"The thickest place is way the other side of Heck Jones's place," Mary said.

"At Seven-Mile Meadow," Polly nodded.

"A powerful long walk," said Larry.

"Who said anything about walking?" I laughed. "You've got your Popcornmobile, haven't you?"

Didn't we get busy! The young'uns fetched all the canning jars in the cellar and bushels of corn for fuel. With a fresh chunk of frozen sunshine in the barrel off they took—spraying popcorn behind them.

I set to work planting tomato seeds. It was full dark, but I could see fine. My dear wife Melissa held up a chicken by the feet—one of those lantern-glowing hens I was telling you about.

Then I began pounding stakes in the ground for the tomatoes to climb up. It was slow work with the wind blowing grit in my eyes.

"I do hope the young'uns don't get lost," my dear wife Melissa said. "It's going to blow a real dust storm by morning."

"Heck Jones had sniffed it coming," I declared. "But lost? Not our scamps. I can hear 'em now. And see 'em too—look!"

They were still a long way off but those headlights glowed bright as sunrise. And that Popcornmobile sounded like the Fourth of July, loud enough to wake snakes.

Jill had taken a turn at the wheel and steered toward the barn. All the kids were waving and laughing. I reckoned that was the best ride they'd ever had.

"That's a jim-dandy machine you built," I smiled.

"And I see you found a lightning bug or two."

"Thicker'n mosquitoes, over at Seven-Mile Meadow," Polly said.

Well, it didn't take long to hang those jars of fireflies on the tomato stakes. And glory be! They lit up the farm bright as day.

It wasn't a moment before the tomato sprouts came busting up through the earth. They broke into leaf and the vines started toward those canning jars. I do believe they preferred that homemade sunshine!

In fact, before we could harvest the crop, pull the stakes and plug the holes, a good many of those tomatoes got sunscald!

We loaded up the Popcornmobile with bushel baskets of tomatoes and I fetched one of the last chunks of frozen sunshine from the icehouse. Will threw a dozen ears of corn into the engine and I went along for the ride.

We made so many trips to Heck Jones's place the popcorn piled up along the road like a snowbank. Finally, minutes before dawn, I hammered at his door.

"Wake up, Heck Jones!" I called.

"Hee-haw!" He began to laugh so hard you'd think he'd swallowed a feather duster. He opened the door and stood there in his nightcap, the legal paper in his hand.

"Told you I'd get your farm one way or t'other, McBroom! It's dawn by the clock and that powerful rich, git-up-and-git acre is all mine!"

"Yup, it's dawn," I said. "No arguing that, Heck Jones. And there's my end of the bargain."

When he saw that crop of tomatoes he just about swallowed his teeth. His mouth puckered up tighter'n bark on a tree.

I took the legal paper out of his hand. "And you bargained to stay off our useless, worn-out one-acre farm, sir. With your hollow cane and your chickens and your muddy shoes and your curled toes. Good day, Mr. Jones."

The young'uns and I all piled into the Popcornmobile to start for home. That's when I saw Princess Prunella. Only she wasn't jumping anymore.

"Merciful powers!" I declared. "Look there! That numbskull cow mistook all this popcorn for snow and has froze to death!"

We got home for a big breakfast and just in time. That prairie dust storm rolled in and stayed for weeks on end. My, it was thick, that dust. Before long our dog was chasing rabbits *up* their burrows. The rodents had dug their holes in the air.

And Heck Jones didn't have any more sense than to climb up on his barn roof and start shingling over the holes Princess Prunella had made. He couldn't see what he was doing until the wind took a shift and the dust cleared. That's when he saw he'd nailed shingles eight feet out in the dust. They all came tumbling down, but he didn't get hurt. Fell into the tomatoes.

Now it's true—I did tell a lie once. That cow of his didn't *really* freeze to death in all that popcorn. But she did catch a terrible cold.

Reader's Response 〜 What do you think was the most outrageous thing in this story? Why?

Hidden WORLDS

Stories can make us take a new look at old surroundings.

What might you see that you never noticed before?

TROPICAL FOREST, *1919, painting by Charles Du Fresne, French, 1876–1938. Musée Nat. d'Art Moderne, Paris. Photo: Art Resource, New York*

Theme Books for
Hidden Worlds

Do you love seeing a rainbow after a rainstorm? Or an animal, wild and free? Take time to look closely. There are hidden worlds all around you.

🐋 In *Charlotte's Web* by E. B. White, a pig named Wilbur learns that he will soon become smoked bacon and ham. That's when Charlotte, a talented spider hidden in the rafters, comes up with a plan to save his life.

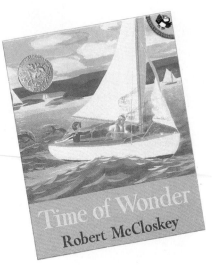

🐋 Explore an island off the coast of Maine in *Time of Wonder* by Robert McCloskey. In this special place you'll sail among the islands, feel the calm of an early morning fog, and batten down the hatches to get ready for a rip-roaring hurricane.

After Jack rescues a seal from the polluted ocean, his life changes forever. When you read *Jack, the Seal and the Sea* by Gerald Aschenbrenner, you'll learn how Jack's love for the sea inspires him to make a difference.

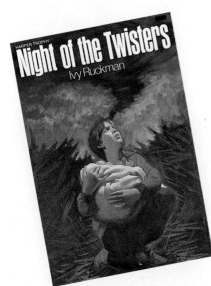

Nature's power is often hidden from us, but it can hit hard when it shows itself. In *Night of the Twisters* by Ivy Ruckman, Dan Hatch and his friends learn firsthand about the terror and destruction of seven whirling tornadoes.

More Books to Enjoy

Raising Gordy Gorilla at the San Diego Zoo
  by Georgeanne Irvine
The Carp in the Bathtub by Barbara Cohen
The Magic School Bus at the Waterworks
  by Joanna Cole
The Great Race of the Birds and Animals
  by Paul Goble

115

The Day Nothing Happened

by Robert H. Redding

Naput and his sister, Nadeen, were hiking on the tundra. It was March and snow covered the ground. For the Eskimo children, March was still a winter month.

"I wish there were something to see," said Naput gloomily.

"So do I," agreed his sister. "This hike isn't much fun."

In the distance the chimneys of their village were smoking. A breeze was blowing, and the children snuggled deeper into their parkas for warmth.

"Father said there are arctic foxes out here," muttered Naput. "I see nothing of the snow dog."

"Maybe their fur is so white it is impossible to see them," said Nadeen.

The children squinted against the sun. For as far as their eyes could reach, there was nothing but the glare of the snow-covered tundra.

"Let's go back," said Nadeen. "Maybe we'll find something interesting to do at home."

The children turned and headed toward the village. Unknown to them, a pair of black eyes watched their every move. The eyes belonged to an arctic fox. She had hurt her foot on the arctic ice and was limping, for the wound was painful.

As the children made their way, the fox managed to keep pace. She was small enough that tundra hummocks hid her. There was a purpose in her vigil. Her injury left her unable to hunt. She couldn't keep up with *nanuk* the polar bear either. Sometimes *nanuk* left scraps from his own hunts, and the fox ate well. But right now the bears were all out on the ocean ice, and the little white fox hadn't followed. She was very hungry. She would perish if she didn't eat in a short while.

There was one immediate hope for the fox. Had the children brought something to eat? The fox had been near humans before and had dined on leftovers. She crouched low and followed with halting steps.

Farther out on the tundra was another animal. It was *kavik*, the wolverine. His fierce, dark eyes glittered as they watched the fox. He, too, was hunting. Lemmings were scarce. There were no rabbits, and *sik-sik*, the ground squirrel, was still underground in his long winter's sleep.

To *kavik*, the fox looked good to eat. He saw that the snow dog was hurt. She would be quick and easy prey.

Naput and Nadeen ambled along. They studied the frozen snow and wondered why it made a crunching sound under their *mukluks*. They thought of exciting things to see on television. Naput remembered his favorite program would be on that evening. The day wouldn't be entirely lost.

The children paused to rest. When they stopped, the fox also stopped. The only one who didn't stop was the wolverine. He advanced craftily, his mind on one thing: Catch the fox: catch his dinner. Belly close to the ground, the wolverine moved forward in his odd, humping gait, and the distance shortened.

Kavik paid little attention to the children. They did not frighten him. Nothing frightened *kavik*, for though he was not large, he was a mighty hunter.

The children started home again, going a little faster. The sun was lowering, and it would be dark soon. They didn't speak, and the silence was great around them, but neither Naput nor Nadeen heard the fox. In spite of her injury, she stepped along as lightly as a bird.

Suddenly the snow dog stopped. She turned swiftly, the hair on her back raised, just in time to meet the wolverine in a head-on clash.

There followed a fierce battle. The wolverine gripped the fox by the tail. At the same time, the fox bit into *kavik's* foot. Then began a fierce tug of war, and as the animals swayed, one fighting for his dinner, the other for her life, they growled deeply.

All at once the tip of the fox's tail came loose, and the wolverine fell back. The fox scampered off a few yards. Her teeth were bared, her eyes bright with hurt and fear.

Kavik gripped the piece of tail firmly in his jaws. Nothing in the world could have pried it loose. He studied the fox for several seconds, then turned away. The snow dog wasn't such easy prey after all. It is possible he could have beaten the fox, but *kavik's* paw throbbed where the fox's teeth had dug in, and the wolverine wanted no more of such treatment. He gave a last growl, then humped off across the tundra holding the bit of white hair and skin in his mouth.

The fox stood like a statue, eyes on her enemy. When she felt safe, she lay down to lick her wound.

Her courage had saved her life, but she was still hungry, and starvation was still waiting. She would rest awhile, then go into the village. Her nose told her food scraps were available. She would have to be careful, because the village dogs were troublesome, but she had to try. It was her last chance for survival.

Naput and Nadeen reached their warm house. Inside, their father, Nilliguk, was carving walrus ivory into a small seal.

"What did you see on the tundra today?" he asked.

"Nothing, father," replied Naput wearily. "We didn't see a thing."

"Sometimes," added his sister, "the tundra can be very boring. Nothing ever happens."

But Nilliguk, wise in the ways of the arctic, smiled and said, "On the tundra it is what you *don't* see that is the most exciting."

Naput scratched his head, puzzled. There were times, he thought, when his father spoke in riddles.

Reader's Response ⌣ What exciting things would you notice or not notice if Naput and Nadeen were hiking with you in a park near your home?

Land of the Midnight Sun

The name *Alaska* comes from the Aleut word *al-ay-es-ka*, meaning "great land." The United States bought Alaska from Russia in 1867. The purchase price was $7.2 million. That worked out to less than two cents an acre!

Alaska is sometimes called Land of the Midnight Sun. During certain times of the year, the sun shines twenty-four hours a day—even in the middle of the night. For example: In Barrow, the Alaskan city closest to the North Pole, the sun rises on May 10 and doesn't set again until August 2—eighty-four days later! The opposite happens between November 18 and January 24, when there are sixty-seven days of total darkness.

In 1959, Alaska was admitted as the forty-ninth state of the United States. It is the largest state in the union. Alaska has three thousand rivers and three million lakes. Because the land is so rugged, flying is the best form of inland transportation. In 1990, one out of every fifty-seven people in Alaska had a pilot's license.

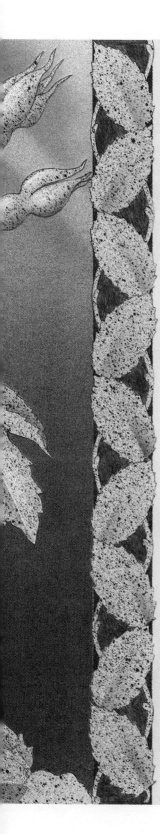

The Secret Song

by Margaret Wise Brown

Who saw the petals
   drop from the rose?
I, said the spider,
But nobody knows.

Who saw the sunset
   flash on a bird?
I, said the fish,
But nobody heard.

Who saw the fog
   come over the sea?
I, said the sea pigeon,
Only me.

Who saw the first
   green light of the sun?
I, said the night owl,
The only one.

Who saw the moss
   creep over the stone?
I, said the gray fox,
All alone.

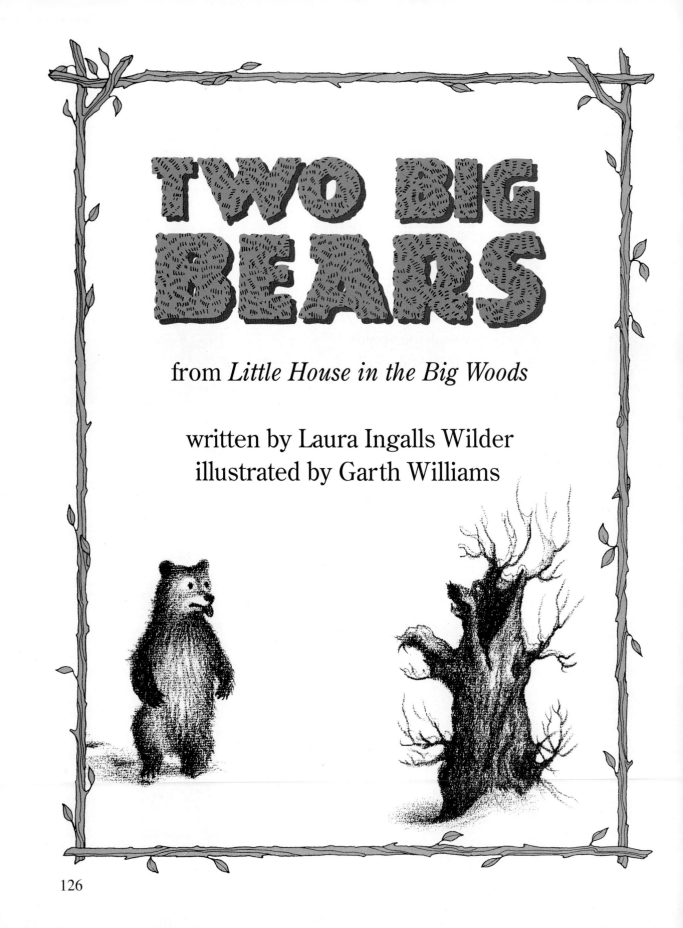

TWO BIG BEARS

from *Little House in the Big Woods*

written by Laura Ingalls Wilder
illustrated by Garth Williams

hen one day Pa said that spring was coming.

In the Big Woods the snow was beginning to thaw. Bits of it dropped from the branches of the trees and made little holes in the softening snowbanks below. At noon all the big icicles along the eaves of the little house quivered and sparkled in the sunshine, and drops of water hung trembling at their tips.

Pa said he must go to town to trade the furs of the wild animals he had been trapping all winter. So one evening he made a big bundle of them. There were so many furs that when they were packed tightly and tied together they made a bundle almost as big as Pa.

Very early one morning Pa strapped the bundle of furs on his shoulders, and started to walk to town. There were so many furs to carry that he could not take his gun.

Ma was worried, but Pa said that by starting before sun-up and walking very fast all day he could get home again before dark.

The nearest town was far away. Laura and Mary had never seen a town. They had never seen a store. They had never seen even two houses standing together. But they knew that in a town there were many houses, and a store full of candy and calico and other wonderful things—powder, and shot, and salt, and store sugar.

They knew that Pa would trade his furs to the storekeeper for beautiful things from town, and all day they were expecting the presents he would bring them.

When the sun sank low above the treetops and no more drops fell from the tips of the icicles they began to watch eagerly for Pa.

The sun sank out of sight, the woods grew dark, and he did not come. Ma started supper and set the table, but he did not come. It was time to do the chores, and still he had not come.

Ma said that Laura might come with her while she milked the cow. Laura could carry the lantern.

So Laura put on her coat and Ma buttoned it up. And Laura put her hands into her red mittens that hung by a red yarn string around her neck, while Ma lighted the candle in the lantern.

Laura was proud to be helping Ma with the milking, and she carried the lantern very carefully. Its sides were of tin, with places cut in them for the candle-light to shine through.

When Laura walked behind Ma on the path to the barn, the little bits of candle-light from the lantern leaped all around her on the snow. The night was not yet quite dark. The woods were dark, but there was a gray light on the snowy path, and in the sky there were a few faint stars. The stars did not look as warm and bright as the little lights that came from the lantern.

Laura was surprised to see the dark shape of Sukey, the brown cow, standing at the barnyard gate. Ma was surprised, too. It was too early in the spring for Sukey to be let out in the Big Woods to eat grass. She lived in the barn. But sometimes on warm days Pa left the door of her stall open so she could come into the barnyard. Now Ma and Laura saw her behind the bars, waiting for them.

Ma went up to the gate, and pushed against it to open it. But it did not open very far, because there was Sukey, standing against it. Ma said, "Sukey, get over!" She reached across the gate and slapped Sukey's shoulder.

Just then one of the dancing little bits of light from the lantern jumped between the bars of the gate, and Laura saw long, shaggy, black fur, and two little, glittering eyes. Sukey had thin, short, brown fur. Sukey had large, gentle eyes.

Ma said, "Laura, walk back to the house."

So Laura turned around and began to walk toward the house. Ma came behind her. When they had gone part way, Ma snatched her up, lantern and all, and ran. Ma ran with her into the house, and slammed the door.

Then Laura said, "Ma, was it a bear?"

"Yes, Laura," Ma said. "It was a bear."

Laura began to cry. She hung on to Ma and sobbed, "Oh, will he eat Sukey?"

"No," Ma said, hugging her. "Sukey is safe in the barn. Think, Laura—all those big, heavy logs in the barn walls. And the door is heavy and solid, made to keep bears out. No, the bear cannot get in and eat Sukey."

Laura felt better then. "But he could have hurt us, couldn't he?" she asked.

"He didn't hurt us," Ma said. "You were a good girl, Laura, to do exactly as I told you, and to do it quickly, without asking why."

Ma was trembling, and she began to laugh a little. "To think," she said, "I've slapped a bear!"

Then she put supper on the table for Laura and Mary. Pa had not come yet. He didn't come. Laura and Mary were undressed, and they said their prayers and snuggled into the trundle bed.

Ma sat by the lamp, mending one of Pa's shirts. The house seemed cold and still and strange, without Pa.

Laura listened to the wind in the Big Woods. All around the house the wind went crying as though it were lost in the dark and the cold. The wind sounded frightened.

Ma finished mending the shirt. Laura saw her fold it slowly and carefully. She smoothed it with her hand. Then she did a thing she had never done before. She went to the door and pulled the leather latch-string through its hole in the door, so that nobody could get in from outside unless she lifted the latch.

She came and took Carrie, all limp and sleeping, out of the big bed.

She saw that Laura and Mary were still awake, and she said to them: "Go to sleep, girls. Everything is all right. Pa will be here in the morning."

Then she went back to her rocking chair and sat there rocking gently and holding Baby Carrie in her arms.

She was sitting up late, waiting for Pa, and Laura and Mary meant to stay awake, too, till he came. But at last they went to sleep.

In the morning Pa was there. He had brought candy for Laura and Mary, and two pieces of pretty calico to make them each a dress.

Mary's was a china-blue pattern on a white ground, and Laura's was dark red with little golden-brown dots on it.

Ma had calico for a dress, too; it was brown, with a big, feathery white pattern all over it.

They were all happy because Pa had got such good prices for his furs that he could afford to get them such beautiful presents.

The tracks of the big bear were all around the barn, and there were marks of his claws on the walls. But Sukey and the horses were safe inside.

All that day the sun shone, the snow melted, and little streams of water ran from the icicles, which all the time grew thinner. Before the sun set that night, the bear tracks were only shapeless marks in the wet, soft snow.

After supper Pa took Laura and Mary on his knees and said he had a new story to tell them.

The Story of Pa
and the Bear in the Way

"WHEN I went to town yesterday with the furs I found it hard walking in the soft snow. It took me a long time to get to town, and other men with furs had come in earlier to do their trading. The storekeeper was busy, and I had to wait until he could look at my furs.

"Then we had to bargain about the price of each one, and then I had to pick out the things I wanted to take in trade.

"So it was nearly sundown before I could start home.

"I tried to hurry, but the walking was hard and I was tired, so I had not gone far before night came. And I was alone in the Big Woods without my gun.

"There were still six miles to walk, and I came along as fast as I could. The night grew darker and darker, and I wished for my gun, because I knew that some of the bears had come out of their winter dens. I had seen their tracks when I went to town in the morning.

"Bears are hungry and cross at this time of year; you know they have been sleeping in their dens all winter long with nothing to eat, and that makes them thin and angry when they wake up. I did not want to meet one.

"I hurried along as quick as I could in the dark. By and by the stars gave a little light. It was still black as pitch where the woods were thick, but in the open places I could see, dimly. I could see the snowy road ahead a little way, and I could see the dark woods standing all around me. I was glad when I came into an open place where the stars gave me this faint light.

"All the time I was watching, as well as I could, for bears. I was listening for the sounds they make when they go carelessly through the bushes.

"Then I came again into an open place, and there, right in the middle of my road, I saw a big black bear.

"He was standing up on his hind legs, looking at me. I could see his eyes shine. I could see his pig-snout. I could even see one of his claws, in the starlight.

"My scalp prickled, and my hair stood straight up. I stopped in my tracks, and stood still. The bear did not move. There he stood, looking at me.

"I knew it would do no good to try to go around him. He would follow me into the dark woods, where he could see better than I could. I did not want to fight a winter-starved bear in the dark. Oh, how I wished for my gun!

"I had to pass that bear, to get home. I thought that if I could scare him, he might get out of the road and let me go by. So I took a deep breath, and suddenly I shouted with all my might and ran at him, waving my arms.

"He didn't move.

"I did not run very far toward him, I tell you! I stopped and looked at him, and he stood looking at me. Then I shouted again. There he stood. I kept on shouting and waving my arms, but he did not budge.

"Well, it would do me no good to run away. There were other bears in the woods. I might meet one any time. I might as well deal with this one as with another. Besides, I was coming home to Ma and you girls. I would never get here, if I ran away from everything in the woods that scared me.

"So at last I looked around, and I got a good big club, a solid, heavy branch that had been broken from a tree by the weight of snow in the winter.

"I lifted it up in my hands, and I ran straight at that bear. I swung my club as hard as I could and brought it down, bang! on his head.

"And there he still stood, for he was nothing but a big, black, burned stump!

"I had passed it on my way to town that morning. It wasn't a bear at all. I only thought it was a bear, because I had been thinking all the time about bears and being afraid I'd meet one."

"It really wasn't a bear at all?" Mary asked.

"No, Mary, it wasn't a bear at all. There I had been yelling, and dancing, and waving my arms, all by myself in the Big Woods, trying to scare a stump!"

Laura said: "Ours was really a bear. But we were not scared because we thought it was Sukey."

Pa did not say anything, but he hugged her tighter.

"Oo-oo! That bear might have eaten Ma and me all up!" Laura said, snuggling closer to him. "But Ma walked right up to him and slapped him, and he didn't do anything at all. Why didn't he do anything?"

"I guess he was too surprised to do anything, Laura," Pa said. "I guess he was afraid, when the lantern shone in his eyes. And when Ma walked up to him and slapped him, he knew *she* wasn't afraid."

"Well, you were brave, too," Laura said. "Even if it was only a stump, you thought it was a bear. You'd have hit him on the head with a club, if he *had* been a bear, wouldn't you, Pa?"

"Yes," said Pa, "I would. You see, I had to."

Then Ma said it was bedtime. She helped Laura and Mary undress and button up their red flannel nightgowns. They knelt down by the trundle bed and said their prayers.

"Now I lay me down to sleep,
I pray the Lord my soul to keep.
If I should die before I wake,
I pray the Lord my soul to take."

Ma kissed them both, and tucked the covers in around them. They lay there awhile, looking at Ma's smooth, parted hair and her hands busy with sewing in the lamplight. Her needle made little clicking sounds against her thimble and then the thread went softly, swish! through the pretty calico that Pa had traded furs for.

Laura looked at Pa, who was greasing his boots. His mustaches and his hair and his long brown beard were silky in the lamplight, and the colors of his plaid jacket were gay. He whistled cheerfully while he worked, and then he sang:

"The birds were singing in the morning,
And the myrtle and the ivy were in bloom,
And the sun o'er the hills was a-dawning,
'Twas then that I laid her in the tomb."

It was a warm night. The fire had gone to coals on the hearth, and Pa did not build it up. All around the little house, in the Big Woods, there were little sounds of falling snow, and from the eaves there was the drip, drip of the melting icicles.

In just a little while the trees would be putting out their baby leaves, all rosy and yellow and pale green, and there would be wild flowers and birds in the woods.

Then there would be no more stories by the fire at night, but all day long Laura and Mary would run and play among the trees, for it would be spring.

Reader's Response ∼ Laura and Ma saw a bear in the barnyard. Pa thought a bear was in the road on his way home from town. Which bear story did you think was more frightening? Why?

Library Link ∼ *This story is from the book* Little House in the Big Woods *by Laura Ingalls Wilder. If you enjoyed the story, you might like to read the entire book to follow Laura and her family on more adventures.*

900 BIRTHDAY CARDS

Laura Ingalls Wilder was surprised in 1932 when her first book, *Little House in the Big Woods*, was an instant success. She had wondered if anyone would be interested in reading about a simple pioneer family who lived in the Wisconsin wilderness in the 1870s. In fact, it was Laura's own daughter, Rose, who convinced her mother to write these stories down.

The author continued to write eight other "little house" books about her family as they moved across Wisconsin, Kansas, Iowa, Minnesota, and the Dakota Territory. She became so popular that on her 84th birthday, she received 900 birthday cards!

Today Laura's books are still loved by many children all over the world and include titles such as *Little House on the Prairie*, *On the Banks of Plum Creek*, *By the Shores of Silver Lake*, and *The Long Winter*.

BLACK BEAR

GRIZZLY BEAR

RABBIT

HARE

ANOLE

CHAMELEON

CROCODILE

hump

BROAD SNOUT

ALLIGATOR

The canine teeth fit into holes in the upper jaw when the mouth is closed.

Alan E Cober

140

ANIMAL LOOKALIKES

**from *The Lookalikes*
by Anne Orth Epple**

Have you ever wondered how a frog was different from a toad? Or a moth from a butterfly? An alligator from a crocodile? A leopard from a jaguar? If you've ever wondered about animals that seem to be both different and alike, then you've played nature's game of "lookalikes."

Many animals from the same large family look alike, and animals of different families may look alike because they find their food in the same way, or because they live in the same kind of surroundings. When we learn how two animals can look alike but at the same time be very different, we understand a little better how these animals survive in the natural world.

When I worked at New York's Bronx Zoo, many visitors asked me questions beginning "What is the difference between...?" I hope that this book will answer some of these questions, and help you to better understand the world of nature's lookalikes.

Grizzly Bear

If a nine-foot-long, 800-pound bear with a blunted head and "dished in" face were to chase you, you could retreat to the nearest tree, for unlike the black bear, the adult grizzly bear is unable to climb. The grizzly bear is the largest bear found in the United States. It lives in the mountains of the American West and up into western Canada and Alaska. While a grizzly's color ranges from yellowish-brown to nearly black, the tips of the hairs, especially on its back, are gray or white, giving it the grizzled effect from which it receives its name.

When standing on its hind legs the grizzly measures eight feet tall. There is a distinctive hump on its back, above the shoulders. The grizzly's slightly curved front claws are long and broad and generally light in color.

All bears are dangerous, but the grizzly is especially so, for it's very unpredictable. While it isn't usually seen along the roadsides, it occasionally comes into a campground at night, like its cousin the black bear, searching for food.

Black Bear

The smallest bear in North America is the black bear, which is found in woods, swamps and mountainous areas throughout most of the United States. The black bear averages about five feet in length and weighs 200-300 pounds, up to an exceptional 500 pounds. Its height at the shoulders reaches three feet. Its color ranges from bluish-black to cinnamon.

The head of the black bear is small and pointed, and its profile is straight, rather than "dished in" like the grizzly's. The front claws of the black bear are short, curved and either black or very dark brown.

The black bear is the common bear seen begging along the roadways in many of our national parks. However, park signs caution against feeding the bears to protect both the public and the bears themselves. (Bears depending on handouts sometimes forget how to obtain their own food.)

The black bear is an excellent climber and will climb trees to obtain fruits and honey.

Rabbits

Rabbits have shorter, narrower ears than those of hares, and their front and hind legs are also much shorter. When chased, rabbits take long hops as they run along.

Baby rabbits are born blind, deaf and hairless, little pink animals that are helpless for about a week and merely snuggle together in their hollowed-out nests in the ground. After about twelve days they have developed enough to leave their nests for short times. Cottontail rabbit babies are a little over four inches long at birth and average about one ounce in weight.

Rabbits prefer to live in bushy clearings or at the edges of woods where, if chased, they can quickly find hiding places. The eastern cottontails and their western cousins are found throughout much of the United States.

Hares

Hares are all ears! Their ears are extremely long and quite wide. Hares also have very long front and hind legs. The powerful hind legs of some hares, such as jack rabbits, which are really hares, are twice as long as their forelegs. All hares are built for speed, some taking giant leaps of up to 20 feet as they bound along.

Like rabbits, mother hares also build nests for their babies. When the babies are born, however, they are covered with hair. They can also see and hear and soon after birth are able to hop about. Jack rabbit babies are six to eight inches long at birth and weigh two to six ounces.

Because speed is their best defense against attackers, hares live in open country, where they won't be slowed down by tall grass or bushes. Some types are common to the American West.

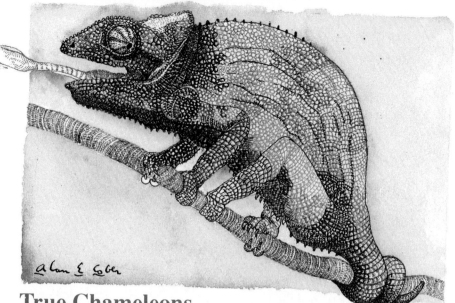

True Chameleons

True chameleons may look like lizards from outer space! The lids of their eyes form cone-shaped turrets. In the center of each turret is a small opening through which the lizards see. When a chameleon's eyes move, the holes move too. And since each of its eyes moves independently, it's possible to see the hole in one eye turret focusing on a spider to the left and the other gazing at a grasshopper to the right.

The bodies of true chameleons are high. With their prehensile, or grasping, tails and their plier-like toes, these lizards move among the treetops in what looks like slow motion. Never moving rapidly, most sway back and forth from time to time as they crawl along.

True chameleons' extremely long tongues are slender sacs with widened sections of sticky flesh at their ends. They shoot out, reach their insect prey nearly six or seven inches away and in an instant return to the chameleons' mouths.

From yellow to yellowish-brown, green, black, gray or some blotched variety of these, true chameleons change colors according to the temperature, sunlight and even their feelings. There are more than eighty species, most less than a foot long.

Anoles

The American chameleons sold in pet stores and at circuses are not true chameleons. These lizards are really anoles. Although the eyes of anoles can move separately, the lack of turrets makes the eye movements less noticeable.

The bodies of anoles are more flattened than those of chameleons. Their tails are not prehensile. Anoles do, however, have special microscopic suction cups under their toes, which enable them to climb up smooth surfaces—even glass—without slipping. They are lively lizards, often jumping from branch to branch, then descending to the ground to hunt insects.

The tongues of anoles are shorter and more slender than those of true chameleons.

Anoles change colors mainly between greens and browns. They are found only in the southeastern United States, south through Mexico and into South America. There are several hundred species. The Cuban anoles are the largest, reaching a length of 16 inches.

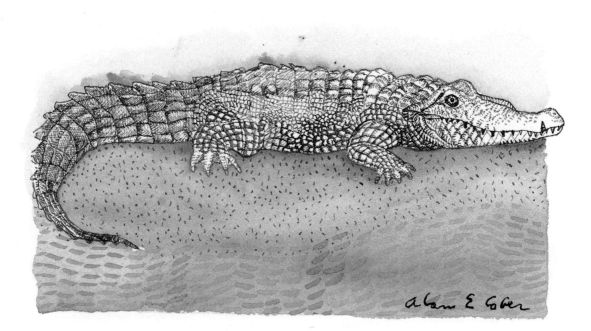

American Crocodile

When Peter Pan and Wendy looked down from the end
of the gangplank, they saw a fourteen-foot crocodile looking
up at them with an expectant grin. They might have known it
was a crocodile and not an alligator because it had a long
narrow snout that tapered at the end to give its head a
triangular appearance.

When an adult crocodile's mouth is closed the large
fourth tooth on each side of the lower jaw sticks out. These
teeth fit into notches on the outside of the upper jaw, giving
the crocodile its grinning expression.

The female American crocodile buries her eggs in a low
mound of sand and generally leaves the nest unguarded.
When it hatches, the young crocodile measures eight to nine
inches long. It has narrow black crossbands or a series of
black spots marking its grayish color. The adult varies in
color from gray to olive-gray.

148

While some crocodiles may live in Never-Never-Land, the American crocodile is found only in the salty marshes of the most southern parts of Florida. Even here it's rarely seen, for these animals are nearly extinct.

American Alligator

If Peter Pan had been looking at an alligator instead of a crocodile, he would have seen a broadly rounded snout, no hungry grin and no large fourth tooth. When the alligator's mouth is closed, its long teeth fit into a pit or pocket inside the upper jaw.

If left alone, an American alligator rarely attacks man. When being captured, though, it whips its tail back and forth with enough force to break a man's leg, snaps its jaws together and thrashes its head from side to side. Even in this state, however, the alligator is usually taken without serious harm to the persons capturing it.

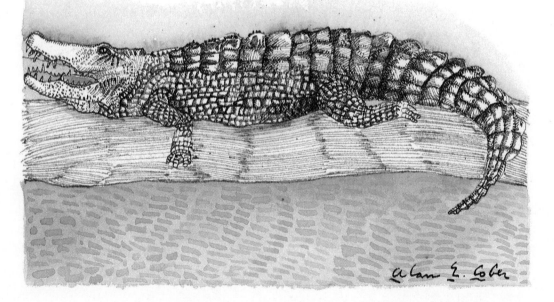

The female American alligator lays her eggs in a nest she builds of decaying vegetation. This mound is sometimes seven feet in diameter and two to three feet high. Usually the female guards the nest from a distance until the eggs hatch. The eight-inch-long baby alligator is black, marked with yellow bands. The adult is all black.

Found throughout many of our southern Atlantic and Gulf states, the American alligator prefers freshwater lakes, swamps and marshes.

Reader's Response ～ You have read about eight kinds of animals—grizzly bears, black bears, rabbits, hares, chameleons, anoles, alligators, and crocodiles. Which would you like to read more about? Why?

Library Link ～ *This article is an excerpt from the book* The Lookalikes *by Anne Orth Epple. If you would like to read about more animal lookalikes, you might enjoy reading the entire book.*

TERN AROUND

The Arctic tern population in Maine had been decreasing in size at a rapid rate. Fortunately for the terns, biologist Stephen Kress had an idea that he thought might lure terns back to their old nesting areas. On Seal Island, where terns hadn't nested in years, he put 50 wooden decoys and added the recorded calls and screeches of a busy tern colony. The decoys and sounds worked, and many terns landed on the island only to fly away once they realized they had been fooled.

But in 1989, the terns stopped leaving. That year 17 pairs of breeding terns stayed on the island and at least 17 chicks were born. In 1991, the number of breeding pairs had increased to 281.

One good tern deserves another!

The Parakeet Named Dreidel

by Isaac Bashevis Singer

It happened about ten years ago in Brooklyn, New York. All day long a heavy snow was falling. Toward evening the sky cleared and a few stars appeared. A frost set in. It was the eighth day of Hanukkah, and my silver Hanukkah lamp stood on the windowsill with all candles burning. It was mirrored in the windowpane, and I imagined another lamp outside.

My wife, Esther, was frying potato pancakes. I sat with my son, David, at a table and played dreidel with him. Suddenly David cried out, "Papa, look!" And he pointed to the window.

I looked up and saw something that seemed unbelievable. Outside on the windowsill stood a yellow-green bird watching the candles. In a moment I understood what had happened. A parakeet had escaped from its home somewhere, had flown out into the cold street and landed on my windowsill, perhaps attracted by the light.

A parakeet is native to a warm climate, and it cannot stand the cold and frost for very long. I immediately took steps to save the bird from freezing. First I carried away the Hanukkah lamp so that the bird would not burn itself when entering. Then I opened the window and with a quick wave of my hand shooed the parakeet inside. The whole thing took only a few seconds.

In the beginning the frightened bird flew from wall to wall. It hit itself against the ceiling and for a while hung from a crystal prism on the chandelier. David tried to calm it. "Don't be afraid, little bird, we are your friends." Presently the bird flew toward David and landed on his head, as though it had been trained and was accustomed to people. David began to dance and laugh with joy. My wife, in the kitchen, heard the noise and came out to see what had happened. When she saw the bird on David's head, she asked, "Where did you get a bird all of a sudden?"

"Mama, it just came to our window."

"To the window in the middle of the winter?"

"Papa saved its life."

The bird was not afraid of us. David lifted his hand to his forehead and the bird settled on his finger. Esther

placed a saucer of millet and a dish of water on the table, and the parakeet ate and drank. It saw the dreidel and began to push it with its beak. David exclaimed, ''Look, the bird plays dreidel.''

David soon began to talk about buying a cage for the bird and also about giving it a name, but Esther and I reminded him that the bird was not ours. We would try to find the owners, who probably missed their pet and were worried about what had happened to it in the icy weather. David said, ''Meanwhile, let's call it Dreidel.''

That night Dreidel slept on a picture frame and woke us in the morning with its singing. The bird stood on the frame, its plumage brilliant in the purple light of the rising sun, shaking as in prayer, whistling, twittering, and talking all at the same time. The parakeet must have belonged to a house where Yiddish was spoken, because we heard it say *''Zeldele, geh schlofen''* (Zeldele, go to sleep), and these simple words uttered by the tiny creature filled us with wonder and delight.

The next day I posted a notice in the elevators of the neighborhood houses. It said that we had found a Yiddish-speaking parakeet. When a few days passed and no one called, I advertised in the newspaper for which I wrote, but a week went by and no one claimed the bird. Only then did Dreidel become ours. We bought a large cage with all the fittings and toys that a bird might want, but because Hanukkah is a festival of freedom, we resolved never to lock the cage. Dreidel was free to fly around the house whenever he pleased. (The man at the pet shop had told us that the bird was a male.)

Nine years passed and Dreidel remained with us. We became more attached to him from day to day. In our house Dreidel learned scores of Yiddish, English, and Hebrew words. David taught him to sing a Hanukkah song, and there was always a wooden dreidel in the cage for him to play with. When I wrote on my Yiddish typewriter, Dreidel would cling to the index finger of either my right or my left hand, jumping acrobatically with every letter I wrote. Esther often joked that Dreidel was helping me write and that he was entitled to half my earnings.

Our son, David, grew up and entered college. One winter night he went to a Hanukkah party. He told us that he would be home late, and Esther and I went to bed early. We had just fallen asleep when the telephone rang. It was David. As a rule he is a quiet and composed young man. This time he spoke so excitedly that we could barely understand what he was saying. It seemed that David had told the story of our parakeet to his fellow students at the party, and a girl named Zelda Rosen had exclaimed, "I am this Zeldele! We lost our parakeet nine years ago." Zelda and her parents lived not far from us, but they had never seen the notice in the newspaper or the ones posted in elevators. Zelda was now a student and a friend of David's. She had never visited us before, although our son often spoke about her to his mother.

We slept little that night. The next day Zelda and her parents came to see their long-lost pet. Zelda was a beautiful and gifted girl. David often took her to the theater and to museums. Not only did the Rosens recognize their bird, but the bird seemed to recognize his former owners.

The Rosens used to call him Tsip-Tsip, and when the parakeet heard them say ''Tsip-Tsip,'' he became flustered and started to fly from one member of the family to the other, screeching and flapping his wings. Both Zelda and her mother cried when they saw their beloved bird alive. The father stared silently. Then he said, ''We have never forgotten our Tsip-Tsip.''

I was ready to return the parakeet to his original owners, but Esther and David argued that they could never part with Dreidel. It was also not necessary because that day David and Zelda decided to get married after their graduation from college. So Dreidel is still with us, always eager to learn new words and new games. When David and Zelda marry, they will take Dreidel to their new home. Zelda has often said, "Dreidel was our matchmaker."

On Hanukkah he always gets a gift—a mirror, a ladder, a bathtub, a swing, or a jingle bell. He has even developed a taste for potato pancakes, as befits a parakeet named Dreidel.

Reader's Response ～ Do you think it was right for David and his family to keep the parakeet when they couldn't find its owner? Explain why or why not.

Library Link ～ *This story is from the book* The Power of Light. *If you enjoyed Isaac Singer's story about Dreidel, you might want to read the entire book.*

Traditions

Isaac Bashevis Singer was born in Poland but came to the United States in 1935. Most of his novels, plays, and short stories are written in Yiddish, the language spoken by many Eastern European Jewish people. Many of Singer's stories describe Jewish traditions.

On Hanukkah, the Jewish Festival of Lights, families gather around a special *Hanukkah menorah*, and light one candle on the first night, two on the second night, and so on, for all eight nights of the festival. A Hanukkah menorah always has holders for nine candles, however, because one candle, called the *shammash* (caretaker), is used to light the other candles. There are songs, stories, presents, and prayers, and children play games with spinning tops called dreidels.

A 16th-century Hanukkah menorah

Pettranella

written by Betty Waterton
illustrated by Ann Blades

Long ago in a country far away lived a little girl named Pettranella. She lived with her father and mother in the upstairs of her grandmother's tall, narrow house.

Other houses just like it lined the street on both sides, and at the end of the street was the mill. All day and all night smoke rose from its great smokestacks and lay like a grey blanket over the city. It hid the sun and choked the trees, and it withered the flowers that tried to grow in the window boxes.

One dark winter night when the wind blew cold from the east, Pettranella's father came home with a letter. The family gathered around the table in the warm yellow circle of the lamp to read it; even the grandmother came from her rooms downstairs to listen.

"It's from Uncle Gus in America," began her father. "He has his homestead there now, and is already clearing his land. Someday it will be a large farm growing many crops of grain." And then he read the letter aloud.

When he had finished, Pettranella said, "I wish we could go there, too, and live on a homestead."

Her parents looked at each other, their eyes twinkling with a secret. "We *are* going," said her mother. "We are sailing on the very next ship."

Pettranella could hardly believe her ears. Suddenly she thought of some things she had always wanted. "Can we have some chickens?" she asked. "And a swing?"

"You will be in charge of the chickens," laughed her father, "and I will put up a swing for you in our biggest tree."

"And Grandmother," cried Pettranella, "now you will have a real flower garden, not just a window box."

Pulling her close, the grandmother said gently, "But I cannot go to the new land with you, little one. I am too old to make such a long journey."

Pettranella's eyes filled with tears. "Then I won't go either," she said.

But in the end, of course, she did.

When they were ready to leave, her grandmother gave her a small muslin bag. Pettranella opened it and looked inside. "There are seeds in here!" she exclaimed.

"There is a garden in there," said the old lady.

"Those are flower seeds to plant when you get to your new home."

"Oh, I will take such good care of them," promised Pettranella. "And I will plant them and make a beautiful garden for you."

So they left their homeland. It was sad, thought Pettranella, but it was exciting, too. Sad to say good-bye to everyone they knew, and exciting to be going across the ocean in a big ship.

But the winter storms were not over, and as the ship pitched about on the stormy seas everyone was seasick. For days Pettranella lay on her wooden bunk in the crowded hold, wishing she was back home in her clean, warm bed.

At last they reached the shores of Canada. Pettranella began to feel better. As they stood at the rail waiting to leave the ship, she asked, "Can we see our homestead yet?"

Not yet, they told her; there was still a long way to go.

Before they could continue their journey her father had to fill out many forms, and Pettranella spent hours and hours sitting on their round-topped trunk in a crowded building, waiting. So many people, she thought. Would there be room for them all?

Finally one day the last form was signed and they were free to go, and as they travelled up a wide river and across the lonely land, Pettranella knew that in this big country there would be room for everyone.

After many days they came to a settlement where two rivers met and there they camped while the father got his homestead papers. Then they bought some things they would need: an axe and a saw, a hammer and nails, sacks of food and seed, a plow and a cow and a strong brown ox, and a cart with two large wooden wheels. And some chickens.

The ox was hitched to the cart, which was so full of all their belongings that there was barely room for Pettranella and her mother. Her father walked beside the ox, and the cow followed.

The wooden wheels creaked over the bumpy ground, and at first Pettranella thought it was fun, but soon she began asking, "When are we going to get there?" and making rather a nuisance of herself climbing in and out of the cart.

Often at night as they lay wrapped in their warm quilts beside the fire, they heard owls hooting, and sometimes wolves calling to one another; once they saw the northern lights.

One day as they followed the winding trail through groves of spruce and poplar, there was a sudden THUMP, CRACK, CRASH!

"What happened?" cried Pettranella, as she slid off the cart into the mud.

"We have broken a shaft," said her father. "One of the wheels went over a big rock."

"Now we'll never find our homestead!" wailed Pettranella, as they began to unload the cart. "We'll make a new shaft," said her father; and, taking his axe, he went into the woods to cut a pole the right size.

Pettranella helped her mother make lunch, then sat down on a log to wait. Taking the bag of seeds from her pocket, she poured them out into a little pile on her lap, thinking all the while of the garden she would soon be making.

Just then she heard something. A familiar creaking and squeaking, and it was getting closer. It had to be—it was—another ox cart!

"Somebody's coming!" she shouted, jumping up.

Her father came running out of the woods as the cart drew near. It was just like theirs, but the ox was black. The driver had a tanned, friendly face. When he saw their trouble, he swung down from his cart to help.

He helped the father make a new shaft, then they fastened it in place and loaded the cart again.

Afterwards they all had lunch, and Pettranella sat listening while the grownups talked together. Their new friend had a homestead near theirs, he said, and he invited them to visit one day.

"Do you have any children?" asked Pettranella.

"A little girl just like you," he laughed, as he climbed into his cart. He was on his way to get some supplies. Pettranella waved good-bye as he drove off, and they set forth once again to find their homestead. "Our neighbour says it isn't far now," said her father.

As they bumped along the trail, suddenly Pettranella thought about the flower seeds. She felt in her pocket, but there was nothing there. The muslin bag was gone!

"Oh, oh! Stop!" she cried. "The seeds are gone!"

Her father halted the ox. "I saw you looking at them

before lunch," said her mother. "You must have spilled them there. You'll never find them now."

"I'm going back to look anyway," said Pettranella, and, before they could stop her, she was running back down the trail.

She found the log, but she didn't find any seeds. Just the empty muslin bag.

As she trudged back to the cart, her tears began to fall. "I was going to make such a beautiful garden, and now I broke my promise to Grandmother!"

"Maybe you can make a vegetable garden instead," suggested her mother, but Pettranella knew it wouldn't be the same. "I don't think turnips and cabbages are very pretty," she sighed.

It was later that afternoon, near teatime, when they found their homestead.

Their own land, as far as they could see! Pettranella was so excited that for a while she forgot all about her lost seeds.

That night they slept on beds of spruce and tamarack boughs cut from their own trees. What a good smell, thought Pettranella, snuggling under her quilt.

The next morning her father began to put up a small cabin; later he would build a larger one. Then he started to break the land. A small piece of ground was set aside for vegetables, and after it was dug, it was Pettranella's job to rake the earth and gather the stones into a pile.

"Can we plant the seeds now?" she asked when she had finished.

"Not yet," said her mother, "it's still too cold."

One morning they were awakened by a great noise that filled the sky above them. "Wild geese!" shouted the father, as they rushed outside to look. "They're on their way north. It's really spring!"

Soon squirrels chattered and red-winged blackbirds sang, a wobbly-legged calf was born to the cow, and sixteen baby chicks hatched.

"Now we can plant the garden," said the mother, and they did.

Early the next morning Pettranella ran outside to see if anything had sprouted yet. The soil was bare; but a few days later when she looked, she saw rows of tiny green shoots.

If only I hadn't lost Grandmother's seeds, she thought, flowers would be coming up now, too.

One warm Sunday a few weeks later, Pettranella put on a clean pinafore and her best sunbonnet and went to help her father hitch up the ox, for this was the day they were going to visit their neighbours.

As the ox cart bumped and bounced down the trail over which they had come so many weeks before, Pettranella thought about the little girl they were going to visit. She will probably be my very best friend, she thought to herself.

Suddenly her father stopped the cart and jumped down. "There's the rock where we broke the shaft," he said. "This time I will lead the ox around it."

"There's where we had lunch that day," said her mother.

"And there's the log I was sitting on when I lost the seeds," said Pettranella. "And look! LOOK AT ALL THOSE FLOWERS!"

There they were. Blowing gently in the breeze, their bright faces turned to the sun and their roots firm in the American soil—Grandmother's flowers.

"Oh! Oh!" cried Pettranella, "I have never seen such beautiful flowers!"

Her mother's eyes were shining as she looked at them. "Just like the ones that grew in the countryside back home!" she exclaimed.

"You can plant them beside our house," said her father, "and make a flower garden there."

Pettranella did, and she tended it carefully, and so her promise to her grandmother was not broken after all.

But she left some to grow beside the trail, that other settlers might see them and not feel lonely; and to this very day, Pettranella's flowers bloom each year beside a country road in Wisconsin.

Reader's Response ∽ If you had been Pettranella, how would you have felt when you lost the special gift?

 **isconsin is...**

- An Indian word with several possible meanings including *gathering of the waters*, *wild rice country*, and *homeland*

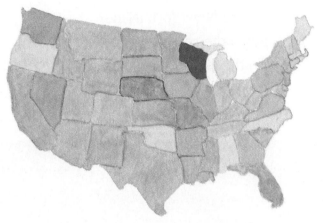

- The land of 15,000 lakes

- Where the Republican party was founded in 1854

- The dairy capital of America

- The birthplace of Frank Lloyd Wright, one of America's most influential architects

- The home of Little Norway, a preserved Norwegian Homestead of the mid-1800s

- Where the Ringling Brothers organized their first circus in 1884

- Called the Badger State because in the 1820s lead miners lived in caves that they dug out of the hillsides. It reminded people of badgers burrowing holes in the ground.

THIS LAND IS

This land is your land,
This land is my land
From California
To the New York island.
From the redwood forest
To the Gulf Stream waters,
This land was made for you and me.

As I was walking
That ribbon of highway
I saw above me
That endless skyway,
I saw below me
That golden valley,
This land was made for you and me.

YOUR LAND

I've roamed and rambled
And I followed my footsteps
To the sparkling sands of
Her diamond deserts,
And all around me
A voice was sounding,
This land was made for you and me.

This land is your land,
This land is my land
From California
To the New York island.
From the redwood forest
To the Gulf Stream waters,
This land was made for you and me.

Woody Guthrie

I'm in Charge of
CELEBRATIONS

written by Byrd Baylor ● illustrated by Peter Parnall

Sometimes people ask me,
"Aren't you lonely
out there
with just
desert
around you?"

I guess they mean
the beargrass
and the yuccas
and the cactus
and the rocks.

I guess they mean
the deep ravines
and the hawk nests
in the cliffs
and the coyote trails
that wind
across the hills.

"*Lonely?*"

I can't help
laughing
when they ask me
that.

I always look at them . . .
surprised.

And I say,
"How could I be lonely?
I'm the one
in charge of
celebrations."

Sometimes
they don't believe me,
but it's true.
I am.

175

I put
myself
in charge.
I choose
my own.

Last year
I gave myself
one hundred and eight
celebrations—
besides the ones
that they close school for.

I cannot get by
with only
a few.

Friend, I'll tell you
how it works.

I keep a notebook
and I write the date
and then I write about
the celebration.

I'm very choosy
over
what goes in
that book.

It has to be something
I plan to remember
the rest of my life.

You can tell
what's worth
a celebration
because
your heart will
POUND
and
you'll feel
like you're standing
on top of a mountain
and you'll
catch your breath
like you were
breathing
some new kind of air.

Otherwise,
I count it just
an average day.
(I told you
I was
choosy.)

177

Friend, I wish you'd been here
for Dust Devil Day.

But since you weren't,
I'll tell you how
it got to be
my first
real
celebration.

You can call them
whirlwinds
if you want to.
Me, I think
dust devils
has a better sound.

Well, anyway,
I always stop
to watch them.
Here, everyone does.

You know how
they come
from far away,
moving
up from the flats,
swirling
and swaying
and falling
and turning,

picking up sticks
and sand
and feathers
and dry tumbleweeds.

Well, last March eleventh
we were all going somewhere.
I was in the back
of a pickup truck
when the dust devils
started
to gather.

You could see
they were
giants.

You'd swear
they were
calling
their friends
to come too.

And they came—
dancing
in time to
their own
windy music.

We all started counting.
We all started looking
for more.

They stopped that truck
and we turned
around
and around
watching them all.
There were seven.

At a time like that,
something
goes kind of crazy
in you.
You have to run
to meet them,
yelling
all the way.

You have to
whirl around
like you were
one of them,
and you can't stop
until
you're falling down.

And then all day
you think
how
lucky
you were
to be there.

Some of my best
celebrations
are sudden surprises
like that.

If you weren't outside
at that
exact
moment,
you'd miss them.

I spend a lot of time
outside
myself,
looking around.

Once
I saw a triple rainbow
that ended in a canyon
where I'd been
the day before.

I was halfway up a hill
standing
in a drizzle of rain.

It was almost dark
but I wouldn't go in
(because of the rainbows,
of course),
and there
at the top of the hill
a jackrabbit
was standing
up on his hind legs,
perfectly still,
looking straight
at that same
triple
rainbow.

I may be
the only person in the world
who's seen
a rabbit
standing in the mist
quietly watching
three rainbows.

That's worth
a celebration
any time.

I wrote it down
and drew the hill
and the rabbit
and the rainbow
and me.

Now
August ninth
is Rainbow Celebration Day.

I have
Green Cloud Day
too.

Ask anybody
and they'll tell you
clouds
aren't
green.

But
late one winter afternoon
I saw
this huge
green cloud.

It was not
bluish-green
or grayish-green
or something else.
This cloud
was
green . . .

green as a jungle parrot.

And the strange thing was
that it began
to take a parrot's shape,
first
the wings,
and then the head
and beak.

High in the winter sky
that green bird
flew.

It didn't last
more than a minute.
You know how fast
a cloud
can change,
but I still
remember
how it looked.

So I celebrate
green clouds
on February sixth.

At times like that,
I always think,
"What if I'd missed it?
What if I'd been
in the house?
Or what if I hadn't
looked up
when I did?"

You can see I'm
very lucky
about things
like that.

And
I was lucky
on Coyote Day,
because
out of all time
it had to be
one moment
only
that
a certain coyote
and I
could meet—
and we did.

Friend, you should have
been here too.

I was following
deer tracks,
taking my time,
bending down
as I walked,
kind of humming.
(I hum a lot
when I'm alone.)

I looked up
in time to see
a young coyote
trotting
through the brush.

She crossed
in front of me.
It was a windy day
and she was going east.

In that easy
silent way
coyotes move,
she pushed
into the wind.

I stood there
hardly breathing,
wishing I
could move
that way.

I was surprised
to see her
stop
and turn
and look
at me.

She seemed to think
that I was
just
another
creature
following another
rocky trail.

(That's true, of course.
I am.)

She didn't hurry.
She wasn't afraid.

I saw her eyes
and she saw
mine.

That look
held us
together.

Because of that,
I never will
feel
quite the same
again.

So
on September twenty-eighth
I celebrate
Coyote Day.

Here's what I do:
I walk
the trail
I walked that day,
and I hum
softly
as I go.

Finally,
I unwrap
the feast
I've brought for her.

Last time
it was three apples
and some pumpkin seeds
and an ear of corn
and some big soft homemade
ginger cookies.

The next day,
I happened to pass
that way again.
Coyote tracks
went all around
the rock
where the food had been,
and the food
was gone.

Next year
I'll make it even better.
I'll bring
an extra feast
and eat there too.

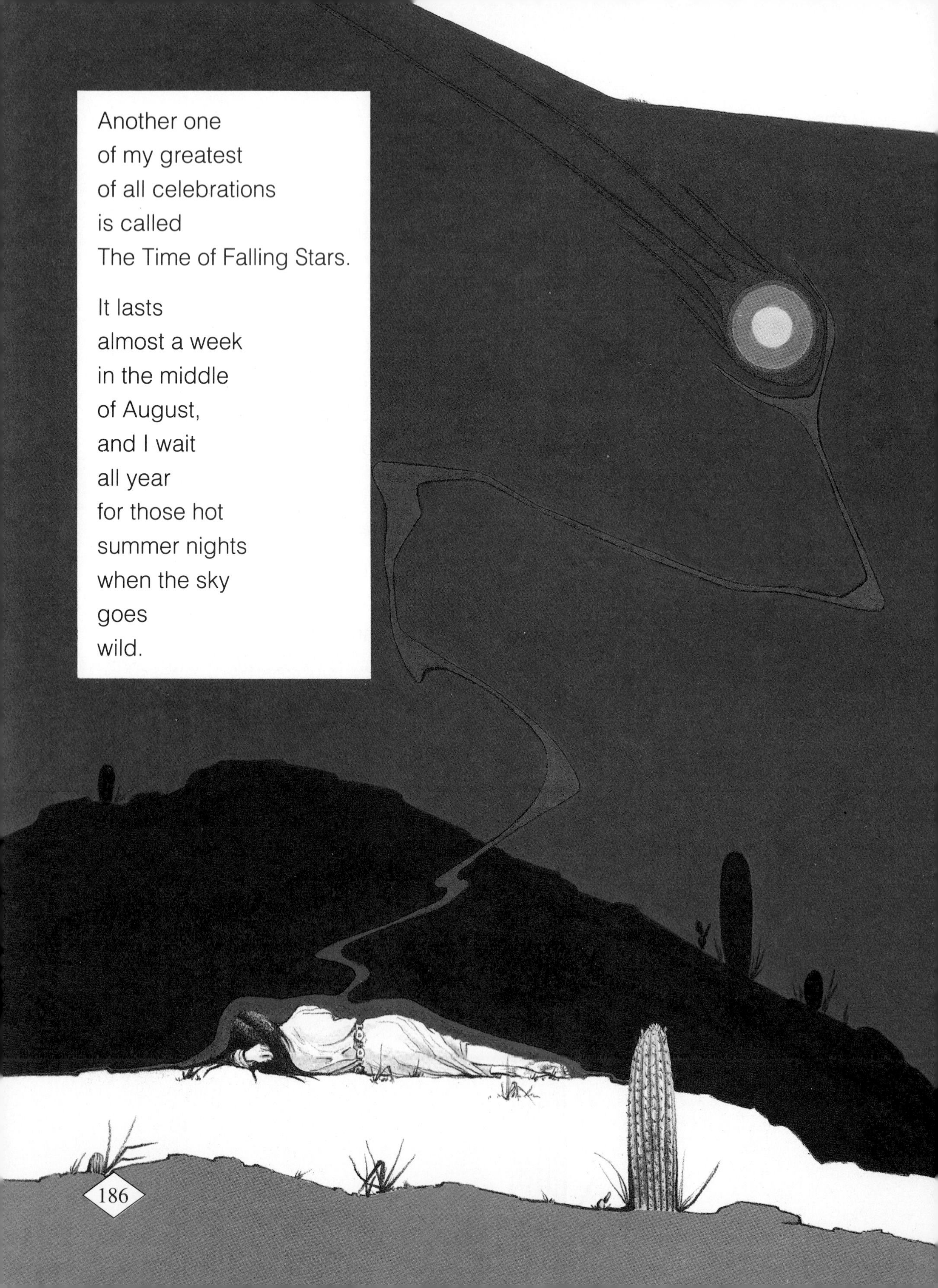

Another one
of my greatest
of all celebrations
is called
The Time of Falling Stars.

It lasts
almost a week
in the middle
of August,
and I wait
all year
for those hot
summer nights
when the sky
goes
wild.

186

You can call them
meteor showers
if you want to.
Me, I like to say
they're
falling stars.

All that week
I sleep outside.

I give
my full attention
to the sky.

And every time
a streak of light
goes
shooting
through the darkness,
I feel my heart
shoot
out of me.

One night
I saw
a fireball
that left
a long
red
blazing
trail
across the sky.

After it was
gone,
I stood there
looking up,
not quite
believing
what I'd seen.

The strange thing was,
I met a man
who told me
he had seen it too
while he was lying
by a campfire
five hundred miles
away.

He said he did not sleep
again
that night.

Suddenly
it seemed
that we two
spoke a language
no one else
could
understand.

Every August
of my life,
I'll think of that.

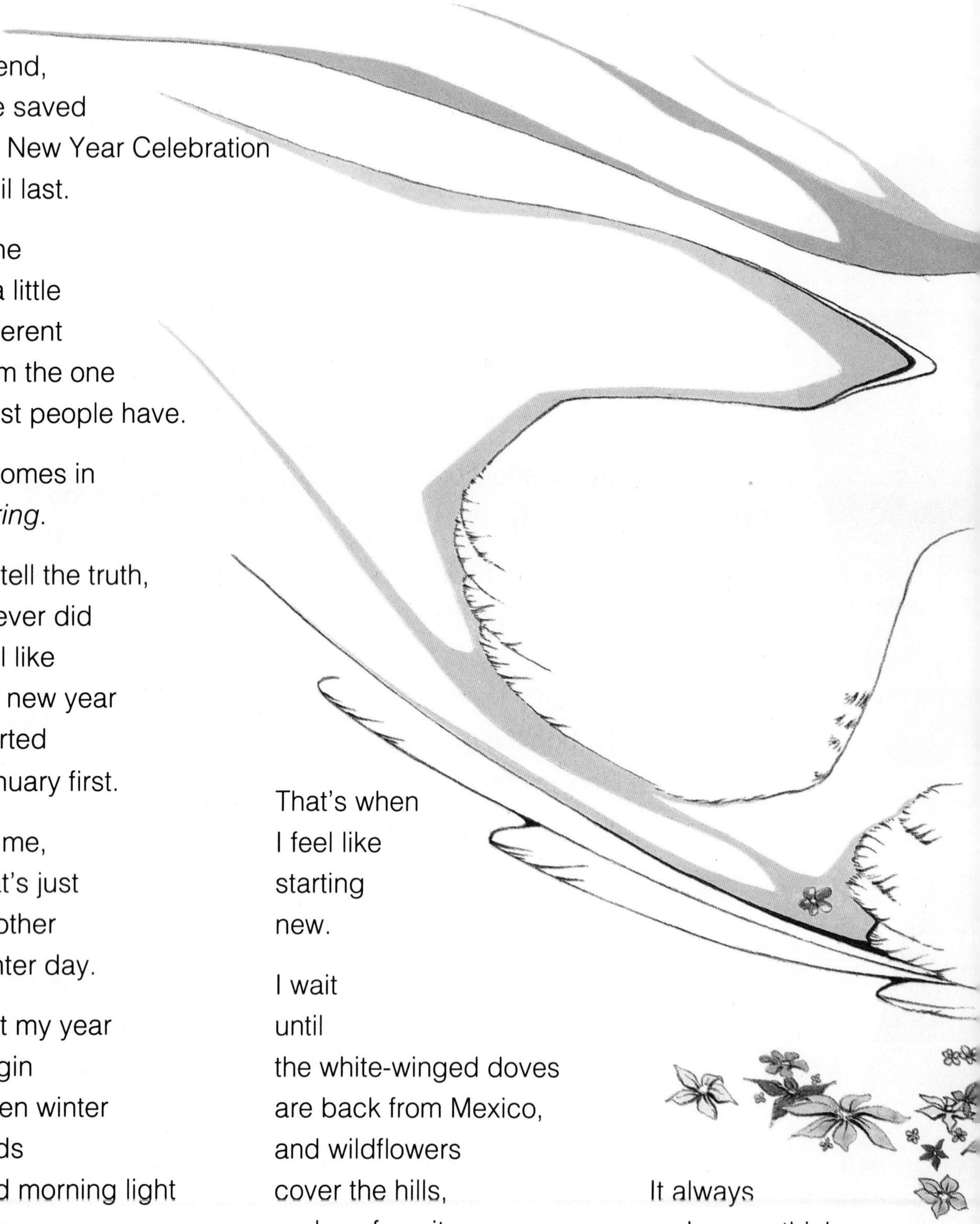

Friend,
I've saved
my New Year Celebration
until last.

Mine
is a little
different
from the one
most people have.

It comes in
spring.

To tell the truth,
I never did
feel like
my new year
started
January first.

To me,
that's just
another
winter day.

I let my year
begin
when winter
ends
and morning light
comes
earlier,
the way it *should.*

That's when
I feel like
starting
new.

I wait
until
the white-winged doves
are back from Mexico,
and wildflowers
cover the hills,
and my favorite
cactus
blooms.

It always
makes me think
I ought to bloom
myself.

188

And
that's when
I start to plan
my New Year
Celebration.

I finally choose
a day
that is
exactly
right.

Even the air
has to be
perfect,
and the dirt
has to feel
good and warm
on bare feet.

(Usually,
it's a Saturday
around the end
of April.)

I have a drum
that I beat
to signal
The Day.

Then I go
wandering off,
following all
of my favorite
trails
to all of the
places
I like.

I check how
everything
is doing.

I spend the day
admiring
things.

If the old desert tortoise
I know from last year
is out
strolling around,
I'll go his direction
awhile.

I celebrate
with horned toads
and ravens
and lizards
and quail. . . .

And, Friend,
it's not
a bad
party.

Walking back home
(kind of humming),
sometimes
I think about
those people
who ask me if
I'm *lonely* here.

I have to
laugh
out
loud.

Reader's Response ～ Copy one of your favorite
verses from this poem. Tell why you chose it.

A New Year's WELCOME

Around the World

Celebrators take bunches of grapes and must eat twelve of them between the first and last toll of the midnight bell. This takes a lot of concentration but promises health and wealth for the New Year.

— from Spain

Many families select long strips of paper for the Kakizome, or "First Writing" of the year. Each person writes a favorite poem or proverb. Well-done Kakizomes hang in a place of honor at home.

— from Japan

During a week of dancing and drumming in every town, the farmers bring in the new yam crop in a big parade, and families taste the harvest. When the yams are in, the New Year has begun.

— from Ghana

The first person to cross the threshold, called the "first footer," foretells the year to come. If the "footer" is tall and dark, the year will be a good one.

— from Scotland

For four days the Seminole Indians celebrate their new corn crop. They eat and play games, and at dusk, everyone dances the Green Corn Dance as a prayer of thanks for the harvest.

— from the Florida Everglades in the USA

This Morning There Were Rainbows in the Sprinklers

This morning
there were rainbows in the sprinklers.
My hollow heels clopped as they wore away the pavement.
Clop, clop, clop.
I sang a worn out folk song
to the steady clop of my heels
wearing out the song
along with my heels
along with the pavement.
I was glad
because I wasn't sleepy anymore
but I yawned
more out of habit than out of sleepiness.
Today it's spring
and the remnants of April crush against my skin
in the wind.
It feels good.
The sky is clear
and I can see last night's quarter moon
like it was etched in the sky with cloud dust.

I time out my song to end
just as I reach my destiny.
I feel like I'm in a movie
a musical
with someone else walking down the street singing too.
I wait to see how the plot ends
because it's my story
and I choose the cast
and I'm directing.

Lorna Dee Cervantes

Green Fun Activities

from *Green Fun*
by Maryanne Gjersvik

So many things that are quick and fun can be done using only leaves, flowers and seeds from the trees and smaller plants growing all around us along sidewalks, in yards, parks and fields. Perhaps you have already learned to make a daisy crown or a milkweed pod boat, or to whistle through a blade of grass, or then again, such tricks may come as a surprise. In any case, I would like to share with you some of the ideas I have collected from my friends and family, from books and from my own memory.

You will have no need for any

tools or equipment. With only patient hands and a little time, you will easily learn of things to make and enjoy in almost any spot made green by grass and leaves. By looking closely at what is growing, you may even begin to discover, on your own, new ways to amuse yourself and interest others that are not even in this book.

To pick a leaf or a flower should not hurt most plants.

You will not be destroying anything if you are careful. That plant will keep on growing more leaves and more flowers and more seeds and giving more pleasure even after you have picked a few here and there. That is the way it should be.

Dandelion Curls

One of the most common of weeds is also one of the first plants to bloom in the spring. Some people think of it as a pest when it invades lawns and gardens. But to others, golden dandelion blossoms look like buttons of pure springtime sun begging to be picked. The name "dandelion" comes from the French, *dent-de-lion*, meaning "lion's tooth."

If you split the flower stems of the dandelion into several strands and dip them in water, the strips will twist into beautiful loops and curls which might turn out to be useful to anyone without curls of his own.

The Dandelion Clock

Dandelion blossoms which are not picked soon change into furry seed-heads. If you blow on one of these heads, the seeds will fly away and float to earth where each seed will have the chance to grow into another plant. If you blow hard enough you may be able to get almost all of the seeds to fly off the head. Some say that you can tell the hour of the day (or how many children you will have) by counting the number of seeds left behind.

A Clover Chain

Long-stemmed white clover can easily become a necklace, or even a long chain. With your fingernail, make a slit in one stem and pull a second stem through the hole. Now slit the second stem and pull a third one through that hole. You can create a chain as long as your patience and your supply of clover. If it is to be a necklace, make a slit in the last stem big enough for the blossom of the first flower to fit through, just as a button fits through a buttonhole.

I understand that children in New Orleans make clover chains that stretch the whole length of a street just for fun.

A Maple Leaf Crown

A summer crown of green maple leaves is something special.

Break the stems off each leaf and save them to use as pins. Put the first two leaves down so that they overlap. Push a single stem pin through the center rib of both.

Keep adding more leaves and pins in the same way until you have a band long enough to reach around the head. When the size is right, connect the first leaf to the last with still another stem pin and your crown is ready to wear.

Flower Faces

Pansies are favorite spring garden plants.

Johnny-jump-ups are their wild cousins whose blossoms are much smaller but still easy to recognize. Both plants seem to have faces in their flowers. Pick a few of different sizes and with different faces, and you will have a whole collection of characters who may remind you of people you know.

197

The Buttercup Test

Some say that you can tell how much anyone likes butter by holding a golden buttercup blossom under a person's chin. If the reflection on his or her chin is a strong yellow, the person is very fond of butter.

Geranium Fingernails

A quick but tricky decoration for fingernails can be made from red geranium petals. Lick the curved-in underside of each petal and quickly stick it on your nail. Do this for as many fingers as you can. I could never decorate all ten fingers because by the time I got about eight petals on, the first would begin to dry and fall off. Perhaps you may do better than I did.

A Cornhusk Doll

The husks around an ear of corn can be turned into a fine figure too. Tear some of the husk leaves into strips for tying the parts together. One of the pieces you have not torn will become the arms. Roll it up and tie a strip around each end. Fold another bigger piece of husk in half over the arms and tie it above and below them to form the head and the waist. You can tuck some corn silk into the fold of the head for hair and tie another piece of husk to the waist for an apron. Or you can divide the bottom of the "skirt" into two bunches and tie each bunch to make legs. A face can be painted on with pokeberry juice, but remember that pokeberries are poisonous to eat.

199

Acorn Finger Puppets

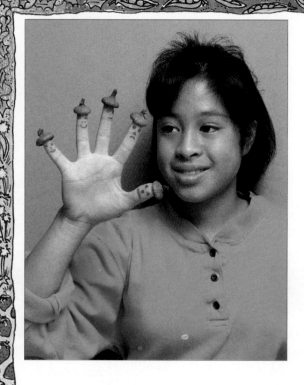

Your fingers themselves will become puppets when you make hats for them with acorn tops. If you want to add eyes and mouths, crushed wild berries, such as pokeberries, will give you the "paint" with which to draw faces, using a soft twig as a brush. American Indians used pokeberry juice to decorate their own faces. They knew, however, that the plant and its berries were poisonous so, like the Indians, never put any part in your mouth.

A Grass Whistle

You can make a very loud whistling squawk using only a wide blade of grass. Hold the grass with two hands between the tips and the base of both thumbs. With your lips against the space just below your thumb knuckles, blow very hard into your hands and onto the blade of grass. Be sure the grass is stretched tightly across the inside of the opening.

Though some people can never make a sound, I have a friend who tells me that her father is able to play the beginning of *My Country 'tis of Thee* on a blade of grass.

Sunflowers

There are many growing things which may be useless to you, though not to birds and animals. The sunflower, for example, is a natural birdfeeder. If you put one of these huge, seed-filled dried flowers where you can watch it, you will be sure to see blue jays and other birds having a feast.

Looking

You don't always have to *do* anything special with growing things. There are many moments when simply looking is most interesting of all. Bees and butterflies are always busy in the flowers. Toadstools and fungi have strange shapes and colors to discover. There is much life to see in the world near the roots of the grass.

Reader's Response ～ Which of the flower activities do you think would be fun or interesting to do?

Library Link ～ *This selection is from the book* Green Fun *by Maryanne Gjersvik. Would you like to know how to make a prickly burr basket decorated with a purple flower tuft? To learn about more things you can do with plants, you should read the entire book.*

The Itchy Three

What grows in most parts of the United States all year round, is filled with a sticky oil, and usually won't bother your pet cat or dog?

a. poison ivy   b. poison oak   c. poison sumac

If you guessed a, b, and c, you are correct. An oil called *urushiol* ($\overline{oo}'$ r$\overline{oo}$ shē ôl$'$) is found inside all three of these "poison" plants that can make your skin red, blistery, and *very* itchy! The oil comes out if the plants get damaged in any way. So if an insect chews a hole in a leaf, or if you tear a plant by brushing it with your leg, or if you break off a stem, it's itch time for you! Should you burn the poison plants? Please, no. Tiny drops of the oil are carried off in the smoke and can cause serious itching if the smoke reaches your eyes or skin or if you breathe it in. So, what can you do about these plants? Enjoy the outdoors and step aside when you see one of the "itchy three."

Poison Sumac

Poison Ivy

Poison Oak

203

THE MOUNTAIN THAT LOVED A BIRD

written by Alice McLerran
illustrated by Eric Carle

There was once a mountain made of bare stone. It stood alone in the middle of a desert plain. No plant grew on its hard slopes, nor could any animal, bird or insect live there.

The sun warmed the mountain and the wind chilled it, but the only touch the mountain knew was the touch of rain or snow. There was nothing more to feel.

All day and all night the mountain looked only at the sky, watching for the movement of the billowing clouds. It knew the path of the sun that crossed the sky by day, and the course of the moon that crossed the sky by night. On clear nights, it watched the slow wheeling of the far-off stars. There was nothing more to see.

But then one day a small bird appeared. She flew in a circle above the mountain, then landed on a ledge to rest and preen her feathers. The mountain felt the dry grasp of her tiny claws on the ledge; it felt the softness of her feathered body as she sheltered herself against its side. The mountain was amazed, for nothing like this had ever come to it from the sky before.

"Who are you?" the mountain asked. "What is your name?"

"I am a bird," replied the other. "My name is Joy, and I come from distant lands, where everything is green. Every spring I fly high into the air, looking for the best place to build my nest and raise my children. As soon as I have rested I must continue my search."

"I have never seen anything like you before," said the mountain. "Must you go on? Couldn't you just stay here?"

Joy shook her head. "Birds are living things," she explained. "We must have food and water. Nothing grows here for me to eat; there are no streams from which I could drink."

"If you cannot stay here, will you come back again some day?" asked the mountain.

Joy thought for a while. "I fly long distances," she said, "and I have rested on many mountains. No other mountain has ever cared whether I came or went, and I should like to return to you. But I could only do so in the spring before I build my nest, and because you are so far from food and water I could only stay a few hours."

"I have never seen anything like you before," repeated the mountain. "Even if it were only for a few hours, it would make me happy to see you again."

"There is one more thing you should know," said Joy. "Mountains last forever, but birds do not. Even if I were to visit you every spring of my life, there might be only a few visits. Birds do not live very many years."

"It will be very sad when your visits stop," said the mountain, "but it would be even sadder if you fly away now and never return."

Joy sat very still, nestled against the side of the mountain. Then she began to sing a gentle, bell-like song, the first music the mountain had ever heard. When she had finished her song, she said, "Because no mountain has ever before cared whether I came or went,

I will make you a promise. Every spring of my life, I will return to greet you, and fly above you, and sing to you. And since my life will not last forever, I will give to one of my daughters my own name, Joy, and tell her how to find you. And she will name a daughter Joy also, and tell her how to find you. Each Joy will have a daughter Joy, so that no matter how many years pass, you will always have a friend to greet you and fly above you and sing to you."

The mountain was both happy and sad. "I still wish you could stay," it said, "but I am glad you will return."

"Now I must go," said Joy, "for it is a long way to the lands that have food and water for me. Goodbye until next year." She soared off, her wings like feathered fans against the sun. The mountain watched her until she disappeared into the distance.

Year after year, when every spring came, a small bird flew to the mountain, singing, "I am Joy, and I have come to greet you." And for a few hours, the bird would fly above the mountain, or nestle against its side, singing. At the end of each visit, the mountain always asked, "Isn't there some way you could stay?" And Joy always answered, "No, but I will return next year."

Each year the mountain looked forward more and more to Joy's visit; each year it grew harder and harder to watch her go. Ninety-nine springs came and went in this way. On the hundredth spring, when it was time for Joy to leave, the mountain asked once more, "Isn't there some way you could stay?" Joy answered, as she always did, "No, but I will return next year." The mountain watched as she disappeared into the sky, and suddenly its heart broke. The hard stone cracked, and from the deepest part of the mountain tears gushed forth and rolled down the mountainside in a stream.

The next spring a small bird appeared, singing, "I am Joy, and I have come to greet you." This time the mountain did not reply. It only wept, thinking of how soon she would have to leave, and of all the long months before she would come again. Joy rested on her ledge, and looked at the stream of tears. Then she flew above the mountain, and sang as she always had. When it was time for her to go, the mountain still wept. "I will return next year," said Joy softly, and she flew away.

When the next spring came, Joy returned, carrying in her beak a small seed. The mountain still wept a stream of tears. Joy carefully tucked the seed into a crack in the hard stone, close to the stream so that it would stay moist. Then she flew above the mountain, and sang to it. Seeing that the mountain was still unable to speak, she flew away once more.

During the weeks that followed, the seed in the crack of the rock began to send down tiny roots. The roots reached into the hard stone, little by little spreading into yet smaller cracks, breaking through the hardness. As the roots found water in the cracks, and drew food from the softening stone, a shoot rose from the seed into the sunlight and unfolded tiny green leaves. The mountain, however, was still deep in sorrow, blind with tears. It did not notice a plant so small.

The next spring Joy brought another seed, and the spring after that another. She placed each one in a protected place near the stream of tears, and sang to the mountain. The mountain still only wept.

Years passed in this way, the roots of new plants softening the stone near the stream of tears. As softened stone turned to soil, moss began to grow in sheltered corners. Grasses and little flowering plants sprouted in hollows near the stream. Tiny insects, carried to the mountain by the winds, scurried among the leaves.

Meanwhile, the roots of the very first seed went deeper and deeper into the heart of the mountain. Above the ground, what had started as a tiny shoot was growing into the trunk of a young tree, its branches holding green leaves out to the sun. At last, the mountain felt the roots reaching down like gentle fingers, filling and healing the cracks in its heart. Sorrow faded away, and the mountain began to notice the changes that had been taking place. Seeing and feeling so many wonderful new things, the mountain's tears changed to tears of happiness.

Each year Joy returned, bringing another seed. Each year, more streams ran laughing down the mountain's sides, and the ground watered by the new streams grew green with trees and other plants.

Now that the mountain no longer wept with sorrow, it began to ask once more, "Isn't there some way you could stay?" But Joy still answered, "No, but I will return next year."

More years passed, and the streams carried life far out into the plain surrounding the mountain, until finally, as far as the mountain could see, everything was green. From lands beyond the plain, small animals began to come to the mountain. Watching these living things find food and shelter on its slopes, the mountain suddenly felt a surge of hope. Opening its deepest heart to the roots of the trees, it offered them all its strength. The trees stretched their branches yet higher toward the sky, and hope ran like a song from the heart of the mountain into every tree leaf.

And sure enough, when the next spring came, Joy flew to the mountain carrying not a seed, but a slender twig. Straight to the tallest tree on the mountain she flew, to the tree that had grown from the very first seed. She placed the twig on the branch in which she would build her nest. "I am Joy," she sang, "and I have come to stay."

Reader's Response ∽ If you had been Joy, what would you have said to the mountain?

THE SWALLOWS OF SPRING

Many years ago, a missionary named Father Junipero Serra established a mission on the California coast and called it San Juan Capistrano. A large stone church was built, but it was destroyed by an earthquake just six years after its completion.

People began to notice that on about the same day each year, thousands of swallows arrive to nest in the ruins of the church. And each year around October 23, the swallows leave to fly south for the winter.

People say that only rarely have the swallows missed their deadline— when storms delayed their arrival.

Father Junipero's mission has been re-created and today people from all over the country gather on March 19 to wait for the swallows— and spring—to return to Capistrano.

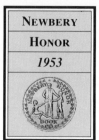

ESCAPE

from Charlotte's Web
written by E. B. White
illustrated by Garth Williams

*The Arable family was pleased when a new litter of
pigs was born; however, one of the piglets was very small.
Fern Arable pleaded with her father to give her the tiny pig
for a pet. He agreed. She named the pig Wilbur. As Wilbur
got bigger, he became more expensive to feed, so Mr.
Arable sold him to Fern's aunt and uncle. Wilbur then
moved to their farm.*

The barn was very large. It was very old. It smelled of
hay and it smelled of manure. It smelled of the perspiration
of tired horses and the wonderful sweet breath of patient
cows. It often had a sort of peaceful smell—as though
nothing bad could happen ever again in the world. It
smelled of grain and of harness dressing and of axle grease
and of rubber boots and of new rope. And whenever the cat
was given a fish head to eat, the barn would smell of fish.
But mostly it smelled of hay, for there was always hay in
the great loft up overhead. And there was always hay being
pitched down to the cows and the horses and the sheep.

The barn was pleasantly warm in winter when the animals spent most of their time indoors, and it was pleasantly
cool in summer when the big doors stood wide open to the
breeze. The barn had stalls on the main floor for the work
horses, tie-ups on the main floor for the cows, a sheepfold
down below for the sheep, a pigpen down below for
Wilbur, and it was full of all sorts of things that you find in
barns: ladders, grindstones, pitch forks, monkey wrenches,
scythes, lawn mowers, snow shovels, ax handles, milk
pails, water buckets, empty grain sacks, and rusty rat traps.

It was the kind of barn that swallows like to build their nests in. It was the kind of barn that children like to play in. And the whole thing was owned by Fern's uncle, Mr. Homer L. Zuckerman.

Wilbur's new home was in the lower part of the barn, directly underneath the cows. Mr. Zuckerman knew that a manure pile is a good place to keep a young pig. Pigs need warmth, and it was warm and comfortable down there in the barn cellar on the south side.

Fern came almost every day to visit him. She found an old milking stool that had been discarded, and she placed the stool in the sheepfold next to Wilbur's pen. Here she sat quietly during the long afternoons, thinking and listening and watching Wilbur. The sheep soon got to know her and trust her. So did the geese, who lived with the sheep. All the animals trusted her, she was so quiet and friendly. Mr. Zuckerman did not allow her to take Wilbur out, and he did not allow her to get into the pigpen. But he told Fern that she could sit on the stool and watch Wilbur as long as she wanted to. It made her happy just to be near the pig, and it made Wilbur happy to know that she was sitting there, right outside his pen. But he never had any fun—no walks, no rides, no swims.

One afternoon in June, when Wilbur was almost two months old, he wandered out into his small yard outside the barn. Fern had not arrived for her usual visit. Wilbur stood in the sun feeling lonely and bored.

"There's never anything to do around here," he thought. He walked slowly to his food trough and sniffed to see if anything had been overlooked at lunch. He found a small strip of potato skin and ate it. His back itched, so he leaned against the fence and rubbed against the boards.

When he tired of this, he walked indoors, climbed to the top of the manure pile, and sat down. He didn't feel like going to sleep, he didn't feel like digging, he was tired of standing still, tired of lying down. "I'm less than two months old and I'm tired of living," he said. He walked out to the yard again.

"When I'm out here," he said, "there's no place to go but in. When I'm indoors, there's no place to go but out in the yard."

"That's where you're wrong, my friend, my friend," said a voice.

Wilbur looked through the fence and saw the goose standing there.

"You don't have to stay in that dirty-little dirty-little dirty-little yard," said the goose, who talked rather fast. "One of the boards is loose. Push on it, push-push-push on it, and come on out!"

"What?" said Wilbur. "Say it slower!"

"At-at-at, at the risk of repeating myself," said the goose, "I suggest that you come on out. It's wonderful out here."

"Did you say a board was loose?"

"That I did, that I did," said the goose.

Wilbur walked up to the fence and saw that the goose was right—one board was loose. He put his head down, shut his eyes, and pushed. The board gave way. In a minute he had squeezed through the fence and was standing in the long grass outside his yard. The goose chuckled.

"How does it feel to be free?" she asked.

"I like it," said Wilbur. "That is, I *guess* I like it." Actually, Wilbur felt queer to be outside his fence, with nothing between him and the big world.

"Where do you think I'd better go?"

"Anywhere you like, anywhere you like," said the goose. "Go down through the orchard, root up the sod! Go down through the garden, dig up the radishes! Root up everything! Eat grass! Look for corn! Look for oats! Run all over! Skip and dance, jump and prance! Go down through the orchard and stroll in the woods! The world is a wonderful place when you're young.''

''I can see that,'' replied Wilbur. He gave a jump in the air, twirled, ran a few steps, stopped, looked all around, sniffed the smells of afternoon, and then set off walking down through the orchard. Pausing in the shade of an apple tree, he put his strong snout into the ground and began pushing, digging, and rooting. He felt very happy.

He had plowed up quite a piece of ground before anyone noticed him. Mrs. Zuckerman was the first to see him. She saw him from the kitchen window, and she immediately shouted for the men.

"Ho-*mer*!" she cried. "Pig's out! Lurvy! Pig's out! Homer! Lurvy! Pig's out. He's down there under that apple tree."

"Now the trouble starts," thought Wilbur. "Now I'll catch it."

The goose heard the racket and she, too, started hollering. "Run-run-run downhill, make for the woods, the woods!" she shouted to Wilbur. "They'll never-never-never catch you in the woods."

The cocker spaniel heard the commotion and he ran out from the barn to join the chase. Mr. Zuckerman heard, and he came out of the machine shed where he was mending a tool. Lurvy, the hired man, heard the noise and came up from the asparagus patch where he was pulling weeds. Everybody walked toward Wilbur and Wilbur didn't know what to do. The woods seemed a long way off, and anyway, he had never been down there in the woods and wasn't sure he would like it.

"Get around behind him, Lurvy," said Mr. Zuckerman, "and drive him toward the barn! And take it easy—don't rush him! I'll go and get a bucket of slops."

The news of Wilbur's escape spread rapidly among the animals on the place. Whenever any creature broke loose on Zuckerman's farm, the event was of great interest to the others. The goose shouted to the nearest cow that Wilbur was free, and soon all the cows knew. Then one of the cows told one of the sheep, and soon all the sheep knew.

The lambs learned about it from their mothers. The horses, in their stalls in the barn, pricked up their ears when they heard the goose hollering; and soon the horses had caught on to what was happening. "Wilbur's out," they said. Every animal stirred and lifted its head and became excited to know that one of his friends had got free and was no longer penned up or tied fast.

Wilbur didn't know what to do or which way to run. It seemed as though everybody was after him. "If this is what it's like to be free," he thought, "I believe I'd rather be penned up in my own yard."

The cocker spaniel was sneaking up on him from one side, Lurvy the hired man was sneaking up on him from the other side. Mrs. Zuckerman stood ready to head him off if he started for the garden, and now Mr. Zuckerman was coming down toward him carrying a pail. "This is really awful," thought Wilbur. "Why doesn't Fern come?" He began to cry.

The goose took command and began to give orders.

"Don't just stand there, Wilbur! Dodge about, dodge about!" cried the goose. "Skip around, run toward me, slip in and out, in and out, in and out! Make for the woods! Twist and turn!"

The cocker spaniel sprang for Wilbur's hind leg. Wilbur jumped and ran. Lurvy reached out and grabbed. Mrs. Zuckerman screamed at Lurvy. The goose cheered for Wilbur. Wilbur dodged between Lurvy's legs. Lurvy missed Wilbur and grabbed the spaniel instead. "Nicely done, nicely done!" cried the goose. "Try it again, try it again!"

"Run downhill!" suggested the cows.

"Run toward me!" yelled the gander.

"Run uphill!" cried the sheep.

"Turn and twist!" honked the goose.

"Jump and dance!" said the rooster.

"Look out for Lurvy!" called the cows.

"Look out for Zuckerman!" yelled the gander.

"Watch out for the dog!" cried the sheep.

"Listen to me, listen to me!" screamed the goose.

Poor Wilbur was dazed and frightened by this hullaba-loo. He didn't like being the center of all this fuss. He tried to follow the instructions his friends were giving him, but he couldn't run downhill and uphill at the same time, and he couldn't turn and twist when he was jumping and dancing, and he was crying so hard he could barely see anything that was happening. After all, Wilbur was a very young pig—not much more than a baby, really. He wished Fern were there to take him in her arms and comfort him. When he looked up and saw Mr. Zuckerman standing quite close to him, holding a pail of warm slops, he felt relieved. He lifted his nose and sniffed. The smell was delicious— warm milk, potato skins, wheat middlings, Kellogg's Corn Flakes, and a popover left from the Zuckermans' breakfast.

"Come, pig!" said Mr. Zuckerman, tapping the pail. "Come pig!"

Wilbur took a step toward the pail.

"No-no-no!" said the goose. "It's the old pail trick, Wilbur. Don't fall for it, don't fall for it! He's trying to lure you back into captivity-ivity. He's appealing to your stomach."

Wilbur didn't care. The food smelled appetizing. He took another step toward the pail.

"Pig, pig!" said Mr. Zuckerman in a kind voice, and began walking slowly toward the barnyard, looking all about him innocently, as if he didn't know that a little white pig was following along behind him.

"You'll be sorry-sorry-sorry," called the goose.

Wilbur didn't care. He kept walking toward the pail of slops.

"You'll miss your freedom," honked the goose. "An hour of freedom is worth a barrel of slops."

Wilbur didn't care.

When Mr. Zuckerman reached the pigpen, he climbed over the fence and poured the slops into the trough. Then he pulled the loose board away from the fence, so that there was a wide hole for Wilbur to walk through.

"Reconsider, reconsider!" cried the goose.

Wilbur paid no attention. He stepped through the fence into his yard. He walked to the trough and took a long drink of slops, sucking in the milk hungrily and chewing the popover. It was good to be home again.

While Wilbur ate, Lurvy fetched a hammer and some 8-penny nails and nailed the board in place. Then he and Mr. Zuckerman leaned lazily on the fence and Mr. Zuckerman scratched Wilbur's back with a stick.

"He's quite a pig," said Lurvy.

"Yes, he'll make a good pig," said Mr. Zuckerman.

Wilbur heard the words of praise. He felt the warm milk inside his stomach. He felt the pleasant rubbing of the stick along his itchy back. He felt peaceful and happy and sleepy. This had been a tiring afternoon. It was still only about four o'clock but Wilbur was ready for bed.

"I'm really too young to go out into the world alone," he thought as he lay down.

Reader's Response ∾ After Wilbur escaped, he had to decide whether he wanted to be free or go back to his pen. Do you agree with Wilbur's decision to go back home? Why or why not?

Library Link ∾ *This story is an excerpt from the book* Charlotte's Web *by E. B. White. If you would like to follow Wilbur and his friends on other adventures, you should read the entire book.*

WORDS WORDS WORDS

WORDS CAN MOVE US TO LAUGHTER OR TEARS.
WHICH WORDS HAVE DONE THIS
TO YOU?

226

Unit 3 Theme

DECOR FOR THE FAIR, SCENES I AND IV, *1947, painting by Alexandre Benois, Russian, 1870–1960. Petrouchka, Art Resource, New York.*

Theme Books for

Words, Words, Words

Have you noticed that words surround you every minute? Words can open your eyes to amazing people, exciting places, and unusual ideas.

❖   What was it like to be a child actor before the days of movies and television? In *An Actor's Life for Me!* Lillian Gish shares the excitement and joy of her childhood days in the theater.

LILLIAN GISH
An Actor's Life for Me!
AS TOLD TO SELMA G. LANES
ILLUSTRATIONS BY PATRICIA HENDERSON LINCOLN

Wind in the Long Grass
A collection of Haiku
EDITED BY WILLIAM J. HIGGINSON
ILLUSTRATED BY Sandra Speidel

❖   What is magic and has seventeen syllables? Haiku! These tiny poems let you see, hear, smell, taste, or feel something special. In *Wind in the Long Grass* you will feast on haiku written by people from around the world.

❖ Mark Twain's life was packed with excitement. When you read *Mark Twain? What Kind of Name Is That?* by Robert Quackenbush, you'll learn how his adventures as a riverboat pilot, gold miner, and frontier reporter inspired him to write books and articles.

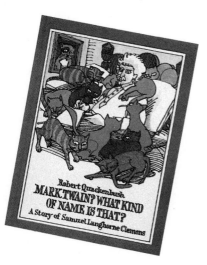

❖ Discover how powerful words can be in *A Taste of Blackberries* by Doris Buchanan Smith. Jamie is full of fun until an accident changes everything. Jamie's best friend tells how he struggles to find the words that can express his feelings.

More Books to Enjoy

Koko's Kitten by Francine Patterson
Murfles and Wink-a-Peeps: Funny Old Words for Kids
    by Susan Kelz Sperling
Handtalk: An ABC of Finger Spelling and Sign Language
    by Remy Charlip and Mary Beth Miller
Unriddling by Alvin Schwartz

The Mysterious ZETABET

written by Scott Corbett

illustrated by Jon McIntosh

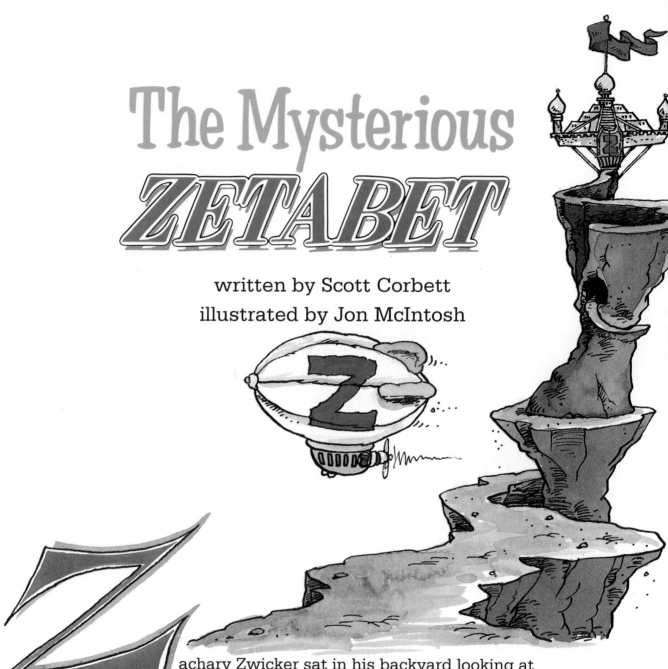

Zachary Zwicker sat in his backyard looking at his homework. It was a long list of words he was supposed to put into alphabetical order.

"The alphabet bores me!" said Zack.

The truth was, a lot of ordinary homework bored him. He liked to learn things, but in his own way. He liked to read books full of strange facts. He even liked to prowl through a big dictionary, looking for unusual words. He especially liked words that began with Z. With a name like his, this was not surprising.

"Besides, I'm hungry!" he complained to himself. But his mother had said he could not have anything to eat until he finished his homework.

Sighing, Zack leaned back against a tree, closed his eyes, and thought about his name and his initials. Z.Z. What wonderful initials for anyone to have. Z.Z. . . . Z-z-z-z . . .

Zack felt himself drifting into space. It seemed to him he was rocking, sort of jerkily, and soon he saw that he was in a cage being carried along a crooked road by four hooded figures. The road twisted back and forth so sharply that he was jolted from side to side against the bars.

Before he had time to do more than feel scared, a tall man in a gaudy uniform came galloping up on an odd-looking animal. He looked down and twisted his large mustache.

"Zounds! You must be the boy our secret police rescued from that terrible place whose name begins with an A!"

Zack supposed he meant "America," but was too frightened to ask.

"I am the X-zalted ruler of this nation, Zyzmund the Zeventh! What is your name?"

"Z-Zachary Z-Zwicker," stammered Zack.

"Zzachary Zzwicker? Four Z's!" said Zyzmund, misunderstanding Zack's pronunciation. "With a name like that you should go far here. Put him down, put him down! Step out!"

When Zack stepped out of the cage he staggered sideways.

"The road twisted so much it made me dizzy," he explained.

"All our roads are zigzag roads. We prefer them that way. Welcome to Zyxland!"

"Where?"

"Zyxland. You are now in the land of the zetabet."

"The what, sir?"

"The zetabet. You haven't learned your ZYX's as yet, but you will, you will. Right now you only know how to say the zetabet backwards, but soon you will learn to recite it properly—

z-y-x-w-v-u-t-s-r-q-p-o-n-m-l-k-j-i-h-g-f-e-d-c-b-a—
every bit as fast as I just said it myself."

Zyzmund leaped down from his steed.

"You will notice I am riding our national animal,
the zebra."

Zack stared. He had studied enough about animals
to know that zebras can never be tamed and ridden.
Zyzmund's "zebra" looked like a horse with black and
white stripes painted on it.

"Are you sure it's a real zebra, sir?" Zack asked.
"I think you got cheated."

"Silence! When I say it's a zebra, it's a zebra!"

"Yes, sir," said Zack, but he still thought it looked
like a horse with a bad paint job.

"Be careful, young Zzwicker," said Zyzmund
sternly. "One of two fates awaits you here in Zyxland.
You will be asked certain questions, and if you
answer them correctly you may choose to become a
Z-Number-One Zyxlander and share our zealous life.
If you fail, you will become our prisoner and we will
turn you into a zombie, like those creatures who were
carrying your cage!"

Zack trembled as the four creatures threw back
their hoods and stared at him with horrible blank eyes
that looked like zeroes.

"Of course, if you succeed, you may also choose
to return to the place where we found you—*providing*
you first do something so impossible that I won't even
waste my time mentioning it," Zyzmund added with a
complacent laugh. "Now listen closely to our rules."

"Yes, sir!"

"It is permissible for ordinary words to begin with the unimportant last letters of the zetabet—l, k, j, i, h, g, f, e, d, c, b, and even a—but important names must begin with important letters. Above all, no A-names are tolerated here. They are forbidden! Do you understand?"

"Yes, sir!"

"Then go. From now on you will travel this road alone—and woe betide you if you answer even one question incorrectly! As soon as I have reviewed a troop of our national soldiers, the Zouaves, I shall fly on ahead and be waiting to meet you—if you are successful, that is—at my palace, the famous Zenith Ziggurat."

"A ziggurat, sir? Isn't that one of those buildings shaped like a pyramid, only with zigzag sides?"

"X-*zack*-ly!" cried Zyzmund, obviously pleased with Zack's description. "Yes, our ziggurats are very much like the ones they used to build in ancient Vabylon."

"Vabylon? Don't you mean Bab—"

"Take care how you babble on!" warned Zyzmund, his eyes flashing. "Mistakes like that can be fatal!"

"I'm sorry! From now on I'll be careful."

"You had better be, young Zzwicker! You had better be. Now go!"

Zigging left, zagging right, zigging left, zagging right, up the road went a nervous Zachary Zwicker. What were the questions he would have to answer? And if he answered them all correctly, what was the impossible thing he would have to do to get away from Zyxland and go home? So far, at least, he did not think he wanted to become a Zyxlander—and certainly not a zombie!

The first place he came to along the road was a shop with flowers in the window and a sign that said,

"What a silly way to spell flower!" he thought. But then he remembered that "f" was at the wrong end of the zetabet.

A man came out of the shop and held up his hand.

"Stop! Before you pass my shop you must tell me the name of our national phlower."

Zack's mind went blank. For a moment he was too nervous to think. But then he made himself concentrate on all the Z-words he had looked up in the dictionary, and one of them came to his rescue.

"I know!" he said. "The zinnia."

"Pass!" said the florist, and Zack zigzagged on ahead.

Soon he came to a shop with rings and bracelets and precious gems in the window and a sign that said,

Even before a woman came outside Zack knew what she was going to ask him.

"Stop! Before you pass my shop you must tell me the name of our national yewel."

A jewel? Which one was it?

"I know!" he said. "The zircon."

"Pass!"

So far he was all right, but could he keep it up? Could he keep on remembering those Z-words? He dreaded the sight of more shops, and his heart sank

when he saw another one ahead of him. It had large maps displayed in the window and a sign that said,

He felt more nervous than ever. Geography was not one of his best subjects. But no one came outside. Zack hoped he could sneak by without being noticed. He was tiptoeing past the shop door when it flew open.

"Stop!"

An important-looking man came out and stood in front of Zack with his arms folded. Zack felt his legs turn to rubber.

"Before you pass my shop you must answer three questions."

"Y-yes, sir." A three-part question! He would never be able to handle that!

"I am Zog the Yeographer, and here is my first question. What are the three Yafrican nations we like best?"

Zack brightened up. One thing he was interested in was Africa.

"I know!" he said. "Zaire, Zambia, and Zanzibar!"

"Right! But now, for the second part, you must tell me the name of Zambia's great river."

"The Zambezi."

"Splendid! You couldn't have done better if you were a Zulu! You must have gotten straight Z's in yeography in school. But now for the third part, and be careful. What are the two greatest rivers in the world?"

Seeing Zog's cunning expression Zack knew he was in dangerous territory now—and he couldn't see his way out. He knew the real answer, all right, but if he gave it he would surely be sent straight to the zombies!

"Well, there's the Mississippi. . . ," he began, stalling for time.

"Yes, yes, but what about the other one?"

Suddenly Zack had it.

"The Yamazon!"

"Pass!"

At that moment they heard the rumble of a motor overhead. They looked up and saw a huge airship.

"There goes Zyzmund the Zeventh zooming back to the Zenith Ziggurat in his zeppelin," said Zog.

"Zowie! I've never seen a zeppelin before," said Zack. "Do you have any other kind of—er—"

He couldn't think of a safe word, so he stopped.

This time Zog helped him out.

"No, you'll never see a nairplane here," he said, "only zeppelins."

Zigzagging on, Zack passed a temple dedicated to Zeus and another temple dedicated to Zoroaster, but fortunately nobody came out to ask him any questions.

Unfortunately, however, this gave him time to realize how hungry he had become. He was famished!

"What's the point of trying to get to the Zenith Ziggurat if I starve to death first?" he said to himself. "I've got to find something to eat!"

So far he had not seen any restaurants—and even if he came to one how could he buy something to eat without any money?

Just as he was thinking about this, along came a fat man wearing a costly-looking coat with a fur collar and carrying a large leather purse.

"Stop!" he said. "Before you pass me you must answer two questions."

He opened the purse and took out a large coin.

"I'll give you a hint," he said, winking. "We use the same name for our money that they use in Poland. Now tell me the name of our national coin."

That was all Zack needed.

"I know!" he said. "It's a zloty."

"Right! And what kind of metal is it made of?"

"Zinc."

"Pass! And just for that you may have the coin, because I'm a very rich man. I'm a zillionaire, I have zillions of zinc zlotys."

"Thank you! Can I buy some food with this?"

"Zertainly! There's a place just a little farther
along."

Zack hurried on, hoping that each zig or zag he
traveled would bring a hot dog stand into sight. But
instead, the next place he came to was a shop with a
sign that said,

"Another shop!" groaned Zack. Just as he feared,
a man came hurrying out to stop him. He was an old
man dressed in a long flowing robe, and he was
carrying a scroll under his arm.

"Stop!"

Zack was too hungry to want to answer any more questions.

"Oh, all right, but please hurry! I'm on my way to get something to eat, and I can't wait much longer."

"Don't be impertinent! You are speaking to a very important person!"

"Oh. Well, who are you?"

"I am Zebulon the Yastrologer, and it is I who first proved the zetabet is supreme! Do you know how I did it? By the sun and the moon and the planets themselves! Their noble names prove we are right, since all of them come from the first part of the zetabet."

"What? How can that be?"

Zack had heard some crazy things, but this was the craziest yet. These Zyxlanders were not playing fair! It made him mad.

"That's impossible!" he cried. "I know all the planets, and some of them are in the wrong part of the alpha—of the zetabet!"

"They are not!" Zebulon unrolled the scroll. "Here they are, in reverse zetabetical order, all but the last one."

Zack stared at the list:

MARS	SATURN
MERCURY	URANUS
NEPTUNE	URTH
PLUTO	VENUS

"Urth?" said Zack.

Zebulon glared at him.

"Surely you know the name of your own planet!"

"Oh! Oh—er—sure!" said Zack.

"Well, I should hope so! Now, then. One planet is missing. You must tell me the name of that planet— the greatest of them all!"

By now Zack had caught on to some of the Zyxlanders' tricks. He was ready for Zebulon this time.

"Yupiter!"

"Pass!"

Zack walked on along the zigzag road, and by now he felt almost faint. He had never been so hungry in all his life.

Then, just as he was turning the corner from a zig to a zag, he saw a huge wall ahead of him, with a great pair of gates in it.

And behind the wall he could see the Zenith Ziggurat, towering up into the clouds. He was almost there!

In front of the wall stood a shop with a sign that said,

It looked even better to Zack than the Zenith Ziggurat!

"Hooray!" he said, and started to run. But he had not run three steps before a merry figure wearing a cap and bells and a zoot suit leaped out from behind a yew tree and sprang into the road in front of him.

"Stop! I am Zany Zephyr, Zyzmund the Zeventh's Royal Yester!"

"I'm pleased to meet you," said Zack. "Why don't you come with me and tell me some jo——some yokes while I'm eating?"

"No! Before you pass me you must answer a question and guess a riddle. First, the question!"

Zany was carrying a large, flat, stringed instrument. He held it up.

"This is our national musical instrument. What is it called?"

Hunger seemed to have sharpened Zack's wits. This time he hardly hesitated.

"I know!" he said. "It's a zither."

"Zumbuddy must have told you!"

"Never mind that, just let me go get something to eat."

"No! First I'm going to zap you with a zinger. Here is my riddle. What has hundreds of teeth and runs up and down all day until it gets caught?"

"A zipper!"

"Pass!" groaned Zany.

The man behind the counter at the znack ztand held up his hand.

"Stop! I am Ziggie, and before you pass my ztand you have to eat my food and pay for it!"

"That's just what I want to do," said Zack, "and I have a zloty to pay with."

"Good. In that case, you may have a bowl of our delicious national food."

Zack stared with horror at the bowl of stewed squash Ziggie set before him.

"Is that what I think it is?" asked Zack.

"What do you think it is?"

"Zucchini!"

"Right!"

"But I can't stand the stuff!"

"What? How dare you say such a thing! It's all we ever eat here in Zyxland, except for an occasional side order of zwieback zandwiches!"

"Zwieback? That dry toast stuff? Why, a sandwich made with that junk would bust into a thousand pieces!"

Ziggie banged his fist on the counter.

"Quiet! You *will* eat zucchini and zwieback, and you will eat them with zest and zeal!"

Now the Zyxlanders had gone too far! Zack was so furious he stamped his feet and banged on the counter with *both* fists.

"I came all this way and answered everyone's silly questions and now I'm starving to death and I don't want a bowl of slop—I want a *hot dog*!"

A thunderous sound behind him made Zack whirl around.

The great gates in front of the Zenith Ziggurat were swinging open.

Ziggie sneered.

"Now we'll see about who's going to eat what," he said confidently. "You just wait!"

Zyzmund the Zeventh came rushing out, followed by a squad of Zouaves.

"Zzachary Zzwicker, eat your zucchini!" he roared.

Zack was too angry to be careful anymore.

"Nothing doing! I *hate* zucchini, and I hate Zyxland! All you do is twist everything around to fit your crazy ideas!" he cried. "I want to go home to America!"

Zyzmund reeled back and howled with rage.

"Now you have committed the unforgivable sin! In my sacred presence you have deliberately used a Forbidden Name—an A-name!"

"I don't care! I want to go back to Auburn—"

"*Another* A-name! Zouaves! Take him away to the zombies! Or better yet, put him back in his cage and take him to the Zoo!"

"No! I answered all your questions right, so I can either be a Zyxlander or go home—and I want to go home!"

"Go home? Don't be ridiculous! To leave Zyxland

you would have to do something so impossible that—"

"What is it? I'll do it!"

Zyzmund chuckled slyly and twisted his large mustache.

"Now we've got you! You must ask a question about the zetabet that we can't answer! And you have one minute to think of your question! Zouaves! Get ready!"

Zack turned pale. What could he possibly ask them about the zetabet that they wouldn't know? Why, the way Zyzmund had rattled it off, it was—

Zack snapped his fingers.

"I've got it!" he cried. "I've got my question!"

Everybody laughed.

"Very well, let us hear it," said Zyzmund, glancing around and winking at his subjects.

"Here it is. Can you quickly recite the zetabet—"

"Why, of course!"

"*Backwards?*"

Now it was Zyzmund who turned pale.

"Er—backwards?"

"Backwards!"

"Oh. Well ... of course I can!" he blustered.

"Then do it!"

Zyzmund cleared his throat. "A-b-c-d-f—No, that's wrong! A-b-c-e-f-g—"

"No, no, sire!" Zany Zephyr came running up the road. "It's a-b-c-d-e-f-h-g—"

"Wrong again!" said Zack. "Well, I'll be going."

"No, wait!" shouted Zyzmund. "A-b-c-d-e-f-g-h-i-m-l—Oh, drat!"

Zack's eyes popped open. Much to his surprise he was back home in his own yard, and very glad to be there—on Appleton Avenue in Auburn, Alabama!

Reader's Response ∽ Would you like to go to Zyxland? Tell what you would like to see and what you would avoid.

All About

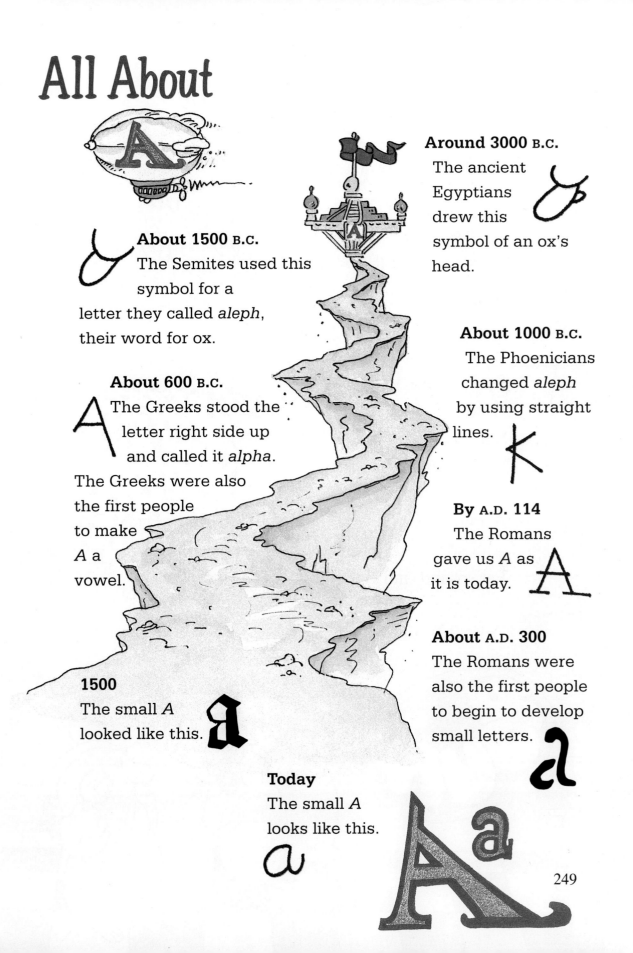

Around 3000 B.C.
The ancient Egyptians drew this symbol of an ox's head.

About 1500 B.C.
The Semites used this symbol for a letter they called *aleph*, their word for ox.

About 1000 B.C.
The Phoenicians changed *aleph* by using straight lines.

About 600 B.C.
The Greeks stood the letter right side up and called it *alpha*. The Greeks were also the first people to make *A* a vowel.

By A.D. 114
The Romans gave us *A* as it is today.

About A.D. 300
The Romans were also the first people to begin to develop small letters.

1500
The small *A* looked like this.

Today
The small *A* looks like this.

249

FEELINGS ABOUT WORDS

Some words clink
As ice in drink.
Some move with grace
A dance, a lace.
Some sound thin:
Wail, scream and pin.
Some words are squat:
A mug, a pot,
And some are plump,
Fat, round and dump.
Some words are light:
Drift, lift and bright.

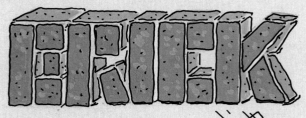

A few are small:
A, is and all.
And some are thick,
Glue, paste and brick.
Some words are sad:
"I never had. . . ."
And others gay:
Joy, spin and play.
Some words are sick:
Stab, scratch and nick.

HAZY preen QUEEN

Some words are hot:
Fire, flame and shot.
Some words are sharp,
Sword, point and carp.
And some alert:
Glint, glance and flirt.
Some words are lazy:
Saunter, hazy.
And some words preen:
Pride, pomp and queen.

SWORD

POINT

Some words are quick,
A jerk, a flick.
Some words are slow:
Lag, stop and grow,
While others poke
As ox with yoke.
Some words can fly—
There's wind, there's high;
And some words cry:
"Goodbye . . .
Goodbye. . . ."

MARY O' NEILL

Pig Latin and Other Secret Languages

from *The Cat's Elbow and Other Secret Languages*

by Alvin Schwartz

Gogeroraloldod Kokisossosedod Mome!

To keep a secret like the one above, use a secret language. It will keep outsiders from eavesdropping. [1]

It also will make you feel mysterious. Some words may sound silly to other people, but *only* you and your friends

---

[1] To translate the secret, see page 260.

will know that "ketchiggityupiggity" means "ketchup" and that "dot hog" means "hot dog."

Children all over the world speak in secret languages, but they are not the only ones. Spies, smugglers, and thieves also do. So do members of secret societies. So do peddlers and shopkeepers. So do lovers. So do parents when they don't want children to know what is being said. In fact, some parents use a secret language they knew when they were young.

Most secret languages aren't complicated—if you know the secret. By adding a special letter to each word, or by moving a syllable or making some other change, you can turn any language into a secret language.

There are hundreds of these languages. There even is one which involves whistling. And there is another one in which people talk by beating on drums.

Many years ago, a town in California had its own secret language. The language was called Boontling. Everybody who lived in that town spoke it. But nobody else could figure it out.

Speaking a secret language isn't hard. All it takes is practice. Just find a friend who wants to learn. Then every day talk to one another in your secret language.

Start by translating a word or phrase in each sentence: "Let's go to the oozay!" "She's a creepbeep!" "You're a dodolollol!" Then try short sentences. Then try longer ones.

In the beginning, you will speak very slowly. You also will not understand everything your partner says. But in a few weeks it will be as easy as iepay. And nobody will understand what you are saying except your fofrorienondod.

1. PIG LATIN

This is one of the best-known secret languages. It also is one of the easiest to learn. People used to say that even a pig could learn it. Which is why it is called Pig Latin.

To speak Pig Latin

1. Move the first letter in a word to the end of the word. Then add "ay."

<u>h</u>amburger   amburger-<u>hay</u>

2. If a word starts with two consonants or more, move these letters to the end of the word. Then add "ay."

<u>ch</u>eese eese-<u>chay</u>

3. If a word starts with a vowel, don't move the vowel. Instead, add "way" to the word.

<u>o</u>nion   onion-<u>way</u>

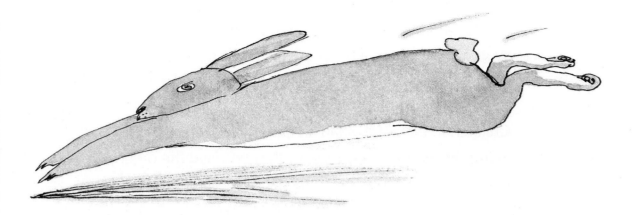

Practice Riddles

What is the best way to catch a rabbit?

Ide-hay ehind-bay a-way ush-bay and-way ake-may a-way oise-nay ike-lay a-way arrot-cay.

What has fur like a coyote, howls like a coyote, and is made of cement?

A-way oyote-cay. I-way ut-pay in-way e-thay ement-cay o-tay ake-may it-way arder-hay.

Why did the traffic light turn red?

Ou-yay ould-way urn-tay ed-ray, oo-tay, if-way ou-yay ad-hay o-tay ange-chay in-way ont-fray of-way all-way ose-thay eople-pay.

What do you call a friendly, helpful monster?

A-way ailure-fay.

(For the solutions to the practice problems, turn to page 262.)

E-thay ext-nay anguage-lay is-way "Inyume-kay."

2. KINYUME

Some children talk backwards when they have a secret to keep. To say a word, they start with the last letter. Then they work their way toward the beginning of the word. In this way, "secret" becomes "t-e-r-c-e-s," and "language" becomes "e-g-a-u-g-n-a-l." But this can get complicated.

Children in East Africa had an easier way of talking backwards. When they said a word, they reversed the order of the syllables. That way, the last syllable was first and the first syllable was last. They called their backwards language Kinyume.

To speak Kinyume

1. If a word has two syllables, move the last syllable to the beginning of the word.

ti<u>ger</u>	<u>ger</u>-ti
li<u>on</u>	<u>on</u>-li
cob<u>ra</u>	<u>ra</u>-cob

2. If a word has more than two syllables, move the last syllable to the beginning of the word. Move the first syllable to the end of the word.

crocodile   dile-o-croc

elephant   phant-e-el

gorilla la-ril-go

3. If a word has only one syllable, move the last letter or sound to the beginning of the word. Move the first letter or sound to the end of the word.

run   n-u-r

chase   se-a-ch

shoot   t-oo-sh

Practice

Tom S. Cat speaks Kinyume:

"I wove this basket," id-sa M-o-t S. ly-i-craft.

"I sing in the choir," id-sa M-o-t S. ly-ful-glee.

"E-b ful-care th-wi at-th e-knif," said Tom S. cuttingly.

"T-ha-w o-d en-sev s-ay-d ke-ma?" asked Tom S. weakly.

E-h-t t-ex-n guage-lan s-i "E-h-t 'S-a t-c Bow-el."

3. THE CAT'S ELBOW

In this language, extra letters are added to each word. The Cat's Elbow is a German secret language. Why does it have such a curious name? It was the name the Germans gave to the funny bone and perhaps to other things they thought were slightly crazy. Of course, cats *do* have elbows. They are the joints in their front legs.

To speak The Cat's Elbow

After each consonant, add the vowel "o," then repeat the consonant. Each vowel remains as it is.

cat   coc-a-tot

mouse   mom-ou-sos-e

purr   pop-u-ror-ror

squeak sos-qoq-uea-kok

pounce pop-ou-non-coc-e

yoy-ou coc-a-tot

Practice

Hard Questions:

There was a goose between two geese,

a goose behind two geese,

a goose ahead of two geese.

How many geese were there?

Tot-hoh-ror-e-e.

How can a cat have three tails?

No cat has two tails.

One cat has one tail more than no cat.

Tot-hoh-e-ror-e-fof-o-ror-e, o-non-e coc-a-tot hoh-a-sos tot-hoh-ror-e-e tot-a-i-lol-sos.

Two fathers and two sons went fishing. They each caught a fish. But together they only caught three fish. How could this be?

Tot-hoh-e pop-e-o-pop-lol-e wow-hoh-o wow-e-non-tot fof-i-sos-hoh-i-non-gog wow-e-ror-e a bob-o-yoy, hoh-i-sos fof-a-tot-hoh-e-ror, a-non-dod hoh-i-sos gog-ror-a-non-dod-fof-a-tot-hoh-e-ror. Tot-hoh-e bob-o-yoy'-sos gog-ror-a-non-dod-fof-a-tot-hoh-e-ror a-lol-sos-o wow-a-sos hoh-i-sos fof-a-tot-hoh-e-ror'-sos fof-a-tot-hoh-e-ror.

SOLUTIONS TO PRACTICE PROBLEMS

Pig Latin

Hide behind a bush and make a noise like a carrot.

A coyote. I put in the cement to make it harder.

You would turn red, too, if you had to change in front of all those people.

A failure.

Kinyume

… said Tom S. craftily.

… said Tom S. gleefully.

"Be careful with that knife …"

"What do seven days make?"

The Cat's Elbow

Three.

No cat has two tails. One cat has one tail more than no cat. Therefore, one cat has three tails.

The people who went fishing were a boy, his father, and his grandfather. The boy's grandfather also was his father's father.

Reader's Response ∾ Which of these languages do you think is the most fun?

Yo-deh-lay-hee-ho!

Pig Latin, Kinyume, and other secret languages aren't the only unusual ways that people communicate. Native Americans used smoke signals to send messages. Sailors traditionally have signaled each other by flying colored and patterned flags. And in the Swiss Alps, people have perfected the art of yodeling.

The word *yodel* probably came from the German *jodeln*, based on the *jo* syllable used as an expression of joy. The yodel is a joyful, wordless song that changes suddenly from deep, low tones to high, shrill ones.

Yodeling probably began when shepherds decided to use their voices instead of alphorns to call their flocks. Although most people think of Switzerland when they hear yodeling, the sounds have been used in American country music and included in country records. And some parents use a kind of yodel when they yell out the back door to call their kids— "Jim*mmmeeeee,* it's dinner time!"

Think about that the next time your mother says she called you till the cows came home.

The Pirates of Sandy Harbor

from *T*A*C*K Secret Service*
by Marvin Miller and Nancy K. Robinson

T*A*C*K is a network of kids. It is not a club. We do not have regular meetings in a clubhouse or anything like that. We do not wear buttons or T-shirts with T*A*C*K written across them.

No one knows about T*A*C*K. We work undercover. Our job is to serve people in the town of Sandy Harbor. We are a secret service.

Let me give you a quick rundown of the T*A*C*K team. The letters stand for our names:

T* for Toria.

That's me. My name is Victoria Gardner, but please call me Toria. I do not answer to Vicky. I am the one writing this journal. No one told me to do it. I just need the practice. You see, I am planning to be a newspaper reporter when I grow up.

A* for Abby.

Abigail Pinkwater is my best friend. Abby moved away last year, but I'd rather not talk about it. Abby is an honorary member of T*A*C*K. She is also our Agent-on-Remote which means "at a distance."

C* stands for Chuck.

Chuck is a trusted member of the T*A*C*K team. He is one of those people you can always count on.

K* is the code name for Will Roberts.

Will is the only one with a code name. Will is special. He is our leader, but he wouldn't want me to say that.

Besides, in a funny way, we are all equal in T*A*C*K.

Will's code name comes from Morse code. In Morse code "K" is dash, dot, dash (–•–). This signal was used in early telegraph language to mean "Switch." SWITCH TO SEND or GO AHEAD, I'M LISTENING...

Will's mind works like a switch. It switches all over the place. He is also a very good listener. He doesn't just listen; he *hears!*

Sometimes Will Roberts hears too well. He gets into trouble. One time our teacher, Miss Miller, asked Will to divide the number eight in half. Right away Will had three answers: four, two zeros, and two threes (one of them backwards).

He showed Miss Miller:

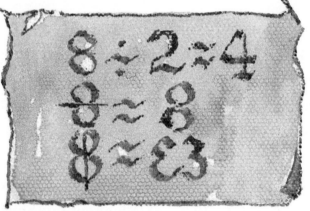

Miss Miller thought he was being fresh. He wasn't. Will Roberts just thinks that way. That is why he is so valuable to T*A*C*K.

Most of our cases are just mysteries, everyday problems and matters of life and death. We don't usually get mixed up in spying or intrigue. But last January the T*A*C*K team suddenly found itself in the middle of the case of The Pirates of Sandy Harbor.

This is what happened ...

"How does this sound?" I asked Chuck. "*Three hundred years ago Sandy Harbor was crawling with pirates. A local boatbuilder named Simon Hawk chased the pirates away. Later he became the founder of the Independent Village of Sandy Harbor.*"

"Sounds great," Chuck said.

Chuck and I were sitting in the town library. This year is the 300th birthday of Sandy Harbor. Everyone in our class has to do a report on local history.

"But Chuck," I said, "that's all I could find on Simon Hawk. There's one dusty old pamphlet in this whole library and our reports are due in two weeks! This won't fill up a whole page. It won't even fill up half a page."

"Write big," Chuck said. I gave him a dirty look. "Sorry, Toria," he said. "I was only kidding. Look, why don't you just add some stuff about pirates in general? You know — about some of the things they did."

"Big deal," I said coldly. "What did pirates do that was so interesting besides killing, torturing, stealing, blowing up ships, and chopping off people's heads?"

Chuck laughed. "Well, maybe you could make it *sound* interesting."

I watched Chuck work. Chuck has collected a lot of material on his subject. He picked the Great Sandy Harbor Flood. That flood happened only thirty years ago, so there are plenty of newspaper articles and pictures.

He also talked to people in town who remember the flood and told him plenty of stories about it.

"What's Will doing his report on?" I asked Chuck.

"Pickles," Chuck said. "He's very excited about it. He says he's working on a recipe that's two hundred years old. He got it from his grandmother. It was never written down so he's testing it."

"Historical pickles?" I asked.

Chuck nodded and turned a page in the old newspaper he was reading. "Wow! Toria, look at this." He showed me a photograph of our main street. It was completely flooded. A small motorboat was tied to a tree in front of our Post Office.

"Amazing!" Chuck said. "I can't believe it! But what am I going to do? I have so much great stuff. How will I ever fit it all into one report?"

"Write small," I said, and I left the library.

After dinner tonight I just sat at my desk staring at a blank piece of paper.

"Anything the matter, Toria?" My father was standing at the door.

I told him about Simon Hawk. "There's nothing on him," I said.

"Why don't you speak to Mr. Hawk?" my father said.

"Very funny, Popsy. Ha. Ha." I was in a terrible mood. "Simon Hawk's only been dead a few hundred years."

"Not Simon," Popsy said. "William Hawk—the director of the Sandy Harbor Historical Society. It's in that little white house behind the library. He's very nice, and I believe his family is related to old Simon."

I was a little nervous when I walked into the Historical Society.

"Mr. William Hawk, please," I said to the lady behind a desk in the front hall.

"Mr. Hawk is in with Mr. Parks right now," the lady said.

"You mean Harrison Parks, the editor of the *Sandy Harbor Herald?*" I asked.

"Yes," the lady sighed. "This place has been a madhouse all morning — after that article in this morning's *Herald.*"

"What article?" I asked.

SEA CHEST FOUND

An old sea chest believed to have belonged to Simon Hawk, the founder of Sandy Harbor, turned up in a local antique shop last week. The chest and its contents were immediately turned over to the Sandy Harbor Historical Society.

There are reports that a note written by Mr. Hawk himself was found in the chest.

Mr. William E. Hawk, director of the society, confirmed that the sea chest belonged to Simon Hawk. He said a monogram on the side is identical to those found on his boat models. However, Mr. Hawk denies there is proof that the note was written by Simon Hawk.

The contents of the note have not been released to the public at this time.

She handed me a copy of the newspaper. "Page four," she said. "Why don't you just take it to the bench outside Mr. Hawk's office." She pointed down the hall.

I sat down and turned to page four.

I read it over again. I could hear voices inside Mr. Hawk's office, but I couldn't hear what they were saying.

Then I noticed a painting hanging on the wall across from the bench. It was full of old sailing ships. I love sailboats. I stood up and went to look at it. It was an old painting of Sandy Harbor! I could recognize Corkhill Island, which is right across the bay from our boat docks. There was a plaque at the bottom. I read it:

Simon Hawk sets sail on his pirate chaser,
The Pemaquid, in pursuit of Captain Horatio Sly.
Captain Sly was attacking *Star of India*,
a cargo ship that had gone aground
on the rocky shoals off Corkhill Island.
(Donated by the estate of Merriwether Stephens)

I looked at that painting for a long time. Then I went and sat down on the bench.

Fifteen minutes went by. I was still waiting. Then an hour. I began to feel sleepy. I stared at the painting.

Suddenly I heard loud voices. The door to Mr. Hawk's office was open. Mr. Parks was on his way out.

"Look, Bill," Mr. Parks was saying, "you know as well as I do what that note proves. It proves that Simon Hawk was working with Horatio Sly. He was working with the pirates!"

"It's too early to say." Mr. Hawk had a quiet, gentle voice. "We need time to study this."

"Well, the way it stands it certainly looks bad for old Simon Hawk. It looks as if he actually *planned* the attack on the *Star of India!*" Mr. Parks sounded very excited. "Now I know you're a fine historian," he said, "but I'm a newspaperman. This is a big story. I'm publishing that note the way it stands!"

"I can't stop you," Mr. Hawk said, "but I feel you are making a terrible mistake. That note was in pieces and the paper is three hundred years old! We can't just fit it together like a jigsaw puzzle."

Mr. Hawk closed the door to his office.

Harrison Parks rushed past me rubbing his hands together.

I jumped to my feet and knocked on Mr. Hawk's office door.

"Yes?" Mr. Hawk opened it. He was tall and very thin. He had lots of soft white hair that fell over his forehead.

I started talking very fast. "Hello, my name is Toria Gardner. I'm doing my school report on Simon Hawk — it's due in two weeks."

I suddenly noticed that Mr. Hawk was staring at me blankly. "Two weeks sounds just fine," he said. "I'll be happy to see you in two weeks," and he closed the door.

For a moment I just stood there.

Now what was I going to write?

All at once I realized I didn't care about my article anymore. I cared about Simon Hawk!

By tomorrow morning the whole town would think Simon Hawk was working with the pirates, that he was just another pirate. *But what if he were innocent?*

I ran as fast as I could to the library. I knew I would find Chuck there.

He stared at my face. "Toria!" he said. "What's wrong?"

"We've got to get Will," I panted.

"Right," Chuck said. "Let's go!" He didn't ask any questions.

Will was in his kitchen. He was wearing a white apron. He was pouring sugar into a big glass jar full of cucumbers and a cloudy liquid. An iron pot was boiling on the stove. Will turned to look at us as we marched in.

"Will," I said grimly. "Drop the pickles. It looks like we have a job for T*A*C*K."

I told Will and Chuck the whole story.

"But, Toria," Will said. "That kind of thing happened a lot. Pirate chasers very often turned into pirates themselves."

"Simon Hawk is innocent until proven guilty," I said.

"Of course," Will said. He took off his apron. "Just tell us where to start."

I thought for a minute. "There's a painting I want you to look at," I said.

Will, Chuck, and I stood in front of the big, dark painting in the Historical Society.

"But Toria," Chuck said. "I don't see anything wrong with that painting."

"Something keeps bothering me," I said. "There's something the matter with it."

Will and Chuck stared at the painting.

"Wait a minute!" I shouted. "I know what it is. The *Star of India* couldn't go aground over there. It's too deep. The rocky shoals are on the other side of Corkhill Island. The painting is crazy. It's all wrong!"

A man was standing behind us, but I was too excited to pay much attention.

"Maybe the bottom of the harbor changed," Will suggested, "in three hundred years."

"Well," I said, "sand can shift around, but rocks don't change much — do they?" I asked the man who was now beside me looking up at the painting.

"No, they don't," he said.

I suddenly realized I was talking to William E. Hawk!

"Oops," I said and I covered my mouth.

"Young lady, do you know that hundreds of people have looked at that painting" — Mr. Hawk seemed pleased — "but you're the only one I've ever come across who noticed that mistake."

"You already knew?" I asked. He nodded.

"Then," I said, "if the painting is wrong, is the whole story wrong — about Simon Hawk chasing the pirates?"

"No," he said. "The artist just wanted an exciting painting. If the *Star of India* were aground in the right place, you wouldn't be able to see it in the painting."

"Wow!" I said. "You can't believe anything, can you?"

Mr. Hawk laughed. "Aren't you the young lady doing some research on Simon Hawk?" he asked me.

"It's due in two weeks," Chuck volunteered.

"That doesn't matter," I said. "Mr. Hawk, I heard you

274

talking to Mr. Parks. I am not going to write a word about Simon Hawk until we know the truth — no matter how long it takes."

"But Toria," Chuck whispered. "You'll fail the assignment."

"I don't care," I said. "It's much more important to know whether Simon Hawk was working with the pirates or not. It's not fair to accuse someone who isn't even around to defend himself — not without definite proof!"

Mr. Hawk was looking at me. He seemed to be making up his mind about something.

Suddenly he clapped his hands. "Come with me," he said. "You too," he said to Will and Chuck. "I want you to take a look at something."

We followed him into his office. On his desk were two sheets of glass stuck together. In between were pieces of paper.

"Remember," Mr. Hawk said, "no one has ever seen Simon Hawk's handwriting."

"THE NOTE!" I gasped. I stood beside Mr. Hawk and read the pieced-together note. It certainly looked bad for Simon Hawk!

"Wasn't this note found in Simon Hawk's sea chest?" I asked Mr. Hawk.

"Yes," Mr. Hawk said.

"Why would Simon Hawk keep his own note?" I asked.

"Good point," Mr. Hawk said. "But I'm afraid it didn't impress Harrison Parks. But that's not the only thing that bothers me. I have a funny feeling about this note. Something's wrong—you know. I feel the same way you felt about that painting."

Chuck and I were standing next to Mr. Hawk. Will was on the other side of his desk.

"Will," I whispered, "come here. You can see it better from here. Will …"

Will didn't move. He just stood there staring at the pieces of paper in the glass. I felt he was being a bit rude.

"Will," I said again, "come over here and look at it the right way!"

Will hesitated. Then he came around to join us.

"Simon Hawk didn't sign that note," Will said. "He found it. That's how he knew when Sly was going to attack!"

Suddenly Will seemed embarrassed. "At least, that's what I think."

"Well, well, well," Mr. Hawk said. "Let's hear your theory."

Simon Hawk didn't sign that note. Will's theory was correct. Can you figure it out?

Will's Solution:

The note was signed by someone with the initial *H*. It was not signed by Simon Hawk. The pieces had been put together wrong. *SIMON* was actually *NOW IS* upside down.

This is how the note really fit together:

Before we knew it, William Hawk was on the phone to Harrison Parks. "Stop the presses, Harrison," he said. "I don't want you to make a fool of yourself. There are some young people I'd like you to meet. Can you drop by?"

Reader's Response ⁓ Would you like to join the T*A*C*K team? Tell why or why not.

Library Link ⁓ *This story is an excerpt from the book* T*A*C*K Secret Service *by Marvin Miller and Nancy K. Robinson. You might enjoy reading the entire book to follow Toria and her friends on new adventures.*

Buried Treasure in the Library

Where do you think treasure hunters begin to look for sunken treasure? If you said the ocean floor, you are only partly right.

One day, when Kip Wagner was walking on the beach near his home in Sebastian, Florida, after a hurricane, he spotted something in the sand. He quickly reached down and picked up a blackened, oddly shaped piece of metal. The date of 1714 and symbols on the metal told him it must be a piece of eight from a Spanish ship. The problem was that he had heard that Spanish ships had sunk in 1715 either north or south of Sebastian. Could all the experts have been wrong?

Kip's friend, Dr. Kelso, went to the Library of Congress in Washington, D. C., to find out. There he found an old book with a map of Florida made in 1775. That map showed the boats had really sunk right off the coast of Sebastian. Just to make sure, Kip wrote to the Archives of the Indies in Spain and received copies of maps and other records of ships that had sailed in 1715.

When they were sure they were right, Kip and Dr. Kelso bought a boat and formed a team called the Real Eight to begin their search. They found over $3 million in treasure, including thousands of silver pieces of eight and hundreds of golden doubloons. Kip would tell you the place to look for treasure is on the ocean floor . . . and in books and libraries.

279

Pippi Finds A
SPINK

by Astrid Lindgren

Pippi and her friends, a monkey named Mr. Nilsson, Tommy, and Annika, have lots of fun together. They follow Pippi on one adventure after another.

One morning Tommy and Annika came skipping into Pippi's kitchen as usual, shouting good morning. But there was no answer. Pippi was sitting in the middle of the kitchen table with Mr. Nilsson, the little monkey, in her arms and a happy smile on her face.

"Good morning," said Tommy and Annika again.

"Just think," said Pippi dreamily, "just think that I have discovered it—I and no one else!"

"What have you discovered?" Tommy and Annika wondered. They weren't in the least bit surprised that Pippi had discovered something, because she was always doing that, but they did want to know what it was.

"What did you discover, anyway, Pippi?"

"A new word," said Pippi and looked at Tommy and Annika as if she had just this minute noticed them. "A brand-new word."

"What kind of word?" said Tommy.

"A wonderful word," said Pippi. "One of the best I've ever heard."

"Say it then," said Annika.

"Spink," said Pippi triumphantly.

"Spink," repeated Tommy. "What does that mean?"

"If I only knew!" said Pippi. "The only thing I know is that it doesn't mean vacuum cleaner."

Tommy and Annika thought for a while. Finally Annika said, "But if you don't know what it means, then it can't be of any use."

"That's what bothers me," said Pippi.

"Who really decided in the beginning what all the words should mean?" Tommy wondered.

"Probably a bunch of old professors," said Pippi. "People certainly are peculiar! Just think of the words they make up—'tub' and 'stopper' and 'string' and words like that. Where they got them from, nobody knows. But a wonderful word like 'spink,' they don't bother to invent. How lucky that I hit on it! And you just bet I'll find out what it means, too."

She fell deep in thought.

"Spink! I wonder if it might be the top part of a blue flagpole," she said doubtfully.

"Flagpoles aren't blue," said Annika.

"You're right. Well then, I really don't know. . . . Or do you think it might be the sound you hear when you walk in the mud and it gets between your toes? Let's hear how it sounds! 'As Annika walked in the mud you could hear the most wonderful spink. '" She shook her head. "No, that's no good. 'You could hear the most wonderful *tjipp'*—that's what it should be instead."

Pippi scratched her head. "This is getting more and more mysterious. But whatever it is, I'm going to find out. Maybe it can be bought in the stores. Come on, let's go and ask!"

Tommy and Annika had no objection. Pippi went off to hunt for her purse, which was full of gold coins. "Spink," she said. "It sounds as if it might be expensive. I'd better take a gold coin along." And she did. As usual Mr. Nilsson jumped up on her shoulder.

Then Pippi lifted the horse down from the veranda. "We're in a hurry," she said to Tommy and Annika. "We'll have to ride. Because otherwise there might not be any spink left when we get there. It wouldn't surprise me if the mayor had already bought the last of it."

When the horse came galloping through the streets of the little town with Pippi and Tommy and Annika on his back, the children heard the clatter of his hoofs on the cobblestones and came happily running because they all liked Pippi so much.

"Pippi, where are you going?" they cried.

"I'm going to buy spink," said Pippi and brought the horse to a halt for a moment.

The children looked puzzled.

"Is it something good?" a little boy asked.

"You bet," said Pippi and licked her lips. "It's wonderful. At least it sounds as if it were."

In front of a candy shop she jumped off the horse, lifted Tommy and Annika down, and in they went.

"I would like to buy a bag of spink," said Pippi. "But I want it nice and crunchy."

"Spink," said the pretty lady behind the counter, trying to think. "I don't believe we have that."

"You must have it," said Pippi. "All well-stocked shops carry it."

"Yes, but we've just run out of it," said the lady, who had never even heard of spink but didn't want to admit that her shop wasn't as well stocked as any other.

"Oh, but then you did have it yesterday!" cried Pippi eagerly. "Please, please tell me how it looked. I've never seen spink in all my life. Was it red-striped?"

Then the nice lady blushed prettily and said, "No, I really don't know what it is. In any case, we don't have it here."

Very disappointed, Pippi walked toward the door. "Then I have to keep on looking," she said. "I can't go back home without spink."

The next store was a hardware store. A salesman bowed politely to the children.

"I would like to buy a spink," said Pippi. "But I want it to be of the best kind, the one that is used for killing lions."

The salesman looked sly as a fox. "Let's see," he said and scratched himself behind the ear. "Let's see." He took out a small rake. "Is this all right?" he said as he handed it to Pippi.

Pippi looked indignantly at him. "That's what the professors would call a rake," she said. "But it happens to be a spink I wanted. Don't try to fool an innocent little child."

Then the salesman laughed and said, "Unfortunately we don't have the thing you wanted. Ask in the store around the corner which carries notions."

"Notions," Pippi muttered to Tommy and Annika when they came out on the street. "I just know they won't have it there." Suddenly she brightened. "Perhaps, after all, it's a sickness," she said. "Let's go and ask the doctor."

Annika knew where the doctor lived because she had gone there to be vaccinated.

Pippi rang the bell. A nurse opened the door.

"I would like to see the doctor," said Pippi. "It's a very serious case. A terribly dangerous disease."

"This way, please," said the nurse.

The doctor was sitting at his desk when the children came in. Pippi went straight to him, closed her eyes, and stuck her tongue out.

"What is the matter with you?" said the doctor.

Pippi opened her clear blue eyes and pulled in her tongue. "I'm afraid I've got spink," she said, "because I itch all over. And when I sleep my eyes close. Sometimes I have the hiccups and on Sunday I didn't feel very well after having eaten a dish of shoe polish and milk. My appetite is quite hearty, but sometimes I get the food down my windpipe and then nothing good comes of it. It must be the spink which bothers me. Tell me, is it contagious?"

The doctor looked at Pippi's rosy little face and said, "I think you're healthier than most. I'm sure you're not suffering from spink."

Pippi grabbed him eagerly by the arm. "But there is a disease by that name, isn't there?"

"No," said the doctor, "there isn't. But even if there were, I don't think it would have any effect on you."

Pippi looked sad. She made a deep curtsy to the doctor as she said good-by, and so did Annika. Tommy bowed. And then they went out to the horse, who was waiting at the doctor's fence.

Not far from the doctor's house was a high three-story house with a window open on the upper floor. Pippi pointed toward the open window and said, "It wouldn't surprise me if the spink is in there. I'll dash up and see." Quickly she climbed up the water spout. When she reached the level of the window she threw herself heedlessly into the air and grabbed hold of the window sill. She hoisted herself up by the arms and stuck her head in.

In the room two ladies were sitting chatting. Imagine their astonishment when all of a sudden a red head popped over the window sill and a voice said, "Is there by any chance a spink here?"

The two ladies cried out in terror. "Good heavens, what are you saying, child? Has someone escaped?"

"That is exactly what I would like to know," said Pippi politely.

"Maybe he's under the bed!" screamed one of the ladies. "Does he bite?"

286

"I think so," said Pippi. "He's supposed to have tremendous fangs."

The two ladies clung to each other. Pippi looked around curiously, but finally she said with a sigh, "No, there isn't as much as a spink's whisker around here. Excuse me for disturbing you. I just thought I would ask, since I happened to be passing by."

She slid down the water spout and said sadly to Tommy and Annika, "There isn't any spink in this town. Let's ride back home."

And that's what they did. When they jumped down from the horse, outside the veranda, Tommy came close to stepping on a little beetle which was crawling on the gravel path.

"Be careful not to step on the beetle!" Pippi cried. All three bent down to look at it. It was such a tiny thing, with green wings that gleamed like metal.

"What a pretty little creature," said Annika. "I wonder what it is."

"It isn't a cockchafer," said Tommy.

"And no ladybug either," said Annika. "And no stagbeetle. I wish I knew what it was."

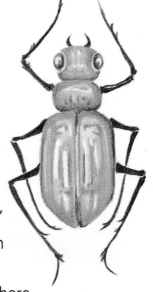

All at once a radiant smile lit up Pippi's face. "I know," she said. "It's a spink."

"Are you sure?" Tommy said doubtfully.

"Don't you think I know a spink when I see one?" said Pippi. "Have you ever seen anything so spinklike in your life?"

She carefully moved the beetle to a safer place, where no one could step on it. "My sweet little spink," she said tenderly. "I knew that I would find one at last. But isn't it funny! We've been hunting all over town for a spink and here was one right outside Villa Villekulla all the time!"

Reader's Response ∼ Pippi's friends and the people in her town seemed to like her very much. Do you think you would like Pippi for a friend? Give a reason for your answer.

Library Link ∼ *This story is from the book* Pippi in the South Seas *by Astrid Lindgren. Here are some other books by the author you might enjoy reading:* Pippi Longstocking; Bill Bergson, Master Detective; *and* Mischievous Meg.

Because It SNOWED
One Day in March

I loved people, I loved nature, and I loved books. In high school, everybody kept telling me that I would be an author someday, and I very stubbornly decided never to write any books.

When Astrid Lindgren's daughter was seven years old and sick in bed, she asked her mother to tell her a story.

"About what?" her mother asked.

"Tell me about Pippi Longstocking," her daughter replied, inventing the name on the spot.

Astrid Lindgren created an odd character to match an odd name. But she had never written down a word about the imaginary Pippi until, years later, when Astrid went for a walk in Stockholm, Sweden, she slipped on the ice and hurt her ankle. With nothing to do but stay in bed for a while, she began to write.

Beginning in 1944, Astrid Lindgren wrote over fifty books, including "Pippi" sequels, plays, and film scripts.

Today, stories about Pippi Longstocking have been translated into more than fifty languages around the world.

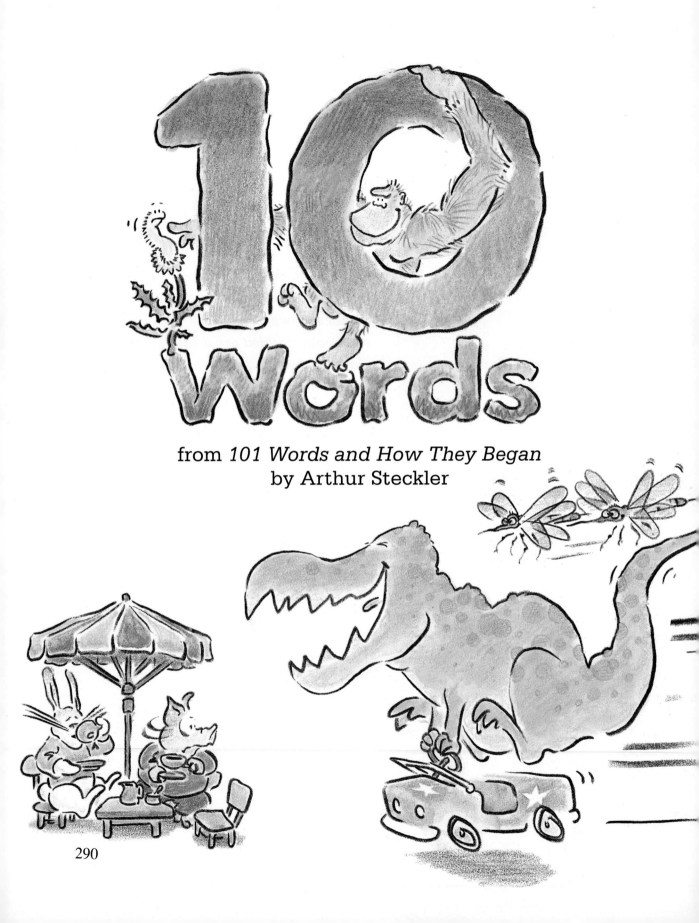

10 Words

from *101 Words and How They Began*
by Arthur Steckler

The words we use have come from many
different sources. Some of them came from languages
thousands of years old. Others came from some of the
almost three thousand different languages that are
spoken today around the world.

Some words came to us from slang, others from
the Bible or from science. Some came from the initials
of other words.

There are words that came from sounds or noises,
like *giggle*, and *gargle*, and *gurgle*, and *rattle*, and
chatter, and *tinkle*, and *hiccup*, and *bubble*, and
shriek, and *buzz*, and *slam*, and *pop*. If you've ever
heard a door *slam*, or a balloon *pop*, you might agree
that these words certainly sound like what happened.
They are called *onomatopoetic* or *onomatopoeic*
words, which is a fancy way to say, "making words
by the sound of the action involved."

There are words that came from the place where
a thing was first used, such as: *dungarees, cantaloupe,*
and *dollar.*

There are some words that are strange for other
reasons. *Sniff* and *sniffle* and *snuff* and *snuffle* and
snout and *snort* and *sneeze* are all words that describe
the nose and its activities. For some strange reason,
all begin with the letters *sn.* No one really knows why.

There are even words which are mistakes, but
which we use anyway, like *kangaroo* and *turkey.*

If you were to read that "a catta pilosa was
crawling on the tooth of a lion when a man of the
forest had him clear away the table," it wouldn't
make much sense. But if you knew that a "catta
pilosa" was a caterpillar, that the "tooth of a lion"
was a dandelion, that "a man of the forest" was an
orangutan, and that the definition of dessert was to
"clear away the table," then the same sentence
would read, "A caterpillar was crawling on a
dandelion when an orangutan had him for dessert,"
which makes more sense to the reader, and maybe to
the orangutan, but certainly not to the caterpillar.

If you have the letter *C* on one of your water faucets, it stands for "cold" in English-speaking countries. But in France, Spain, and Italy, it stands for "hot," because the French word for hot is *chaud,* the Spanish word for hot is *caliente,* and the Italian word for hot is *caldo.* (So if you visit France, Spain, or Italy, be careful when you turn on the cold water faucet, or you'll find yourself in hot water.)

A name is a word by which a person, place, or thing is known. And just as words can have interesting beginnings, so can names.

Giuseppe Verdi was a famous composer of music. If you translate his Italian name into English, it becomes just plain Joseph Green, because Giuseppe is the Italian for Joseph, and Verdi is the Italian for Green.

Probably the most common masculine name is John. Yet as we go from country to country and language to language, see how it changes:

Italy .... Giovanni
Turkey .... Yuhanna
Spain .... Juan
Ireland .... Sean
Denmark .... Jens
France .... Jean
Brazil .... Joaninho
Morocco .... Yahya
Switzerland .... Johann
India .... Zaid
Holland .... Jan
Greece .... Ioannes
Thailand .... Yohan
Japan .... Yohana-den
Russia .... Ivan
Austria .... Hansel

If you asked an airline agent for a ticket from "Red Stick" to "White House," there's no telling what he might think, or where you might end up. But if you knew that Baton Rouge, the city in Louisiana, when translated from French to English, becomes "Red Stick," and that Casablanca, in Morocco, when translated from Spanish to English, becomes "White House," you would at least know where you were going, even if you didn't want to go there.

There are many, many words that seem to play tricks or games on us.

Words About the Animal World

dinosaur

Two animals, both from olden times, one that is extinct and another that still exists, are named after lizards. The name of the extinct one, the DINOSAUR, came from the language of the ancient Greeks. Their word *deinos,* which means "fearful," and *sauros,* which means "lizard," were combined to name the fearful lizard known as the DINOSAUR.

alligator

ALLIGATORS, which of course still exist, were also named after lizards, but their name came from Latin to Spanish, and eventually to English. Early Spanish settlers, when they first saw an ALLIGATOR, called it *el lagarto,* which meant, "the lizard," or "the great lizard." *El lagarto* later became *alligarta.* When it entered the English language, it became ALLIGATOR, which is what it remains today.

mosquito

Going from very big to very small members of the animal kingdom, we find the word MOSQUITO. The Latin word *musca* and the Spanish and Portuguese word *mosca* both mean a fly. By adding *ito* to the end of *mosca,* it became a little fly. The name of the capital of Ecuador is Quito, from the Quitu Indians of that area. Since Ecuador gets its name from the hot, steamy equator, where it is situated, and where there must be many mosquitoes, it seems fitting that the name of the capital and the word MOSQUITO are so similar.

Words About Things We Eat and Drink

hamburger

If you think the word HAMBURGER comes to us from Hamburg, Germany, you're right, just as frankfurters are named for Frankfurt, Germany. Originally the HAMBURGER was known as a Hamburg steak, and it was introduced to this country in 1884 when numbers of German settlers came to the United States.

ketchup

When we think of HAMBURGERS, we usually think of KETCHUP. Yet they come from completely different origins. Long ago in China, the Chinese people enjoyed a pickled fish sauce, which they called *ke-tsiap.* Over the years, this sauce changed, and so did its name, which became *kechap* in the Malayan language. Soon *kechap* became KETCHUP.

coffee

We get our word COFFEE from the Turkish and Arabic languages. *Qahveh* is the Turkish word for COFFEE, just as *qahwah* is the Arabic. Later, the French called it *café.* Their word for COFFEE also became their word for a coffee shop. *Café* became our word *cafeteria,* which, of course, is a self-service restaurant, although *cafeteria* comes from the Mexican Spanish *cafetería.*

Words About Things We Ride

jeep

In the U.S. Army the letters G.P. stand for "General Purpose," and were applied to lots of equipment, including vehicles. *G.P.* sounds a bit like JEEP. Also, the comic strip "Popeye" had a little animal called Eugene the JEEP, who made the sound "jeep, jeep." So the car we know as a JEEP, which is certainly an American idea, came from two American sources: the U.S. Army and the "Popeye" comic strip.

blimp

Every so often we see a BLIMP flying over a football stadium. Now, we know that BLIMPS are big bags full of gas that is lighter than air, and that they do not have a rigid skeleton or inside framework. During World War I, several varieties of these "soft" airships were tested. Since they were the limp rather than rigid type, the first one was called "A-limp," the second "B-limp," and so on. Eventually the "B-limp" model was adopted, and the term *B-limp* became simple BLIMP.

298

Words About Things We Use

window

If someone tried to tell you about "an eye for the wind," you probably wouldn't know what he meant. But that's how the word WINDOW came about. In the Scandinavian languages, there was a word *vindauge,* which was made up of two other words, *vindr,* meaning "wind," and *auga,* meaning "eye." By combining "an eye to let the wind in," another word was invented.

lasso

The Spanish word *lazo* means a rope with a sliding noose at one end. This became our word LASSO. Yet many people confuse a LASSO with a lariat, which is from the Spanish *la reata,* meaning "the rope," and is used to tie or hobble cattle. LASSO and lariat may both be made of rope, but they have different meanings. Both words were adopted by our cowboys from Spanish cowboys and the Spanish language.

Collecting and learning about words is, in a way, somewhat like collecting and learning about sea shells, or stamps, or butterflies. Except, of course, that most people don't put collections of words on shelves, or frame them and hang them on walls. Yet a collection of words goes with us wherever we go; it can grow and be strengthened every time we talk with someone; and it can help us in one of the most important things in life: communicating with others.

Reader's Response ∿ You have just read how ten words came into our language. Which word do you think has the funniest or most interesting story behind it? Explain why you chose that word.

Library Link ∿ *This article is an excerpt from the book* One Hundred and One Words and How They Began *by Arthur Steckler. You might enjoy reading the entire book to find out about the other ninety-one words.*

Speaking of Words...
Who Chooses Names for Hurricanes?

SCIENTISTS from all over the world suggest names. Then the World Meteorological Organization makes up the lists.

There are **TWO** sets of hurricane-name lists—one for the East Coast and one for the West Coast. Each is listed in alphabetical order.

When the **FIRST STORM** of the season hits the Atlantic coast, it is given an "A" name. The second storm in the region gets a "B" name, and so on.

Both the East Coast and West Coast have **SIX** lists of names—one for each year in a six-year period. After six years, the names are recycled.

Some names only get used once. The names of destructive storms—like **HUGO**—are retired. Another H name will take Hugo's place when the 1989 Atlantic storm list is used again in 1995.

Will you ever hear of a hurricane named **QUINCY** or **ZELDA**? No. There are not enough names that begin with Q, U, X, Y, or Z.

The Terrible Leak

retold
by Yoshiko Uchida

One rainy night, long, long ago, a small boy sat with his grandmother and grandfather around a charcoal brazier. Warming their hands over the glowing coals, they told stories and talked of many things. Outside, the wind blew and the rain splattered on the thatched roof of the cottage.

The old man looked up at the ceiling saying, "I surely hope we don't have a leak. Nothing would be so terrible as to have to put up a new thatched roof now when we are so busy in the fields."

The little boy listened to the lonely wail of the wind as it whipped through the bamboo grove. He shivered,

and turned to look at his grandfather's face. It was calm
and smiling and unafraid.

"Ojii-san," the little boy said suddenly. "Is there
anything you're afraid of?"

The old man laughed. "Why, of course, lad," he said.
"There are many things a man fears in life."

"Well then," said the little boy, "what are you *most*
afraid of in all the world?"

The old man rubbed his bald head, and thought for a
moment as he puffed on his pipe.

"Let me see," he said. "Among human beings, I
think I fear a thief the most."

Now, at the very moment the old man was saying this, a thief had climbed onto the roof of the cowshed, hoping to steal one of the cows. He happened to hear what the old man said, and he thrust out his chest proudly.

"So!" he thought to himself. "I am the very thing the old man fears most in all the world!" And he laughed to think how frightened the old man and woman would be if they only knew a thief was in their yard this very minute.

"Ojii-san," the little boy went on. "Of all the animals in the world, which one are you most afraid of?"

Again, the old man thought for a moment, and then he said, "Of all the animals, I think I fear the wolf the most."

Just as the old man said this, a wolf was prowling around the cowshed, for he had come to see if there were some chickens he might steal. When he heard what the old man said, he laughed to himself. "Ah-ha!" he said. "So I am the animal the old man fears the most," and wiggling his nose, he sniffed haughtily.

But inside the house, the little boy went on. "Ojii-san," he said, "even more than a thief or a wolf, what are you the most, most, *most* afraid of?"

The old man sat thinking for a long while, and thoughts of ogres and demons and terrible dragons filled the little boy's head. But the old man was listening to the rain as it splashed and trickled in rivulets of water around the house. He thought again how terrible it would be to have a leak in his roof. He turned to the boy and said, "Well, the one thing I fear most of all right now is a leak! And I'm afraid one may come along any minute!"

Now when the thief and the wolf heard this, they didn't know the old man was talking about a leak in the roof.

"A leak," thought the thief. "What kind of terrible animal could that be? If the old man fears it more than a thief or a wolf, it must be a fearsome thing!"

Down below, the wolf thought the same thing. "A leak must be a dreadful creature if the old man fears it more than me or a thief," he thought. And he peered into the darkness, wondering if a leak might not spring out of the forest, for the old man had said one might come at any moment.

Up on the roof of the cowshed, the thief got so excited he slipped and tumbled down into the darkness. But instead of falling to the ground, he fell right on the back of the wolf.

The wolf gave a frightened yelp. From somewhere above him in the dark night, something had leaped on his back and was clutching his neck. "This must be the terrible leak the old man talked about," thought the wolf, and with his tail between his legs, he ran pell-mell into the woods.

Now the thief did not know he had landed on the back of a wolf. He knew he had fallen on the back of something large and cold and full of fur. What's more, it had given a wild yelp and begun to run. The thief was so frightened he couldn't even call for help. Instead, he clung to the neck of this creature that seemed to be flying through the night into the forest.

"I must be on the back of the terrible leak the old man talked about," he thought fearfully, and closing his eyes tight, he hung on. The harder the thief clung to the wolf's neck, the faster the wolf ran.

As they got deeper and deeper into the forest, branches of trees swung low and scratched the thief's face. Finally, when he felt a big branch sweep past, he caught it and swung himself up into a tree. But the wolf did not know what had happened, and he ran on and on until he came to his cave at the farthest end of the forest. When he finally stopped, he realized the thing on his back was gone.

"Ah, the leak has dropped off somewhere!" he thought, and he sighed a great sigh of relief.

Early the next morning, the wolf went to see his friend, the tiger.

"Mr. Tiger, Mr. Tiger! What a terrible fright I had last night," he said, panting at the very thought of it. "Do you know what kind of creature a leak is?"

The tiger shook his head. "Why, I don't believe I've ever heard of anything called a leak," he said. "What is it?"

"It is something human beings fear more than anything else in this world," said the wolf. "And do you know, one of those terrible creatures jumped on my back last night? I ran all night through the forest with this leak hanging onto my neck, for it clutched at me and almost choked me to death!"

The tiger grunted sympathetically. "Ah, how terrible that must have been," he said.

The wolf took a deep breath and went on. "The leak dropped off somewhere after I got into the forest, but I'm sure it must still be here. If we don't capture it, none of us will ever be safe again. Will you help me to find it?"

The tiger nodded. "Certainly, I'll help," he said. "Besides, I'd like to see what a leak looks like. I wonder if it has two heads?"

And so the tiger and the wolf set off to look for the terrible leak. As they prowled through the forest, a monkey sitting in a tree peered through the leaves and saw them below.

"Say, Mr. Tiger! Mr. Wolf!" he called. "Where are you going with such worried frowns on your faces?"

"We are searching for a thing called a leak," they answered. "It is something so terrible that human beings fear it more than a thief or a wolf. It must surely be the most fearsome thing in the world, and we cannot live safely in this forest until we capture it."

The monkey listened carefully. "A leak?" he asked. "Why, I've never heard of such a creature. Surely, you must be mistaken."

But the wolf shook his head. "No, no! I am not mistaken, for this very creature clutched at my throat and rode on my back all the way into the forest last night. It dropped off somewhere, and must be hiding near us this very minute!"

Now the monkey had seen the wolf running through the forest the night before, with the thief hanging on to his neck. He suddenly realized that this terrible thing they feared was only a human being, so he said in a loud, bragging voice, "Why, if that is the thing you are searching for, I can tell you where he is. He is sitting on one of the branches of the tree over there. In fact, I shall go and capture him single-handedly if you want me to."

The tiger and the wolf looked over at the tree where the monkey pointed. Sure enough, there, on one of the branches, sat a creature looking somewhat like a human being. The tiger growled and bared his long, sharp teeth. The wolf looked up at the sky and howled a long, piercing yowl. The thief heard their cries, and trembling with fear, he fell off the branch and went tumbling into a hole in the trunk of the tree.

As the three animals saw him fall, they ran over to the tree and stood around the hole where the thief was hiding.

"Now, how shall we go about capturing this leak?" they said to one another.

"Whoever captures him will become king of the forest," the tiger said. "For he will surely be the bravest and strongest of all."

"That is an excellent idea," said the monkey. Then, because he knew this leak was only a human being who was frightened himself, he marched right up to the hole in the tree trunk. He thrust his tail inside and flipped it about saying, "Are you in there, Mr. Leak? Are you inside?"

The thief had heard the animals as they talked outside the tree. "It will never do to let them capture me," he thought. "For if they catch me, they will surely kill me."

He decided he must do something to frighten them away, so he grabbed the monkey's tail and pulled as hard as he could. Then, he growled and shouted fiercely, trying to sound more terrible than the tiger and the wolf put together.

"Help!" shouted the monkey as he felt his tail being pulled.

The thief pulled hard, but the monkey pulled even harder, for he didn't want to be dragged into the hole in front of the tiger and the wolf. They both pulled so hard the monkey's tail broke off with a snap, and the monkey went sprawling onto the ground.

"My tail, my tail! My beautiful tail!" he shrieked, and he ran off into the forest, disappearing into the leaves of a tall cedar tree.

"The leak is certainly a fearful thing," said the wolf, shaking his head, and with a great howl he ran off into the woods after the monkey.

"It is best to leave such fearful things alone," said the tiger in a soft voice, and he went slinking off into the woods after the monkey and the wolf.

When all the animals had gone, the thief crept out of the tree trunk. He looked about carefully to make sure that nothing was following him, and then he ran as fast as he could out of the forest.

The thief never learned that what he thought was the terrible leak was only a frightened wolf. And the wolf never discovered that what he thought was the most terrible thing in all the world was only a frightened thief.

And the little boy and his grandmother and grandfather didn't have to be afraid of a leak in the roof after all, for in the stillness of the night the rain stopped, the moon came out bright and clear, and the next days were full of the promise of sunshine.

Reader's Response ∼ Did this story teach you something about communicating with others? What did it teach you?'

TV AND Tokonoma

What would your house be like if you lived in Japan? . . .
Paper-panelled sliding doors leading to a garden? TV, stereo,
VCR? Most Japanese homes combine traditional and modern
ways of life. Your house might have one room with
carpeting, but *tatami*, or straw mats, would still cover most
of the floors. You would still take off your shoes, and perhaps
put on your slippers, before entering. Your parents might
cook dinner on a gas or electric stove, but you are likely to sit
on a cushion when you eat—at
a low table, only inches off the floor. After
dinner your family might watch TV, or listen
to the stereo, but they would still get out
quilts or special pads, called *futons*, and
spread them on the floor to sleep.

Whether you lived in a wooden
house or an apartment building,
one room would be sure to
have a special nook, called a
tokonoma (tō k ə nō´ m ə).
The tokonoma is decorated
with flowers and a scroll
painting—to show
the beauty of
nature.

JUAN GETS HOME

from *How Juan Got Home*

by Peggy Mann

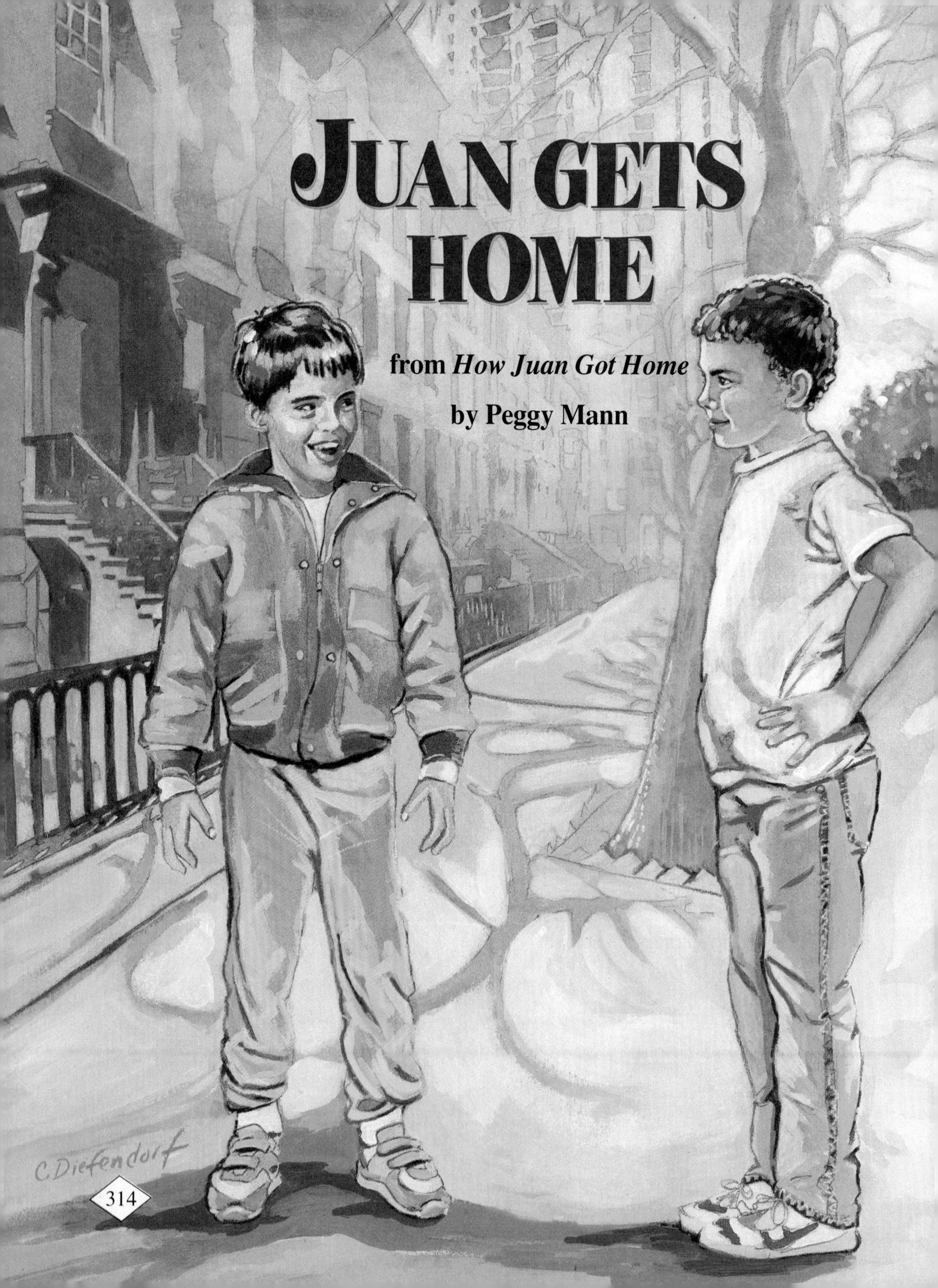

Juan *recently arrived in New York City from Puerto Rico. He lives with his uncle in a neighborhood where families speak English, not Spanish. Since Juan speaks very little English, he wishes he could return to Puerto Rico— until he meets Carlos, a Hispanic boy his own age.*

They made two trips from the Bodega Rivera to the basement of the brownstone rooming house where Carlos lived. Juan kept talking almost nonstop all the way. He had so much talk inside him it seemed he just couldn't get it all said.

Carlos spoke very little. When they had finished piling the boxes in a corner of the basement, Carlos explained why he always answered Juan in such short sentences. He knew very little Spanish.

Juan stared at him through the basement gloom, astounded. A *puertorriqueño* who didn't know Spanish?

315

Carlos shrugged and explained that he'd come to the mainland when he was three years old to live with his grandmother. He'd been brought up on English, in the streets and in school. In fact, the only Spanish he knew came from talking to his grandmother. And since she was an old lady of sixty-two he didn't spend much time talking to *her*.

Juan nodded. He felt he had found a friend—only to lose him. What was worse, he felt like a fool. Here he'd been jabbering away to this boy all about Barranquitas and his house and his mother and sisters and friends and his Hot Wheels collection and the Piñonas River and his school and the TV programs he watched at home. And all the time

Carlos had hardly understood a single word!

"As a matter of fact," Carlos said in English as he started up the basement stairs, "you'll find that most of the Spanish kids on this street don't speak Spanish. At least, their Spanish is nothing to speak of!" Then, having made a kind of pun, Carlos laughed.

But Juan trudging up the stairs behind him did not laugh. He had not understood a word Carlos said.

Carlos turned then and repeated the sentences in a stiff and inaccurate Spanish.

Juan nodded glumly. He felt betrayed. Even if he took the bus over here every day to play with the *puertorriqueño* kids on Columbus Avenue, it would be no good. He would still be a stranger—among his own people. Only they weren't his own people anymore. They were *americanos*.

When they reached the street Carlos said, in Spanish, "Well, thanks for helping me out."

And, in Spanish, Juan replied. "That's okay." Then he added, "I better say good-bye now. I'll be going back home at the end of the week."

"To the island?" Carlos said, in some surprise.

Juan nodded.

"You must be pretty rich," Carlos said, "to come hopping all the way over here just for one week. How much is the plane fare?"

Juan explained that the trip home wouldn't cost him anything. Pan American Airways would fly him home free. Carlos frowned. He did not understand. "Free? How could that be?"

Juan, speaking in slow careful Spanish as though he were addressing a very small child, explained how Pan Am had promised to send him home free the night he arrived. So since he hadn't taken them up on their offer then, he would do so at the end of the week.

"Listen, you stupid kid," Carlos said. "Sure they were going to send you home free when your uncle didn't show up. I mean they can't let a little kid like you just be hanging around the airport at night all alone. But your uncle *did* show up. So the offer's over. Now you're *his* worry.

Not theirs. How could they ever make any money if they kept dealing out free tickets to anyone wanting to make a trip back home?"

He spoke now in English. Juan kept nodding. Then he said, "*No entiendo*. I not onnerstan'."

So, with some effort, Carlos repeated it all in Spanish. Juan nodded again. This time he understood all too well, and knew with certainty that Carlos was correct. In fact, this very thought had been lurking in the back of his mind. But he hadn't allowed it to come forward before. Because he didn't want to know the truth. The truth that he *could* not go home.

"Listen, kid," Carlos said suddenly, in Spanish, "since you helped me with the boxes, how'd you like a free box seat for the game tomorrow afternoon?"

"What kind of game?" Juan asked.

"Stickball."

"What's stickball?"

"Stickball's what it says it is," Carlos said. "You hit a ball with a stick. Want me to show you?"

Juan nodded.

"C'mon," Carlos said. "I got my equipment upstairs." He shoved open the front door and Juan followed him into the hallway. The place smelled strongly of cats and rancid cooking oil and the garbage which sat outside each doorway in overflowing pails or paper bags.

Juan felt like holding his breath and holding his nose. Who would want to live in such a place when they could be back in the fresh mountain air of Barranquitas where the only smell one noticed was that of flowers?

When they reached the third floor Carlos took a ring of keys from his pocket and started unlocking one of the doors. "We got three different locks," he explained to Juan, "because we been robbed five times."

Juan was impressed. Carlos must live in a pretty big place with some valuable things in it for anyone to bother robbing his apartment *five* times. After all, even though the hallways smelled, that didn't mean the apartments weren't beautiful inside.

But inside there was nothing much either. Just one room with a flowered curtain drawn across the middle. The whole place was not much bigger than the bedroom he shared at home with his two sisters. There was a wooden table and four wooden chairs all painted bright green. There was a picture of the Virgin Mary tacked to the wall. And in the corner a small stove and a large sink, stacked with dishes. Sunlight fell in through the open window and lay in a long oblong pattern across the worn green linoleum on the floor. There was a flower box on the windowsill with some geraniums in it.

Not a bad place, Juan thought. At least it looked friendly. He'd a lot rather live here than in Uncle Esteban's fine basement apartment where all the windows had bars like a jail.

Carlos meanwhile had gone behind the curtain. He came back with a small rubber ball and a broom. "Of course," he said, "the bat we play with is a mop handle without the mop. But our captain keeps that in his house. I'm the manager of the team," he added, with an edge of pride in his voice. "That means I set up the games and arrange everything. The big game we got on tomorrow is against the Young Princes. Blacks against Spanish. Come on. I'll show you how we play."

Juan followed Carlos into the hallway again, waited while his new friend locked the door with three different keys, and went down the stairs after him, taking two at a time as Carlos did. In the street Carlos waited until a few cars had gone by. Then, when there was a lull in the traffic, he stepped out, threw the ball into the air, swung the broom handle hard. And missed.

Shamefaced, he picked up the ball. "Well, I myself am not so hot at this game," he said in English. "I'm better at organizing than playing. But the idea is, if you hit the ball past the first sewer that's pretty good. If you hit it past the second sewer, that's sensational. And if you hit it past the third sewer, that's impossible. The third sewer's right down at the end of the street. You can hardly even see it from here."

Juan nodded. He had barely understood a word that Carlos said.

But he was embarrassed to ask his friend to repeat it all over again in Spanish. So he asked instead, "I try?"

"Sure," Carlos said and threw him the broom which Juan caught in one hand. Then Carlos threw the ball which Juan caught in the other hand. And stepped out into the street.

"Hey! *Watch it!*" Carlos screamed in English.

Juan stepped back just as a yellow taxi sped by his toes.

He'd been so intent about showing Carlos that he could hit this ball with the broom that he forgot about everything else—including getting run over. His heart now started thudding with fear at his narrow escape.

"Listen!" Carlos said sternly. "They got such things as cars in this city and don't you ever forget that!"

Juan nodded. He looked carefully up and down the street.

"It's okay now," Carlos said. "Nothing coming."

But still Juan felt afraid.

"Hurry up! *Avanza!*" Carlos said. "Take your chance while you got it."

So Juan, his heart still pounding, stepped out into the street, threw the rubber ball into the air, and hit it with the broom handle. Hard.

He watched the ball proudly as it sped through the air.

Carlos screamed again. And again Juan rushed back to the safety of the sidewalk. But this time there were no cars coming. This time Carlos screamed for another reason. "You hit three sewers!" he kept screaming. "Man, don't you understand, you hit *three sewers*!"

"Yes," said Juan. "I onnerstan'."

He did not know what "three sewers" meant. But he did understand that Carlos was impressed at how he had hit the ball.

"Listen," Carlos said. "You must be puttin' me on, man. Telling me you never played stickball before." He repeated the question in Spanish. The words were charged with suspicion. "You sure you never played stickball before?"

Juan shook his head. "No," he said. "I have never played stickball before." He saw no reason to explain that he had been playing stick-stone ever since he was seven years old. Hitting a stone with a stick across the Piñonas River in the Contest game he had invented.

"Listen, kid," Carlos said suddenly. "How'd you like to play on our team tomorrow afternoon?" Then, slowly, carefully he tried the words in Spanish. "*¿Vas a jugar con nosotros mañana?*"

Juan grinned. "Sure, man," he said in English. "Hokay!"

When he got home Juan burst into his uncle's apartment and announced the news. *He* was going to play on the team against the Young Princes!

Uncle Esteban seemed mightily pleased. He gave Juan a resounding thwack on the back and raised the boy's arm in the manner of a winning boxer. Then he asked, "Where are the *plátanos* and the *gandules* and the *ajíes*?"

Juan gasped and clapped his hand over his mouth. He had left the groceries somewhere. But where?

"I'll go back," he told his uncle. "I'll find them!"

Uncle Esteban laughed. "Never mind," he said. "You've already found something a lot better."

The next afternoon, which was Saturday, Uncle Esteban paid a replacement to take over for him so that he could come and watch his nephew in the big game. "Also," said Uncle Esteban, "I may find a few friends myself. Who knows?"

They arrived early. Carlos was sitting on the stoop of his house, waiting. But as soon as he caught sight of Juan he raced down the street to welcome him.

"Man!" he said to Juan breathless. "Am I glad to see you! I been telling the team all about you. How a little kid—what are you, seven, eight years old?—can hit three sewers!"

Juan understood some of the sentences. He drew himself up with dignity. "I am ten years old."

"Oh," Carlos said. "So you're little for your age, that's all. But no matter how old you are—or how little—you're the first kid on this street that's hit three sewers all summer long." Then he looked at Juan and frowned. "What I'm wondering now is, was it just a lucky accident? Do you think you could ever do such a thing again?"

Since Juan did not understand, he merely grinned and nodded.

The game was scheduled for four o'clock. By three thirty the entire neighborhood, it seemed, was out on the street. The steps of the brownstone stoops were crowded as bleachers. The box seats set out by the areaways and the alleyways were all taken. Some people had even brought camp chairs and stools to sit out on the sidewalk. And the windows facing the street were filled with spectators gathered to watch the big game.

Voices rose like a wall of sound.

From the other end of the block came the loud tinkly music of "Mary Had a Little Lamb." It blared forth from the loudspeaker of a Mister Softee truck which was surrounded by children buying ice cream.

Juan had never in his life felt so nervous. It was one thing to hit a stone with a stick across the Piñonas River with only his friends, Ricardo and Eduardo and Julio and Ramón, watching. It was quite something else to try to hit a three-sewers run under the eyes of all these staring strangers. Fervently he wished he had never ventured forth from his uncle's apartment to buy the things they needed for the special Spanish supper.

Uncle Esteban was chatting with some men who were setting out a card table on the sidewalk. He seemed to have forgotten all about Juan.

"C'mon," Carlos said. "I gotta be sure you know the rules of the game." He took Juan by the arm and brought him over to a very tall boy called Pee-Wee. This boy spoke good Spanish, and carefully explained to Juan about the pitcher, the catcher,

the first, second and third bases. And how to run from one to the next. "*¿Alguna pregunta?*" said Pee-Wee then. "Any questions?"

The only question Juan had was how had he gotten into this mess. And how could he get himself out of it, and go back home to his uncle's house. But he managed to grin as though everything was fine and calm inside and he said, "I onnerstan'."

When it came his turn to stand up and bat he felt faint with fear. All the eyes on the street seemed to be boring into him. As he stood at home plate holding the sawed-off mop handle silence spread down the block. An exploding silence. Pee-Wee had told him that the word had gone around. This little kid had hit three sewers. Could he do it again? They all were watching; all were waiting.

The pitcher was a tall black boy. "Batter up, champ," he called. "You the midget miracle man they been crowing about?"

Laughter rose from the Young Princes and from people watching the game. Hooting, derisive laughter.

Anger clenched inside Juan's chest like a hard fist. Why were they making fun of him? Because he was a stranger? Because he was little for his age?

When the ball came flying toward him he slammed at it with all his strength, and watched then with stunned satisfaction as the ball sped down the street.

Everyone was screaming at him. "Run . . . . Run!" But he did not know what the word meant. Some kind of English *¡Bravo!* maybe. He smiled at the standing, scream-ing sidewalk crowd and raised one hand over his head in a victory

sign, as his uncle had done at home.

Pee-Wee ran up, began shaking him. "*¡Corre! ¡Corre!*"

And suddenly Juan remembered the rules and started racing toward first base: the fender of a parked car. The screams of the crowd grew louder. He made it to second base, a chalked circle in the middle of the street. Pee-Wee was racing along beside him. "Keep going!" Pee-Wee shouted in Spanish. "The ball went under the Softee truck. Keep running!"

He reached third base: the fire hydrant. And then the sprint back. He slid onto home plate, his breath coming in hard gasps.

Carlos and Pee-Wee and the rest of his teammates were all around him, slapping him on the back and shouting, "Man, you got home! You made a home run! You got home!"

Pride swelling inside him, he sat on the curb, Carlos on one side of him, Pee-Wee on the other. Carlos instructed Pee-Wee to ask whether Juan would come over again and play on their team. And Juan instructed Pee-Wee to say sure, he would come! He'd come over here every day to play. Even when school started in September, he'd keep coming.

Pee-Wee translated these words, and Carlos clapped Juan on the knee. "Man," he said. "You're in!"

Juan was up at bat four more times that afternoon. He hit no more home runs but that didn't seem to matter. He had done it once, so there was always the hope he might do it again. Each time he stood up at bat an expected hush of anticipation spread down the street. They were with him, he knew. Even those on the other team.

He was in! He belonged. And between his times at bat he sat on the curbstone, Carlos on one side, Pee-Wee on the other. At first he spoke only to Pee-Wee, spoke only in Spanish. But by the end of the afternoon he was shouting and cheering like all the others as one of his teammates hit the ball and raced down the street.

"Come on, man! Move it!" Loud and proud he yelled the words— words of the English language.

Reader's Response ∼ Did it seem real to you that Juan had a hard time feeling as if he belonged in his new home? Why?

Library Link ∼ *This story is an excerpt from the book* How Juan Got Home *by Peggy Mann. You might enjoy reading the entire book to learn more about Juan's experiences in his new home.*

GAMES
IN ANY
LANGUAGE

jan ken pon

You move your arm up and down three times and then make a fist, which stands for rock, or hold your hand out straight to stand for paper, or—you guessed it— spread two fingers to mean scissors. Sound familiar?

from Japan

alak do lak

This game has been played for hundreds of years by children and adults in Iran. One person hits a short piece of wood into the air with a bat. Other players try to catch the flying piece before it hits the ground. Hm-m-m. What does this game remind you of? . . .

from Iran

da ga

The person chosen to be Da Ga (The Big Snake) tries to catch another player. The person caught must join hands with the "snake" and help chase other players. The Da Ga grows longer and longer until there is no one else to catch. You may not have played Da Ga–or have you?

from Nigeria

327

Nathaniel's Rap

It's Nathaniel talking
and Nathaniel's me
I'm talking about
My philosophy
About the things I do
And the people I see
All told in the words
Of Nathaniel B. Free
That's me
And I can rap
I can rap
I can rap, rap, rap
Till your earflaps flap
I can talk that talk
Till you go for a walk
I can run it on down
Till you get out of town
I can rap

I can rap
Rested, dressed and feeling fine
I've got something on my mind
Friends and kin and neighborhood
Listen now and listen good
Nathaniel's talking
Nathaniel B. Free
Talking about
My philosophy
Been thinking all day
I got a lot to say
Gotta run it on down
Nathaniel's way
Okay!
I gotta rap
Gotta rap
Gotta rap, rap, rap
Till your earflaps flap

Gotta talk that talk
Till you go for a walk
Gotta run it on down
Till you get out of town
Gotta rap
Gotta rap
Rested, dressed and feeling fine
I've got something on my mind
Friends and kin and neighborhood
Listen now and listen good
I'm gonna rap, hey!
Gonna rap, hey!
Gonna rap, hey!
I'm gonna rap!

Eloise Greenfield
Jan Spivey Gilchrist, *Illustrator*

A Grain of Wheat

from A *Grain of Wheat*: A *Writer Begins*
by Clyde Robert Bulla

*Clyde Robert Bulla knew he wanted to become a writer
when he was about seven years old. His love of books began with
the Christmas books his mother read to him when he was just a
little boy.*

The three Christmas books were read to me until I knew
them by heart. From the ABC book I learned the letters—"A
is an apple pie, B bit it, C cut it," and all the rest. From
Mother Goose I learned about verses and rhymes. And *Peter
Rabbit* was a good story with good pictures.

I held the books in front of me and pretended to read. I
made pencil marks in a tablet and pretended I was writing.

My mother taught me to write *Clyde*.

"Now when you go to school, you'll know how to write
your name," she said.

I wanted to read and write, but I didn't want to go to
school. Someone had told me tales of what went on at school.
They must have frightened me.

331

Those were the days of country schools. Ours was the Bray School. My sister Louise had taught there before she was married. My sister Corrine had just finished high school and was ready to take Louise's place.

Corrine was teaching for the first time. I was going to school for the first time.

It was a two-mile walk to school. We started off together. Almost always it rained on the first day of school, but this was a sunny September day. I had my new dinner bucket. There was a beef sandwich in it, and a boiled egg and a banana and a piece of cake. But that gave me no joy.

I said, "I know I'll get a whipping."

"I'll be the teacher," Corrine said. "*I'm* not going to whip you."

Later we learned to cut across pastures and through woods to make the way shorter. On this day we took the road. Past Otis King's, past John King's and Mag Elliott's, over the iron bridge and up the clay hill, past George Haynes's, and there was the school lane.

On one side of the lane was a pasture. On the other side was a row of hedge trees. An odd kind of fruit grew on them. Hedgeballs, we called them. They looked like big green oranges and were good for nothing except to throw at fence posts or roll down hills.

At the end of the lane was the schoolyard, with the schoolhouse in the middle. The schoolhouse was white with a red-brick chimney. It had only one room. The blackboard was up front, along with the teacher's desk and the library. The library was a tall green cupboard with a door.

There were rows of seats and desks for the boys and girls. In the back of the room was a big iron stove.

Corrine and I were the first ones there. She wrote

Welcome on the blackboard. Boys and girls began to come from the farms in the neighborhood. There were nine boys and nine girls. Two or three rode horses to school, but most of them walked.

I was in the first grade with three other boys—Leonard, Lawrence, and Harold. Later Lawrence and Harold moved away, but Leonard and I were in school together for years.

When we were called up for our first class, we sat on a long bench in front of the teacher's desk. The teacher asked a question. What would we buy if we had a hundred dollars? I've forgotten what Lawrence and Harold answered. Leonard said he would buy a horse. That was a good answer for a farm boy. I said I would buy a table.

The older boys and girls had been listening. They all laughed at my answer.

Corrine said, "Why would you buy a *table*?"

I said I didn't know.

On the playground, girls and boys said, "A table—a table! What are you going to do with your table?"

And I knew I must guard against saying stupid things.

Still, I liked school. I was surprised at how much I liked it, although I was sometimes sorry my dog couldn't be there. Every day he started off with me. Every day I had to send him back.

It took our whole school to make two baseball teams. Besides baseball, we played ante-over, kick-the-can, dare-base, and Indian. In winter we played fox-and-geese in the snow.

George Haynes's pond was near the school. It was a good place to skate when the ice was smooth and thick enough. Our skates were the kind that clamped onto our

shoes. The clamps fastened with a key, and I could never get mine tight enough. My skates kept coming off.

When there was snow, we brought our sleds to school. Each sled had a name. Mine was "The Flying Arrow." Wayne King, who lived across the road from me, had one named "King of the Hills." Coasting down a hill was like flying. Not so much fun was the walk back up, dragging our sleds behind us.

Once during every school-year the boys made what we called a hut. It was a lean-to against the side of the coal-house. We made it of boards, logs—whatever we could find. Tall grass grew under the hedge trees. It dried stringy and tough. We pulled it up until we had a big stack, then we covered the outside of the hut with it. The idea was to cover the hut until it was completely dark inside.

The hut was for boys only. We told the girls they couldn't come in. I can't remember that any of them ever wanted to.

In first grade we had spelling, numbers, reading, and writing. I was slow at numbers, better at spelling. What I really liked were reading and writing. I wanted to learn new words. I wanted to write them and put them together to see what I could make them say. I would write *apple*. It could be "*an* apple" or "*the* apple." It could be on a tree or in a dish. It could be green, red, or yellow.

Words were wonderful. By writing them and putting them together, I could make them say whatever I wanted them to say. It was a kind of magic.

Reading was a kind of magic, too. In a book I could meet other people and know what they were doing and feeling and thinking. From a book I could learn about life in other places. Or I could learn everyday things like tying a knot or building a birdhouse.

By the time I was ready for the third grade, I had read most of the books in our school library. There weren't many. I wanted more. Except for my three Christmas books, we had no children's books at home. I began reading whatever I could find in the family bookcase.

There was a thick book called *Oliver Twist*. It had words I didn't know, but there were many I *did* know, and I was able to read the story all the way through.

Lee, the soldier who married my sister, went to California. Louise followed him, but for a time she was in Missouri while he was far away by the Pacific Ocean. I wrote this poem about them:

California and Missouri

> Hand in hand,
> Over the sand,
> Down by the sea,
> And there sits Lee.
>   'Tis California.
>
> Go out and romp
> In the swamp
> And pick some peas.
> There sits Louise.
>   'Tis Missouri.

It was my first poem.

I started to write a story, but it was never finished. I called it "How Planets Were Born." This is the way it began: "One night old Mother Moon had a million babies. . . ."

Now I knew why I had said, in the first grade, that I wanted a table. Even then I wanted to be a writer. And didn't writers sit at tables or desks when they wrote?

I wanted to be a writer. I was sure of that.

"I'm going to write books," I said.

My mother said, "Castles in the air."

"What does that mean?" I asked.

"It means you're having daydreams," she said. "You'll

dream of doing a lot of different things, but you probably won't do any of them. As you get older, you'll change."

I went from the second grade to the third to the fourth, and I hadn't changed. I still knew what I wanted to be.

I thought about writing and talked about it. I talked too much.

My father told me he was tired of listening to me.

"You can't be a writer," he said. "What do you know about people? What have you ever done? You don't have anything to write about."

When I thought over what he had said, it seemed to me he was right. I stopped writing. But not for long.

The city nearest us was St. Joseph, Missouri. Our newspaper came from there. In the paper I read about a contest for boys and girls—"Write the story of a grain of wheat in five hundred words or less." First prize was a hundred dollars. There were five second prizes of twenty dollars each. After that there were one hundred prizes of one dollar each.

I began to write my story. It went something like this: "I am a grain of wheat. I grew in a field where the sun shone and the rain fell."

I didn't tell anyone what I was doing. When my story was finished, I made a neat copy. I mailed it in our mailbox down the road.

Time went by. I began to look for the newspaper that would tell who had won the contest. At last it came.

There was a whole page about the contest. I saw I hadn't won the first prize. I hadn't won a second prize either. That was a disappointment. I had thought I might win one of the second prizes.

I read down the long list at the bottom of the page—the names and addresses of the boys and girls who had won the one-dollar prizes. Surely my name would be there. It *had* to be!

I read more and more slowly. Only a few names were left.

And one of them was mine! "Clyde Bulla, King City, Missouri."

"I won!" I shouted.

My mother looked at my name. "That's nice," she said. *Nice?* Was that all she could say?

I started to show the paper to my father. There was something in his face that stopped me. I could see he wasn't happy that I had won a prize.

My sister Corrine was there. I could see she wasn't happy either. She was sorry for me because all I had won was a dollar.

Didn't they know it wasn't the dollar that mattered?

I had written a story that was all mine. No one had helped me. I had sent it off by myself. How many other boys and girls had sent their stories? Maybe a thousand or more. But my story had won a prize, and my name was here in the paper. I was a writer. No matter what anyone else might say, I was a writer.

Reader's Response ∽ How did reading about Clyde Robert Bulla's struggle to become a writer make you feel?

Library Link ∽ *This story is an excerpt from the book* A Grain of Wheat: A Writer Begins. *You might enjoy reading the entire book to find out more about its author, Clyde Robert Bulla.*

Bread, Bread, Bread

Wheat is the world's most important cereal crop. In many countries throughout the world, bread made from wheat or other grains—corn, oat, or rye, for example— appears in some form at almost every meal.

A Peruvian boy enjoys a taste of the bread his mother makes to sell in the market. ▶

◀ Pizza is bread, too! Americans popularized pizza with pepperoni on top.

◀ Tortillas are flat circles of bread that people in Mexico bake.

◀ Fill a pita bread pocket with vegetables or meat and you'll have a Middle Eastern lunch or dinner.

341

Mika's Apple Tree

from *Mika's Apple Tree: A Story of Finland*
by Clyde Robert Bulla

*One day after school, Mika and his mother stopped
to buy a basket from a woman who made and sold
baskets. The woman lived in a small gray house. Next to
the house was an apple tree. Mika thought the tree was
beautiful and sat looking at the tree while his mother
went inside to buy a basket. As they were leaving, the
woman gave Mika an apple from the tree.*

Mika ate the apple the woman had given him.
It was a good apple, full of juice and not too sweet.

"I wish we had an apple tree by *our* house," he said.

"So do I," she said, "but it can't be."

"Why?" he asked.

"You know why," she said.

The farm was shaped like a piece of pie. The wide
part was on the other side of the road. The barn was
there, and the pasture and the field, the garden, and the
woods. The farm came to a point where it reached out

into the lake. The point was all rock, and the house was on the point. Mika's grandfather had built it there long ago.

"Why did Grandfather build our house out here?" asked Mika.

"He thought a house built on rock would be strong," said Mother. "And there was another reason. When your grandfather was young, he stayed at home to take care of his mother and father, but he always wished he could have been a sailor. He liked to be near the water. He used to say he wanted to live where the waves came up to the front door."

"They almost do," said Mika.

"You like our house, don't you?" asked Mother.

"Yes," said Mika, "but I'd like it more with an apple tree here."

"An apple tree growing out of rock—that would be the greatest tree in all Finland!" said Mother, and she went inside to make supper.

Gulls were crying overhead. They had seen Mika eating and they were waiting for what might be left.

343

He threw the apple core away. A gull swooped down for it. And then a thought came to Mika.

"Shoo!" he shouted.

The gull screamed and flew away.

Mika picked up the core and put it into his pocket.

That night, in his room, he took the seeds out of the core. Some had been lost, but three were left.

The next day he found a saucepan in the trash barrel. There was a hole in it, and Mother had thrown it away.

He took the saucepan to the woods and filled it with dirt. He brought it back to the house.

"What are you doing?" asked Mother.

"I'm going to plant my apple seeds," he said.

She laughed. "Are you going to grow apple trees in the saucepan?"

"I'll *start* them in the saucepan," he said.

He planted the seeds and set the saucepan on the window sill. He kept the seeds watered.

Every day after school he looked at the saucepan. One seed began to grow, but the little plant curled up and turned brown. One seed did not grow at all. But the third seed sent up a sprout. The sprout sent out a leaf.

Winter had come. Snow fell. Mika stopped riding his bicycle to school. He went on his skis instead.

In the short winter days he kept the saucepan in the south window where the plant might catch a little sun. Through the long nights he kept the plant near the fire.

One day when he came home from school, a man was there.

"Father!" shouted Mika.

The man picked him up and swung him about the room.

"Am I bigger?" asked Mika.

"Yes!" said Father. "I can hardly lift you."

"Are you going to stay a long time?" asked Mika.

"Three days," said Father. "There's a lot we can do in three days. Guess what we're going to do first."

"What?" asked Mika.

"We're going to have a sauna," said his father.

They went out to the bathhouse. They left their clothes in the small room just inside the door. They went into the larger room. It was ready for the sauna bath.

Father had made a fire in the oven. There were stones on top of the oven. The stones were crackling hot.

Father took a dipperful of water from the tub by the door. He threw it on the stones. There was a hissing noise, and clouds of steam filled the room.

At first Mika could hardly breathe. Still, he liked the feel of the heat and steam.

He and Father sat on one of the seats along the wall. They beat themselves with sticks from a birch tree. The sticks had leaves on them.

"These leaves still smell fresh," said Father, "and I cut the sticks last summer."

Mika liked the smell of the leaves. He liked the way his skin tingled under the birch sticks.

Father brought a pail of water and a cake of soap. He said as they scrubbed themselves, "This is something I think about when I'm at sea. I miss my sauna."

They sat there, talking. Father wanted to know what had happened at school.

"Your mother says you talk about what you'll be when you grow up," he said.

"Sometimes," said Mika.

"What are you going to be?" asked Father.

"I keep thinking," Mika said, "but I don't know yet."

"Isn't there anything you want to be?" asked Father.

"Yes," said Mika, "but no *one* thing."

"Well," said Father, "there's no hurry, is there?"

"No," said Mika, "but at school everybody knows but me."

They dressed and went into the house. Supper was ready. They had cabbage soup with rye bread and butter. They had pancakes with jam.

A storm came up across the lake. The wind shook the windows.

"It's a good evening to be in our house," said Mother.

"Yes," said Father. "I'll remember this when I'm back on my ship."

Mika wished his father would never go back to the

ship. But he did not say it. He sat and listened and said nothing at all.

Spring came. Mika's apple tree was small, but it had lived through the winter.

"You should plant it now," said Mother. "Then it will have a good start before next winter. Do you know where you want it?"

"Yes," said Mika.

"By the barn?" she asked.

"No," he said.

"By the potato patch?" she asked.

"No," he said.

"Where then?" she asked.

"I want it here by the house," he said.

"Mika, you're like your grandfather," she said. "When we told him something couldn't be done, that was the thing he wanted to do! Even grass doesn't grow here on the point. How could you make a tree grow?"

"I have an idea," said Mika.

He walked around the house. Near one corner was a wide, deep hollow in the rocks. Sometimes water stayed there for a long time after a rain.

He looked into the hollow. Then he took a bucket and a shovel, and went to the woods.

He filled the bucket with dirt. He carried it back to the house. He poured the dirt into the hollow.

The bucketful of dirt had been heavy. Yet at the bottom of the hollow he could hardly see it.

The next time he took two buckets to the woods. When they were full of dirt, they were too heavy for him to carry. He brought the wood cart out of the barn. It held both buckets.

He pulled the cart across the road and onto the point. He poured the dirt into the hollow.

Mother came out of the house. She asked, "What *are* you doing?"

"I'm filling the hollow," he said.

"Mika," she said, "don't you know that will take you all summer?"

"Yes," he said.

She said again, "You're like your grandfather." She went back into the house.

And Mika hauled another load of dirt.

When school was out in June, he had more time for his work. Day after day he carried dirt to the hollow.

One afternoon four boys from up the road came to help him. But they played more than they worked. They threw dirt and pushed one another into the hollow. Mika did most of the work alone.

The day came when the hollow was filled to the top.

Father was at home that day.

He said, "So much dirt for such a small tree."

"There has to be room for the roots," said Mika. He brought the saucepan out of the house.

Very carefully he lifted out the little tree. Very carefully he planted it in the hole he had dug.

Every day he looked at it to make sure no bugs were eating the leaves. He put heavy rocks about it so that no wandering dog would dig it out.

One evening in autumn he felt the damp east wind against his face. He smelled snow in the air.

He thought of the little tree under a drift of snow. He found the saucepan that Mother had thrown away again. He turned it upside down over the tree.

In the morning the ground was white.

That winter was long and cold, with one snow after another.

On the day before Christmas Eve, Father came home. He went to the woods and brought back a Christmas tree. Mika put candles and tinsel on the tree. Mother showed him how to make stars and crowns out of golden straw. He put them on the tree, too.

The house was clean and shining. The Christmas baking was done. Mother had baked ginger cookies, prune tarts, and little round fruitcakes. And on Christmas Day there were presents. Mother and Father gave Mika two books, a blue knitted sweater, and a new pair of skis. Mika had presents for them, too. At school he had carved a big wooden spoon for them, and he had made them a bird feeder to put outside the window.

Father stayed until the fourth day after Christmas. Just before he went away, he and Mika took shovels and made paths in the snow.

Mika said, "I want to dig down and see my tree."

"No, don't," said Father. "The snow keeps it from the cold."

By the end of winter, white drifts were high against the house. Mika kept thinking of his tree. He wished he had waited until it was bigger and stronger before he planted it. He wished he had waited another year.

In the spring Father came home for a week. While he was there, two visitors came. They were his two brothers.

One of them, Mika's Uncle Olli, was a lumberman in the far north. The other, Uncle Paavo, made furniture in the great city of Helsinki. For the first time in years the three brothers were together.

They sat at the table and talked for hours. They

walked about the farm. They met Mika coming from school, and they all walked home together.

As they sat in the kitchen, Uncle Olli said, "So this is the boy who doesn't know what he is going to be when he grows up."

"Can't you make up your mind, Mika?" asked Uncle Paavo.

Mika shook his head.

"You could come with me," said Uncle Olli. "I'll take you to the forests—our green gold, we call them. We'll cut trees and float them down the rivers. While we're there, I'll show you the reindeer. How would you like to ride in a sled with a reindeer pulling you over the snow?"

"I'd like it," said Mika.

"And on a clear night you could see the Northern Lights—great rays of light all across the north sky," said Uncle Olli. "It's a sight, I can tell you.... What do you say? Will you come with me?"

"No," said Uncle Paavo. "Mika is coming with me. We'll go to Helsinki and make furniture in my factory. I'll show him how we make the chairs and tables we send out all over the world. In the city there are always good times. We can see the best plays and hear the best music—"

"Be quiet, you two," said Father. "When Mika is old enough, I'll take him to sea with me."

"I think he'd rather go with me," said Uncle Olli.

"No, he'd rather go with me to Helsinki," said Uncle Paavo.

They were laughing, yet it seemed to Mika that it was more than a joke.

"What do you say, Mika?" said Father. "You're really going to sea with me, aren't you?"

"I'll have to think about it," said Mika.

Mother had opened the door to let the sun shine in.

Mika went outside. He breathed the spring air. Then he saw that the snow had melted until the top of the old saucepan was in sight.

He knelt in the snow. He lifted the saucepan. The little tree stood there like a small, straight stick.

For a moment he thought it was frozen. He touched the stem. He bent it gently toward him.

The tree was not frozen. It was cool and alive. He could feel its life in his fingers.

He ran into the house.

"Have you made up your mind?" asked Uncle Olli. "Are you going with me or your Uncle Paavo or your father?"

They were still laughing, yet Mika still had a feeling it was more than a joke.

He said, "I'd better stay here. I'd better stay—to take care of my tree."

"Your tree?" said the two uncles.

"He planted it by the house," said Father. "He worked hard all summer to make a place for it."

The men were quiet for a while.

Uncle Olli said, "Could it be we have a farmer here?"

"That's how it looks to me," said Father.

"Is that right, Mika?" asked Uncle Paavo.

Mika did not answer, but he was saying to himself, A farmer—I think that's what I *will* be!

"You don't have to make up your mind now," said Father. "There's plenty of time. You know that, don't you?"

"I know it," said Mika, but he kept thinking, A farmer—a farmer! And suddenly he felt very happy.

He went back outside. He sat for a long time, looking at his tree and the shadow it made on the ground.

Reader's Response 〜 How did you feel about Mika's effort and determination in this story?

Why do we like stories about people who do what they set out to do?

MAKE IT HAPPEN

People can do the most amazing things.

Unit 4 Theme

LAWRENCE, Jacob (American, born 1917): "The migrants arrived in great numbers," panel 40 from THE MIGRATION OF THE NEGRO, *(1940–41). Tempera on gesso on composition board, 12 x 18". Collection, The Museum of Modern Art, New York. Gift of Mrs. David M. Levy.*

355

Theme Books for
Make It Happen

*S*ometimes reaching a goal is hard to do. What is it that makes people persist and accomplish what they set out to do?

✜ In *Stone Fox* by John Reynolds Gardiner, the only way Willy can save Grandfather's farm is by winning the annual dogsled race. But how can he compete against champion racer Stone Fox? Is Willy's determination enough to win the race?

✜ When British Redcoats capture Philadelphia, Annie MacDougal wants to show her loyalty to the Revolutionaries. In *The Sign Painter's Secret* by Dorothy and Thomas Hoobler, her chance, though risky, comes sooner than she thinks.

❖ Learn about life in medieval times in *A Tournament of Knights* by Joe Lasker. Baron Orlando calls a tournament to honor his son, Lord Justin, who has just become a knight. When Lord Justin faces Sir Rolf in a jousting match, will he prove his honor— or his fear?

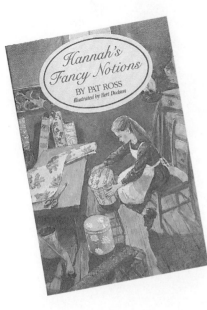

❖ Because Rebecca must work hard all week in the distant mills of Lowell, Massachusetts, Hannah wants to make something extra special for her sister's birthday. Find out how Hannah's idea changes her family's fortune in *Hannah's Fancy Notions* by Pat Ross.

More Books to Enjoy

Phoebe the Spy by Judith Berry Griffin
The Legend of the Bluebonnet by Tomie dePaola
Justin and the Best Biscuits in the World
    by Mildred Pitts Walter
Harriet the Spy by Louise Fitzhugh

The Bicycle Racer

from *Bicycle Rider*
by Mary Scioscia

"Out of the way! Here I come! I'm winning!" shouted Marshall, pedaling his bicycle as fast as he could.

Walter laughed. "But I just won, Shorty. That line back there in the sidewalk is the finish line."

"I almost won," said Marshall, pulling up beside his big brother.

As they entered the kitchen, Mama said, "I'm glad you're home, boys. Walter, we need more wood for the stove. Marshall, please get me a bucket of water from the well. Supper is nearly ready."

Big sister Pearl stirred a huge pot of stew on the iron cookstove. Geneva popped a pan of biscuits into the oven. Carlton carried the eighth chair to the table. Ruth cuddled the baby in her arms as they went back and forth in the rocking chair. Papa stood in the hallway, brushing his red coachman's jacket. Walter set down an armload of wood beside the stove. Marshall brought Mama a bucket of water.

"Supper is ready," said Mama.

The Taylor family sat down together. They all bowed their heads; Papa said grace. Gaslights flickered above the table, making dancing shadows on everyone's face.

"Papa, I almost beat Walter today when we raced home from his job," said Marshall.

"It's true," Walter said as he passed the biscuits. "I'm glad I gave him my old bike."

"I declare," said Mama, "if that boy isn't faster than any horse and carriage in Indiana."

"I'm going to be just like you, Marshall, when I get big," whispered Carlton.

"Papa," said Marshall. "I want a job."

"You're too little to have a job," said Ruth. "You're one of the younger children."

"I'm the oldest of the younger children," said Marshall. "I can't be a carpenter yet, like Walter, or a coachman, like Papa, but I have my bike, and I'm a fast rider. I can deliver packages for a store."

"Maybe," said Papa.

"Can I try this Saturday?"

Papa looked at Mama. "What do you think?" he asked.

Mama nodded. "He's short," she said, "but he's a good bicycle rider, and dependable."

"Yes. You may try to find a job, son," said Papa.

"Not this Saturday," said Carlton. "You promised to take me to the bicycle store, Marshall, and to teach me the bicycle tricks you made up."

"Those tricks? They don't amount to a hill of beans, Carlton."

"Marshall, you promised," complained Carlton.

"All right. We'll go to the bicycle store *after* I look for a job. And I'll teach you the bicycle tricks, too."

On Saturday morning Marshall biked downtown. Mercer's dry goods store was the biggest store on Main Street. Rolls of brown wool and pink and yellow flowered calico were arranged behind gleaming scissors and brightly colored spools of thread in the store window. Inside the store, Mrs. Mercer stood behind the counter.

"Can I help you?" she asked Marshall.

"Yes, ma'am. I want a job. I have my own bicycle. Do you need someone to deliver packages?"

"Dear me, no," she said briskly. "We do everything ourselves. My husband delivers packages on his way home every night."

Next Marshall tried Caldwell's grocery store.

"Mr. Caldwell, sir," said Marshall. "I want a job as an errand boy. I have a bicycle. I'm a fast rider, and I can deliver groceries."

Mr. Caldwell was arranging a pyramid of oranges. Slowly, he placed each orange in the design. When he put the last orange carefully at the top of the pyramid, he stepped back to admire the arrangement. He patted his stomach.

"Well, young fellow," he finally drawled. "Caldwell's has its own delivery wagon drawn by two fine brown horses. Grocery orders are too big to go out on a bicycle. Come back another year, when you're bigger. We might be able to use you somewhere else in the business."

"Thank you, sir," said Marshall.

Grocery orders might be too big to go on a bicycle, but medicines were always in small boxes. Marshall went to Smith's drugstore. Mr. Smith was making a chocolate soda for a woman and her little girl. Marshall stood waiting politely till he finished.

"What would you like?" asked Mr. Smith after he had served the woman and girl.

"I want a job, sir. Could I deliver medicines for you? I have my own bicycle, and I ride fast."

"Right now a high school boy named Roger does that for me. Come back next year, when Roger goes to college," said Mr. Smith.

At home for his midday meal, Marshall was downcast. "Shucks. Job hunting is hard. Everyone thinks I'm too small."

"Don't worry. Next year, when you're bigger, you'll get a job," Mama answered him.

In the afternoon, Carlton got up on the bicycle behind Marshall. They rode down Main Street to Hay and Willit's bicycle store.

"That's my favorite," said Marshall, pointing at a shiny red racing bicycle in the center of the window.

Carlton liked the funny one beside it with a big front wheel and a tiny back wheel. They both admired the sparkling gold medal pinned to a black velvet stand.

"Read me that sign," Carlton said.

" 'Hay and Willit's bicycle store. Best in Indianapolis. This gold medal will go to the winner of the ten-mile race. May 10, 1892,' " Marshall read.

"I bet you could win that race," said Carlton.

"Not me," said Marshall. "I'm not that fast. Even though I am almost as fast as Walter. Hey, Carlton. Look how wide the sidewalk is here in front of the store. Want me to show you some of the bike tricks now?"

Carlton clapped his hands. "Yes. Show me, Marshall."

Marshall lay on the bicycle seat and pushed the pedals with his hands. He helped Carlton do the same trick. People walking past the store stopped to look.

Marshall squatted on the bicycle seat and juggled three pennies. Carlton tried squatting on the seat, too. He couldn't do it. Marshall did the trick again.

More people stopped to watch.

A tall thin boy said, "That's a stupid trick. I bet you fall on your head."

A small girl said, "George Pepper, mind your manners."

"Go lay an egg!" said George Pepper.

More people stopped to watch. A coachman pulled his carriage over to the curb to see Marshall's tricks.

Marshall did a headstand on his bicycle seat. Then he rode his bicycle backward. Suddenly, the bicycle shop door opened and Mr. Hay stood in the doorway.

"Now you're in for it," jeered George Pepper. "You're in real trouble now!"

"Young man," called Mr. Hay. "I want to speak to you."

Marshall walked the bicycle over to Mr. Hay.

"Yes, sir?" said Marshall.

"Where did you learn those tricks?" asked Mr. Hay.

"I made them up, sir. I was just showing my little brother. He likes to see them."

"I don't wonder," said Mr. Hay.

"I'm sorry, sir, if we disturbed you."

"Disturbed us! Not at all! Those are the best bicycle tricks I've ever seen. My partner and I could use a boy like you. How would you like a job? We need someone to dust and sweep the store every day and to put coal in the potbellied stove. You could come here after school and on Saturdays to do these jobs. And if there is time, you could do your bicycle tricks in front of our store. It will make people want to come to this bicycle shop."

"Yes, sir!" cried Marshall.

"Start Monday after school," said Mr. Hay.

"I'll be here!" said Marshall.

Carlton climbed up behind Marshall on his bicycle.

As Marshall pedaled home, Carlton said, "It's funny. When you looked for a job, you didn't get one. When you didn't look for a job, you got one!"

365

Epilogue

Marshall Taylor became the fastest bicycle rider in the world. Nicknamed Major Taylor because he stood so straight, he was the first **black** person to participate in national bicycle races that were integrated. His first professional race in 1896 was at Madison Square Garden in New York City. During the years from 1896 to 1910 he raced in the U.S.A., Europe, and Australia. Several times he won American and World Championships.

Bicycle racing was a major sport in the late 1800's and early 1900's. Huge crowds would go to see any race Major Taylor rode in. All the newspapers would cover the event.

Taylor was especially loved by his fans for his remarkable riding skills and for his fairness and good sportsmanship.

Reader's Response ～ Of all the things Marshall Taylor did in this story, which one did you most admire? Why?

Library Link ～ *This story is an excerpt from the book* Bicycle Rider *by Mary Scioscia. You might enjoy reading the entire book to learn more about Marshall Taylor.*

Rules
of the
Road

When Marshall Taylor entered his first professional race in 1896, bicycles were the fastest wheels on the road! Many people complained that they frightened horses and were dangerous to riders and pedestrians.

Then, as now, riding a bicycle was a responsibility. An Indiana newspaper published these safety tips in 1894:

1. Be courteous to pedestrians. Always give them the right of way.
2. Keep a good distance behind any carriage.
3. Slow down and look right and left at crossroads.
4. Make certain that your cycle is in working order.
5. Never do stunts with your cycle.
6. Never try to hitch a ride by holding on to a wagon.
7. Never ride two on a bike unless it is a tandem.
8. Steer straight; don't weave.
9. Watch for dogs, other small animals, and young children.
10. Ride on the right and in a straight line. Stay close to the side of the road. Ride single file if in a group.

How many of these safety rules still apply today?

The World

10 PAGES.   NEW YORK, MONDAY, OCTOBER 10, 1887.   10 PAGES.

NELLIE BLY

Remarkable Story of the Successful Female Reporter

by Polly Carter

One hundred years ago, if you were a girl, nobody even thought of asking you what you wanted to be when you grew up. Women were expected to stay at home. When Elizabeth Cochrane decided in 1885 that she was going to be a reporter, she knew she would have to fight for herself as well as for all the people whose stories she wanted to tell.

Elizabeth was a born reporter. Her father, who was a judge in Pittsburgh, Pennsylvania, sent her around as his scout when he had a case to decide. She talked to the people involved and tried to find useful information that might not turn up in court. Judge Cochrane trained Elizabeth to think for herself and to draw up reports on what she had learned.

When her father died, Elizabeth's six brothers wanted her to be an old lady's companion or a children's governess. But she liked adventure. She decided to make her own plans.

In Pittsburgh's main newspaper, the *Dispatch,* Elizabeth read an editorial called "What Girls Are Good For." It said that women had "inferior brains" and should stay at home where they would not be in men's way.

Elizabeth boiled over. Inferior brains indeed! She would show that editor.

She wrote a furious answer to the *Dispatch* but didn't sign it. Her anonymous letter was so good that George Madden, who had written the editorial, thought it had been sent by a man. He wanted someone with so much talent to work for his newspaper.

In an advertisement, Madden offered a job to "the gentleman who wrote a letter to the Pittsburgh *Dispatch,* criticizing our editorial." When the gentleman turned out to be Elizabeth, he nearly refused to see her.

Luckily, Elizabeth was as good a talker as she was a writer. Even though she was only eighteen, it was obvious that she had talent, ideas, and courage. Madden knew he was taking a big risk, but he hired her.

Because women in those days were not supposed to do anything so unladylike as work for a newspaper, Madden decided to protect Elizabeth and her family by giving her a pen name. He chose "Nellie Bly," the name of a Stephen Foster song which everyone was singing at the time.

And it wasn't long before Nellie Bly the reporter was as well known as the song. Nellie wanted to help the poor and downtrodden, and she fought for them with her pen.

She went into the slums and wrote about the horrible conditions there: dirt, sickness, and suffering. She went into tenements and factories and wrote angrily about landlords and factory owners who let people live and work in cold, dark, rat-infested rooms. The people of Pittsburgh who read her articles began to get angry, too.

Next, Nellie had the idea of pretending she needed a job. She went to work in one of the darkest, coldest, most rat-infested factories she could find. Her fellow workers were half-blind, shivered with cold, and often fainted from having to stand and twist wires as quickly as they could for twelve hours a day.

Nellie was fired after one hour for getting a drink of water.

The story Nellie wrote about this factory made its owners angry. They threatened to ruin Madden's newspaper by pulling out all their advertisements. Madden asked Nellie to write about music and art, instead of slums. He hoped she would settle down.

But Nellie didn't want to settle down. She decided to work in New York instead.

"Why go to New York?" Nellie's family asked her. The answer was simple. New York had the biggest, most important newspapers in the country.

Nellie had been drawn into the lives of the poor people whose stories she told in her *Dispatch* articles, stories of suffering and hardship met with quiet strength and sharing. Nellie decided to give these people voices.

But she soon found that it wasn't easy to speak up for others when she couldn't be heard herself. The New York newspaper publishers were so big and important that they didn't have time to listen to her. For weeks Nellie tramped the pavements looking for a job.

Finally, in desperation, she decided to stand outside a publisher's door until he took notice of her. This was a bold move, and she boldly chose the greatest and most important editor of all, Joseph Pulitzer of the *World*.

For three hours she stood outside his office. At last, impressed by her determination, the managing editor let her in to see Mr. Pulitzer.

Nellie knew she had to talk quickly and talk well. She remembered that Madden had decided to hire her because she had interesting new ideas and the courage to carry them out.

She told Pulitzer, "I have a good idea for a new story. I'll find out what Blackwell's Island for the insane is really like, from the inside."

"How?" said Mr. Pulitzer.

Nellie gulped. "I'll have to pretend I'm insane, too."

By pretending she had lost her memory, Nellie found it was easy to get to Blackwell's Island. It was not so easy to stay there. Before she went, she had been afraid of how the real patients would treat her, but she soon found she had more to fear from the cruel and careless nurses.

After lining up with all the other patients to be washed in the same tin tub of dirty, ice-cold water, she was dressed in a thin slip marked LUNATIC ASYLUM BIH6. Shivering, she ate her moldy bread and stringy meat. Ten days later a lawyer from the *World* came to rescue Nellie. She had seen so many suffering patients and ignorant nurses that she was almost sick herself. But she rushed home and sat down to write a whole series of articles.

Her opening story, "Behind Asylum Bars," took up almost the entire front page of the newspaper. This was the first time anyone had thought of writing an I-was-there story about such an important subject. Everyone was so interested in what Nellie had to say that the *World* had to print thousands of extra copies that day. Nellie felt proud, but she was even prouder when the city raised a large sum of money for better food, better clothing, and better nurses at Blackwell's Island.

This was only the beginning. Nellie pointed the way for many other reforms and rescued countless people from misery and injustice in the abominable factories, jails, and workhouses. Whenever she discovered that someone had become rich and powerful by cheating and stealing, she did not hesitate to write about it.

"Don't hire a small, pretty girl if you have something to hide," people joked. "She may be Nellie Bly, and then you'll be in trouble."

When Nellie wanted to relax, she wrote articles that made people laugh. Even these stories came out of her own experience. Dancing in a chorus line was almost as hard for Nellie as going to Blackwell's Island, but she and her readers had fun.

One evening, curled up by the fire with a popular new book, Nellie had the most fun idea of all.

She was reading *Around the World in Eighty Days,* by the French writer Jules Verne. She smiled at the hero, Phileas Fogg, and his idea of going around the world in two months and two weeks just to prove it could be done. Then she laughed.

It was a good idea. Why shouldn't somebody *really* go around the world in eighty days?

Joseph Pulitzer agreed with Nellie. The publisher saw his chance to increase his newspaper's circulation and to

show all the world what America and Americans could do. Nellie took only two dresses with her for the whole trip. On shipboard a gentleman who had nineteen trunks himself asked her to marry him because he admired a woman who could travel with just one bag and who didn't think about clothes all the time.

Nellie's route was slightly different from Phileas Fogg's, partly because she stopped in France to meet Jules Verne and have tea with him. She finally arrived back in New York Harbor after 72 days, 6 hours, 11 minutes, and 14 seconds. Her two dresses were both in shreds. A small monkey she had found in Singapore sat chattering on her shoulder.

Nellie was the biggest story of the day in newspapers throughout the world. Her own paper's front page headline proudly announced, "FATHER TIME OUTDONE!"

But her best story was what she made out of her own life. She showed that the pen really is mightier than the sword and she led the way for women into journalism. Nellie had become a part of history, a legend in her own time, because she had new ideas and the courage to carry them out.

Reader 's Response ⁓ Elizabeth Cochrane had many exciting reporting jobs. Which one do you think was the most interesting? Why?

IN NELLIE'S DAY

1873 **Riveted Denim Blue Jeans** were first patented by Jacob Davis and Levi Strauss.

1876 The first clear transmission of human speech by **Telephone** was made by Alexander Graham Bell.

1886 **Coca Cola®** was invented and first sold by Dr. J. Pemberton.

1893 An early version of the **Zipper** was patented by W. L. Judson.

1895 Welcome to the movies! The **First Moving Picture Show** projected onto a screen was shown by the Lumiere brothers.

1901 The **Great Spindletop Oil Field** was discovered near Beaumont, Texas.

1906 W. K. Kellogg started a company to sell a **Cereal** he had invented in 1898. Can you guess the cereal's name?   Answer: Corn Flakes!

1914 An electric **Traffic Light** (red and green only) was put up in Cleveland, Ohio.

If you had lived in Nellie's day, which events might have influenced you the most?

The
GIFT

written by Helen Coutant
illustrated by Vo-Dinh Mai

Anna left the house at the usual time that morning. It would take her five minutes to run down the hill to where the school bus waited. If she was fast, she could stop by old Nana Marie's house. By now, Nana Marie might be back from the hospital. She had disappeared without warning more than a week ago. For two days, no one had answered when Anna knocked on the door after school. By the third day, Anna could scarcely eat she was so worried. Had they taken Nana Marie to one of those homes for very old people? But the next afternoon the daughter-in-law, Rita, who took care of Nana Marie, had opened the door an inch. It was just enough so that Anna could hear her voice over the blare of the TV.

"You here to see Nana Marie? She's in the hospital." That was all Anna found out.

Now, rounding a bend in the road, Anna could see Rita standing by the gate in front of Nana Marie's house. Rita's loud voice rang out. "She's coming home today! Home from the hospital! Nana Marie!"

Nana Marie was coming home. Anna's heart gave a joyful leap.

"We're throwing a little party," Rita went on. "Just a few neighbors on the hill to welcome her back, cheer her up. Drop by after school. She'll be looking for you."

A party. That meant Anna would have to share Nana Marie with everyone else. Rita's voice, suddenly lower, caught Anna's attention.

"She won't really be looking for you, Nana Marie won't. But come to see her anyway. She'll need your company now that she's blind. . . ."

Blind? Rita's voice rattled on, but Anna heard nothing more. Her heart seemed to have stopped on the word *blind*. How could Nana Marie suddenly be blind? There had been nothing wrong with Nana Marie's eyes. In fact, it was those extraordinary warm eyes, a cornflower blue, that had drawn Anna to Nana Marie in the first place. A small, choking noise escaped from Anna's throat.

Rita cocked her head and looked down, waiting for Anna to speak; then resumed her monologue. "Just happened, just like that," she said, shaking her head. "It's a pity. It's terrible. But you come by this afternoon for the party. We'll cheer her up, give Nana Marie some little presents to help her forget. Can I count on you?"

Count on her! Had Anna ever missed a chance to visit Nana Marie in the last six months, ever since the two had discovered each other one balmy September afternoon?

"So you come!" Rita repeated, her voice rising. Anna couldn't answer. She pulled back, nodding, and turned away. She walked carefully around the puddles in the road. Her whispered "good-bye" floated up unheard by Rita, who was already going in the house, shivering from the February cold.

When the door banged, Anna took off, propelled by anger and sorrow. Her heart was pumping "blind, blind, blind" faster and faster. Blind without any warning. How could it happen? And yet it had.

She got to the foot of the hill just in time to see the school bus disappear around the curve. It had gone without her. The tears she had been holding back came to her eyes. There was no way she could get to school. Her mother was already at work. Not wanting to go back to the empty house, Anna headed for her favorite path, which led upward into the woods. The day was hers to do as she pleased.

There must be something she could do for Nana Marie. Rita had said something about a present. But what present could ever console a person who had become blind?

Anna remembered a time she had imagined being blind. Once in the middle of the night she had opened her eyes thinking it was morning. The unexpected blackness pressed down on her. She turned her head this way and that and saw nothing, as if she had been buried. Just when she was ready to scream, her hand shot out and touched the light, nudging it on. The brightness, which then appeared so suddenly, dazzled her eyes. The patchwork quilt shone. The yellow walls glistened as if they had been freshly painted, and the air rushed out of her lungs in relief. Now she wondered how Nana Marie had felt waking up blind.

Anna broke into a trot. Ahead was a place she often came, a small, deep spring in the woods. When she knelt to gaze into the bottomless pool, at first she saw nothing but darkness. Then as the sun came out, the water seemed to open up, reflecting the bark of silver beeches, shining like armor. The reflection of luminous silver reminded her of Nana Marie. She sat back on her heels, remembering.

Six months ago, at the end of summer, Anna and her parents moved to the house just up the hill from Rita's.

A week later Anna started school. She didn't know anyone and found it hard to make friends with the other fifth graders. She was very lonely until one afternoon when she had looked up and saw Nana Marie's welcoming smile.

There was a small moving van outside Rita's house that day. From a safe distance, half concealed by bushes, Anna watched it being unloaded. There were only a half dozen pieces of furniture, all a lovely dark wood, highly polished. Rita stood by, directing the operations. Anna could see the simple delight on Rita's face and wondered where this furniture was coming from.

As Anna watched, Rita's husband got out of his car, walked around it, and opened the door by the front seat.

Then there was a long wait. Finally a white head emerged. Haltingly, as though every movement took a great deal of thought, a very old woman rose and holding on to her son's arm, began to walk toward the house. Halfway to the steps, she paused for breath. Then, as if she felt Anna's eyes on her, the old woman looked up. Their eyes met, and Nana Marie smiled.

The next afternoon when Anna came home from school, she saw Nana Marie sitting in a rocking chair on the front porch. Slowly Anna approached, her school shoes raising little puffs of dust.

The moment Nana Marie saw her she smiled, and the next thing Anna knew she was sitting cross-legged at Nana Marie's feet. Then they began to talk as if they had known each other for years. On and on till supper time they talked, "like old friends reunited," Nana Marie said. They even found out they had birthdays the same month and only two days apart.

Every day after that, when the school bus let Anna off at the bottom of the hill, she raced up to Rita's house to keep Nana Marie company. As long as the afternoons were warm they sat on the porch until twilight. They never ran out of things to talk about. Nana Marie pointed out the fat groundhog scavenging for corn in the stubble of the field below Rita's house, and the flock of wild geese whose perfect "V" cut the sky as they flew south with haunting cries. And always, if she told Anna to listen, from far away would come the hollow *clack-clack* of a woodpecker at work on a tree. Anna would linger, enchanted, until there was just enough light left for her to run home. Sometimes an autumn moon, perfectly round, lit her way.

When cold weather arrived, Anna climbed the steep stairs to Nana Marie's room. Sitting by the window, they could see the world just as well as from the porch. They watched the trees on the top of the mountain turn bare and black, while there was still a wide strip of deep yellow at the foot of the mountain. Day by day this strip shrank until one day, after heavy rains, it was gone. Next came the snow, pure magic seen from Nana Marie's window.

Although most of Nana Marie's polished furniture was downstairs in Rita's living room, it was still cozy in Nana Marie's room. There was a bed, a table, a large chest of drawers, and a trunk. As soon as Anna arrived, she would put her books on the trunk and boil water on the hot plate in one corner. Then the two of them would have tea and share the events of the day.

As the weeks passed, Anna learned that every object in Nana Marie's room had a meaning and a story. One by one, Anna learned the stories.

The silver hairbrush and matching hand mirror that lay on the chest of drawers had been an engagement present from Nana Marie's husband. A large *MK* with many curlicues was engraved on the back of each piece. Next to the hairbrush was a battered red and yellow cigar tin that said *The Finest Turkish*. When Anna opened the lid, she found a large round watch that dangled from a chain. The watch ticked once or twice when Anna moved it, then stopped. It had belonged to Nana Marie's father. An Indian goddess carved out of wood gazed thoughtfully at the box. On the trunk was a very shiny bright-blue clay bowl overflowing with odds and ends. One side of the bowl was crooked, and it tipped when Anna touched it. It had been a present from Nana Marie's grandson when he was seven. Boxes of letters and photographs completely covered the table. Anna loved best the teapot with its two Chinese pheasants. Its spout was stained brown from all the tea that had been poured, and Nana Marie said the teapot was six times as old as Anna.

Finally, what at first had seemed to Anna only a small, cluttered room expanded to become a history of Nana Marie's life, of her joys and sorrows and memories stretching over almost a century.

Gazing deep into the shining pool again, Anna decided that Nana Marie was like this spring. Each day of her old age she had quietly caught and held a different reflection. Stored in her depths were layers of reflections, shining images of the world. Many of these she had shared with Anna. But now that she was blind, would these images be gone, the way water became dark when there was no light? What would her days be like?

Anna's thoughts moved to the party that Rita would hold in the afternoon. She knew what the neighbors were likely to bring: candy, scarves, flowers. She could do the same, yet none of these gifts would express what she felt for Nana Marie. And could any of them really make Nana Marie feel better?

Lost in thought, Anna continued to follow the path up the mountain. Even though her sneakers were wet from the soft thawing soil of the woods, she decided to stay there until school was out. Maybe by then she would know what to bring Nana Marie.

Slowly the world about her drew Anna in, just as if she had been with Nana Marie. The wan February sun was swallowed by a thick mist, which the mountain seemed to exhale with each gust of wind. Although the air was damp, it had an edge of warmth that had been absent in the morning. It felt almost like the beginnings of spring. As the hours passed, Anna picked up objects she thought Nana Marie would like: a striped rock, a tiny fern, a clump of moss, an empty milkweed pod. None of them, on second thought, seemed a proper gift for Nana Marie. Other days, she would have loved them. But now Anna thought they could easily make her sad, for in touching them, Nana Marie would be reminded of the things she would never see again. There had to be a way to bring the whole woods, the sky, and the fields to Nana Marie. What else would do? What else would be worthy of their friendship?

Suddenly Anna knew what her gift would be. It would be like no other gift, and a gift no one else could bring. All day long Anna had been seeing the world the way Nana Marie had shown her. Now she would bring everything she had seen to Nana Marie.

Her wet feet, her damp jeans and jacket, no longer mattered. Eagerly she turned and began the long trudge back to Nana Marie's house. Her hands were empty in her pockets. But the gift she carried in her head was as big as the world.

Just as the sun went over the mountain, Anna emerged from the woods. Ahead of her was the road and Nana Marie's house. She looked at Nana Marie's room, the window directly over the front door. A light should be on by now. But the blinds were down as they had been all week, and the window was so dark it reflected, eerily, the reddish glow of twilight. Everyone must be downstairs at the party. Probably Rita hadn't even bothered to go upstairs and raise the blinds. Yet downstairs the windows were dark too. What had happened? Where was Nana Marie?

Anna stopped to catch her breath. Her entire body was pounding. She ran around Rita's car to the kitchen door. She hesitated, biting her lip, before she rapped softly on the glass part of the door. There was no answer. She could see a light in the living room, the TV set was turned on. She knocked again, louder, then put her hand on the doorknob. It opened from the other side, and Rita stood there in her bathrobe. The kitchen table was covered with the remains of the party: tissue paper, stacked plates and cups. So the neighbors had come and gone. Anna was too late for the party, but Nana Marie must be there!

"Well, here at last," Rita said. "I figured you went home and forgot. The party ended half an hour ago. I told Nana Marie it wasn't any use waiting up for you longer. I expect she's asleep by now. She was real disappointed you didn't come, though she got lots of nice things from everybody. Why don't you come back tomorrow when she's rested."

"Please, I can't," Anna said. She bent, tearing at her wet shoelaces. "I have a present for Nana Marie. It won't take long. I'll take my shoes off and go upstairs to her room."

Rita shrugged. She seemed anxious to get back to her TV show. At the door to the living room she called back,

"Don't go waking her up. I just got her settled. You can leave the present on her table. I'll tell her about it tomorrow."

Nodding, Anna headed for the stairs on tiptoe. The world of Rita dropped away as she climbed toward Nana Marie's room. The landing at the top of the stairs was dark, and the door to Nana Marie's room was closed. Anna paused and let her breath out slowly. What did blind people look like? What if the doctors had taken out Nana Marie's eyes and only two black holes were left? Anna's hand hesitated on the doorknob.

Then she opened the door and shut it behind her.

Nana Marie's room was pitch black. There was no sound at all. Was the room empty? The window was straight ahead. Anna ran to it, groping for the cords. The blinds clattered up, crashing in the darkness. Rita was sure to come up. Then a faint light flowed into the room. Outside, in the winter twilight, a small frozen moon was wandering upward.

"Anna," Nana Marie was calling her name. She was not asleep after all. "Anna," Nana Marie said, and now there was surprise and joy in her voice. Nana Marie was sitting in her

rocking chair. Her eyes were open and as blue as they had always been, like the sky on a summer morning.

"Oh, Nana Marie!" Anna exclaimed. She patted the old warm skin of Nana Marie's cheek.

"You came," Nana Marie said. "I thought maybe you were getting tired of having such a very old lady for a friend."

"I brought you a present," Anna said. "I'm late because it took me all day to get it."

"Gracious," said Nana Marie. "You shouldn't have done that! All the nice people who came this afternoon brought me presents as if I could see and were still of some use to someone!" She chuckled, gesturing toward the table and a new stack of boxes.

"Mine is different," Anna said. "I brought you a last day."

"A last day…" Nana Marie's voice trailed off. At the hospital someone had arranged her hair in soft waves. She put her hand up as if to touch them, but halfway there her fingers stretched out, reaching for Anna. She took Anna's hand and held it firmly.

"You didn't have a last day to look at the world," Anna said. "So I brought it to you. Everything I saw today. Just as if you saw it with me. The way you would see it. And tomorrow I'll bring you another—and the next day another. I'll bring you enough seeing to last forever. That's my present, Nana Marie."

Nana Marie was silent for a minute. Then she added softly, almost to herself, "Bless you, child, how did you ever think of that?" She leaned back in the rocking chair. One hand held on to Anna's. With the other she gestured toward a chair. "Pull it up right here, Anna," she said, "so we can look out over the valley and the moonlight together. The moon is out, isn't it, Anna? I can feel it." She closed her eyes.

Anna pulled Nana Marie's hand into her lap and held it with both of her own as she described the silver beeches reflected in the spring, the yellow mist breathing in and out, the pale sun—everything she had seen that day.

When Anna was finished, Nana Marie sat up and turned toward her. Nana Marie's blue eyes shone with contentment. "Thank you, Anna," she said. "That was beautiful." She paused briefly and when she continued it was almost as though she was speaking to herself. *"This* is a day I'll always remember."

Anna sat holding on to Nana Marie's hand until the moon disappeared over the house. Even though something as terrible as going blind had happened to Nana Marie, she really hadn't changed. She could still marvel at the world, she could still feel the moonlight. Anna knew she was going to be all right.

Reader's Response 〜 Did you think Anna's choice of a gift was a good one? Why or why not?

TWO CULTURES ONE DREAM

Vo-Dinh Mai grew up in Hué, the old capital of prewar Vietnam. Before coming to America, he lived in France and studied literature, philosophy, and drawing. Most of all, he loved to paint.

Helen Coutant was born in Washington, D. C., and grew up on Long Island, New York. She went to the University of California and Columbia University in New York City. Helen wanted to teach and write stories for children.

Today Mai's paintings are exhibited in the United States, Europe, and Vietnam. Helen teaches English. Together they have written and illustrated books for children that combine both Eastern and Western cultures—including *First Snow, The Magic Drum*, and *The Gift*.

Besides writing and illustrating, Helen Coutant and Vo-Dinh Mai enjoy translating Vietnamese stories into English, to promote the understanding of Southeast Asian culture and the dream of world peace.

391

BASKETBALL STAR

When I get big
I want to be the best
basketball player in the world.
I'll make jumpshots, hookballs
and layups
and talk about dribble—
mine'll be outta sight!

Karama Fufuka

DREAMS

Hold fast to dreams
For if dreams die
Life is a broken-winged bird
That cannot fly.

Hold fast to dreams
For when dreams go
Life is a barren field
Frozen with snow.

Langston Hughes

392

The Lizard LETDOWN

by Christine McDonnell

On his way home from school Leo often stopped to look in the pet store window. Sometimes there were puppies tumbling over each other or curled up in balls, sleeping. Sometimes there were kittens—striped ones and spotted ones—so little, they looked as if they had just opened their eyes. At Eastertime the window was filled with fat white rabbits. And once there was a parrot who sat on a stand and screamed, "Hello, Mac."

When he stopped to look on Wednesday, the window was filled with guinea pigs: a round brown one, a sleek black one, an orange one, a fluffy white one, and a little one with patches of every color, mixed up like a crazy quilt. The patchwork pig had an orange spot covering one eye and a brown spot circling the other. His back was a mixture of white, brown, black, and orange. Two feet were black, one was orange, and the other white. Leo laughed when he saw him. When the patchwork pig noticed Leo standing at the window with his nose pressed up against the glass, he began to make noise. "Wink, wink, wink-wink-wink," he said. His nose twitched like a rabbit and his round black eyes shone.

"Wink, wink, wink," Leo said in return. Then he looked around quickly to make sure no one was passing nearby. The sidewalk was empty. "Wink, wink," Leo bleated some more. The guinea pig answered back.

Leo stepped back from the glass to read the signs on the window.

Six dollars is a lot, Leo thought. Much more than I've got. Maybe a chameleon would be better.

Leo had read about chameleons. They could change colors to match whatever you put them on. Only $3.75.

I'd like a chameleon, he thought. I could carry him around and put him on top of different things and watch him change colors. Only $3.75.

Leo put his hand into his pocket and pulled out his change. Only thirty-five cents, and he had been planning to buy a chocolate crunch bar at the drugstore. There was no money left in his bank either.

He started home with his hands in his pockets, looking carefully at the sidewalk in hopes of finding some change. He picked up a penny in front of the barber shop and a nickel by the fire station. He checked every parking meter on Main Street, but there were no stuck coins. He checked the pay phones on the corner, but no one had forgotten any change. When he turned down his own block, after skipping the chocolate bar, he had forty-one cents in his pocket.

Not enough, thought Leo.

He was still thinking of the chameleon when he reached his own yard. I bet that lizard could turn red and yellow just like all these leaves, he thought. Leaves! Leo looked down at the sidewalk. It was covered with leaves. So was the yard. And the yard next door at Mrs. Rider's house. I'll rake up the leaves and earn enough to buy that little lizard, Leo decided.

He dropped his knapsack on the back porch and found the rake in a corner of the garage. Mrs. Rider was likely to pay more than his parents, who would probably tell him that his allowance was payment enough. He went next door and rang Mrs. Rider's bell.

"Hello, Leo," said Mrs. Rider, taking her reading glasses off her nose.

"Want me to rake for you, Mrs. Rider?"

The old lady looked out at her yard. "Those leaves have fallen down in earnest, haven't they now? It must have been the rain last night. I don't remember there being so many before."

She scrutinized Leo with a frown. "You want to rake for me, do you?" She paused. "Well, Leo, I don't know. Do you remember what happened last year?"

Leo blushed and scratched the back of his knee with his foot. Last year he had agreed to rake for Mrs. Rider. He had raked all the leaves into a gigantic pile in the middle of the front yard. But before he could stuff the leaves into the big green plastic garbage bags, Bulldog Nelson, Tony Rosa, and two other older boys had come along.

"Hey, let's jump in those leaves," Bulldog yelled to the others.

"Wait. Wait a minute." Leo tried to stop them. But Tony just pushed him out of the way. "Step aside, short stuff," he said.

The four big boys jumped in the leaf pile again and again until the leaves were scattered all over the yard. Hearing their loud hoots and yells, Mrs. Rider came out of her house. She hated to have children playing in her front yard. "They'll ruin my azaleas," she always said.

"Get away from here, you boys. Get away. Right now," she said, walking stiffly down the front path, leaning on her cane. She stopped and pointed the cane at Leo.

"And you, young man. What have you got to say for yourself? Letting those hoodlums run all over this yard. You've done more harm than good."

Leo tried to explain, but he tripped over his words and felt foolish. He didn't want to admit that he was afraid of Bulldog and his friends. So he apologized, raked up the leaves again, and went home without collecting any pay.

"But that was last year, Mrs. Rider. I'm older now. You can trust me. Those big guys can't push me around now." Then an idea popped into Leo's mind. "Besides, this time I'll rake all the leaves into the backyard and nobody will be able to see the pile from the street."

Mrs. Rider peered at him closely once more. Then she smiled, and her stern expression thawed. "Very well, Leo. You may have a second chance. Let's say two dollars for the front and back yards, and another dollar if you'll bring in a supply of firewood from the garage and pile it neatly by the wood stove in the den. I like to keep warm when I read."

Leo quickly agreed. Three dollars. That made $3.41. With this week's allowance he'd have enough to buy that chameleon on Saturday.

He raked all the leaves into a pile in the backyard. They were wet and slippery from last night's rain, so he wasn't even tempted to jump into the pile himself. When he bundled the leaves together, they filled six garbage bags. Leo lugged them one at a time to the side of the house where the garbage cans stood.

The wood was heavy too. Leo made at least ten trips from the garage, piling the wood neatly by the wall in the bright-yellow den. Mrs. Rider's wing chair stood between the window and the stove. Bookcases filled the opposite wall. It was a cheerful, sunny room, and the wood stove made it cozy. No wonder she likes to read in here, he thought.

Mrs. Rider offered Leo a glass of cold cider when he was finished. "Good work," she said as she gave him three dollar bills. Leo thanked her, put the money in his pocket, and headed home.

Only three days until he could buy the chameleon, he thought as he lay in bed that night. Tomorrow he would build a cage. There was leftover screening and wood in the basement. It wouldn't be hard. He would put in a branch for the lizard to climb on and a bed of moss for a soft place to lie. His paint dishes would be good for food and water.

I wonder what a lizard eats, he thought before he fell asleep.

He finished the cage on Thursday afternoon. His sister, Eleanor, got a look at it as Leo carried it up to his room.

"What's that?" she asked.

"A cage."

"I can see that, dopey. What's it for?"

Leo hesitated. He hadn't asked his parents about the lizard. If Eleanor made a fuss, maybe they wouldn't let him buy one.

"It's a cage for an animal."

"I figured *that*. It's too small for you."

Leo knew he couldn't stall any longer. Eleanor was getting irritated.

"It's for the new pet I'm buying on Saturday."

Eleanor eyed the construction. It didn't look very sturdy.

"It's escape-proof," Leo added.

"I've heard that one before. Like the time you brought your class mouse home."

It had taken Leo three weeks to find the mouse after it got loose.

"What kind of nasty little beast are you bringing home this time?"

Leo had to tell her. "It's a chameleon."

"Ugh! One of those creepy lizards? Why do you want to waste your money on something disgusting like that?"

"It's neat," protested Leo. "It turns colors. It won't bother you at all. I promise. So don't make a big deal out of this, okay?"

"You mean, with Mom and Dad?" Eleanor hesitated for a second, calculating her advantage. "I'll help you out if you promise not to tell that I've been keeping my light on late every night."

Leo had seen the light in Eleanor's room when he got up to go to the bathroom at night. He knew she was staying up, reading.

He agreed happily, thinking he had gotten the best of the bargain. His parents did not protest too much.

"Are you sure that this is what you want?" his mother asked.

Leo was sure he was sure.

On Friday he spent the afternoon finding different-colored things to test his chameleon on. He made a pile on his bed.

First there was his red-plaid bathrobe. It was a deep red, with lines of green, yellow, and white in it. The chameleon would look like a Scotch lizard when he landed on the bathrobe, Leo thought.

Next he borrowed the pink blotter from Eleanor's desk. She never used it anyway. It had come in a set that Grandma had sent, a pink desk set that said JUNIOR MISS on it in gold letters. Eleanor hated it.

Then he thought of his blue-and-yellow-striped tie, the one he had to wear for Christmas dinner and visits to his grandmother's. At least it will be good for something fun for a change, Leo thought. In Leo's imagination his chameleon could turn every color of the rainbow.

On Saturday morning Leo collected his allowance from his father and headed downtown. The sign was still up in the pet shop window. The guinea pigs were still there too. At least three were—the shiny black one, the orange one, and the patchwork one.

Leo didn't stop to say "Wink, wink," this time. He rushed right inside. The chameleons were crawling around in a tank on the counter.

"One chameleon, please," Leo said to the pet store owner.

"Three seventy-five," said the man, assembling a little square white box with a wire handle.

Leo counted out his money and put it on the counter.

The man reached inside the tank.

"Is there one in particular that you want?"

They all looked alike. But one blinked his eyes twice and Leo decided that he must be signaling him.

"That one," he said, pointing to the lizard that had blinked.

The pet store man picked up the chameleon and put him in the box. It looked like a container of Chinese food. Boy, wouldn't somebody be surprised if he opened this up expecting egg foo young, Leo thought.

"Do you know how to take care of this lizard?" asked the man.

Leo shook his head.

"Fresh water, lettuce, and mealy worms. You can grow them yourself. Here are the instructions and a bunch to start with."

They were disgusting! Little white worms crawling in a heap. Ugh! Who ever thought chameleons would eat anything so awful-looking.

"You put these worms on some oatmeal and they'll start reproducing. You'll have a colony in no time," said the man cheerfully.

And my mother will have a fit, Leo thought.

He took the bag with the lizard, the worms, and a care-and-feeding sheet and thanked the man. Then he stopped by the window on his way out. The patchwork pig seemed to recognize him right away.

"Wink. Wink-wink," he bleated, and raced around in a circle.

"Wink-wink, yourself," Leo answered. "I bet you don't eat worms."

He put the bag in his bike basket and headed home.

Up in his room Leo set the chameleon container on his desk and opened the top of the cage. Then he lifted the flaps of the white box. The lizard was moving around in the bottom, trying to climb the sides. His claws rasped against the cardboard. Leo tentatively reached a finger into the box to feel the lizard's skin. It was cool, dry, and bumpy; not slimy but still a little creepy. The lizard squirmed away, not enjoying the encounter any more than Leo.

Leo decided not to pick the chameleon up just yet.

Instead, he upended the box and slid the surprised lizard
into his new home. He landed on the moss but quickly
scampered up the branch and perched there quivering,
his eyes darting around the cage.

Leo dumped a blob of worms into the food dish and
watched his chameleon for a while. But the lizard did not
move, and finally, feeling slightly disappointed, Leo went
down to lunch.

"Wash your hands well if you've been touching that
animal," said Leo's mother as she put Leo's sandwich in
front of him.

"I only touched him with one finger," Leo said.

"That's enough. Wash up."

Leo decided not to mention the mealy worms during lunch. It was probably not table talk, as his mother always said.

After lunch he went back upstairs. The chameleon had not moved. Maybe it wouldn't be so hard to pick him up after all. Leo spread his bathrobe on the bed. Next to it he placed the pink blotter. Then, finally, he draped his tie across the bedspread.

"Time to experiment," he announced. "Introducing the rainbow lizard."

The chameleon sat on the branch in his cage, so still that he didn't seem alive. Leo carefully opened the top and reached in. Just as his hand came down on the chameleon, it whisked away to the other side of the cage.

"Oh-ho! Tricky, eh?" Leo reached again and missed.

He finally cornered the lizard between the screen and the branch and picked him up. The chameleon wiggled madly for a second and then was very still. Quick, abrupt moves were his specialty. Leo kept his hand firmly around him even though he didn't like the way he felt.

"Time to see what you can do."

He placed the chameleon on top of the red-plaid bathrobe, making a fence around him with his legs. The lizard sat there, blinking. He turned his head so one beady little eye was staring straight at Leo. Leo watched and waited. The chameleon was brown. The bathrobe was a bright-red plaid. Leo waited and watched carefully to see the transformation.

Nothing happened.

The chameleon remained brown. He didn't turn even the slightest bit red.

Maybe plaid is too hard to start with, Leo thought, beginning to feel worried about his investment. He probably has to start off on something easier. Leo pushed the lizard farther over until he was standing on the pink blotting paper and watched carefully. The lizard stuck out his tongue, but it was red, not pink. His skin stayed brown. He was definitely not cooperating with the experiment.

After waiting for a few minutes, Leo decided to try the tie.

"Maybe these bright colors are too difficult for you," he said to the chameleon, moving him over onto the tie. "If you can't do the stripe, at least try to turn blue."

The chameleon remained a dull brown.

"What a gyp! What good are you, anyway?"

He picked up the little lizard and put him back in the cage, setting him down on the moss. This time the chameleon stayed there instead of climbing the branch. Gradually he turned from a dull brown to a dull green.

Leo watched the change. "Okay. At least you can do something. Brown and green. Is that all?" He was very disappointed. "I wonder if those are the only colors you turn." Maybe the rainbow lizard existed only in his imagination.

There was a set of encyclopedias in Eleanor's room. Leo found what he was hunting for in volume three. It even had a little drawing that looked exactly like his

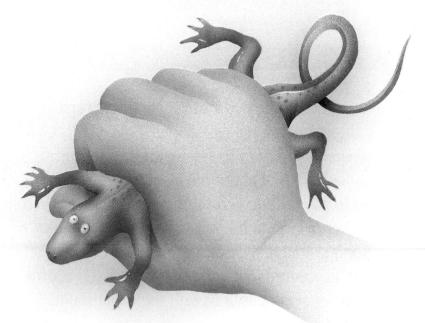

lizard. The description said that they only turn colors for camouflage, and can become green or brown depending on their surroundings.

"What a gyp," Leo repeated. "Three dollars and seventy-five cents, and he doesn't know any good colors. And I have to grow his disgusting old worms."

He went back into his room to look at his pet. There wasn't really anything he could do with the lizard. He wasn't any fun to play with. He didn't make any noises. He wasn't even good to pet.

The white box was still standing next to the cage. In a flash Leo decided what to do. He trapped the lizard again and lifted him out. Then he dumped him back into the container and folded down the top. He looked at the clock. Three forty-five. Plenty of time to get downtown.

The pet store was still open when Leo pulled up on his bike. And the patchwork pig was still in the window. Leo crossed his toes inside his sneakers for luck as he waited at the counter.

"Back already?" said the pet store man when it was Leo's turn.

Leo put the chameleon container on the counter. "Do you think I could trade this lizard in?"

"Trade it in for what?"

Leo glanced back at the window. "For the guinea pig with all the different colors. I know I need another two twenty-five, but I'll earn that by Monday. Could you take this lizard back and keep my three seventy-five as a down payment on a guinea pig?"

Leo held his breath as he waited for the answer.

The man opened the box and looked at the chameleon. "Looks none the worse for wear," he said.

He dumped the chameleon back into the cage with the others. It darted around until it found a space behind a piece of bark.

"Which guinea pig did you say?"

"The spotted one with all the different colors."

"Oh. The patchwork pig. All right, I'll hold it for you."

Before he left, Leo reached in and gave the patchwork pig a pat. His fur was soft and his nose was cold. His whiskers tickled as he sniffed Leo's hand.

"I'll call you Patches."

Leo spent Sunday raking leaves in three other yards. By dinnertime his arms ached, but he had made five dollars. Enough for the guinea pig, a book on how to care for him, and the water bottle that he needed for drinking.

He went by after school on Monday to pick him up. The man put the guinea pig in a large white box with air holes. Leo carried him home carefully. The pig did not make a sound the whole trip. Not a single "wink."

"Don't be scared," Leo said in a soft voice.

Up in his room Leo set the box softly on his bed. Then he emptied out all of the moss and branches from the cage. He lined the bottom with a thick layer of newspaper and bunched soft pieces of towel in the corner.

"That's for your bed," he said to the guinea pig, who was still in the box.

Next Leo fastened the water bottle to the side of the cage. "All set," he said as he opened the box.

The guinea pig looked up with his shiny round eyes. His nose twitched. Leo gave his soft fur a pat with his finger. Then he reached underneath and picked him up. The guinea pig was surprisingly heavy. Leo could feel his heart beating against his side.

"Hey, don't be scared," he said again.

He set the guinea pig down gently in his new home.
The animal waddled around the edges of the cage
sniffing the corners. He licked the spout of the water
bottle. Then he lay down on the towel.

Leo watched him closely, anxious to make sure he
was comfortable. "Welcome home, Patches," he said. "I
bet you're hungry."

He raced downstairs and scrounged in the
refrigerator vegetable bin. He found two carrots that
were starting to shrivel and started back upstairs. When
he reached the top step, Patches began to make noise.

"Wink, wink. Wink-wink," he bleated when he heard
Leo coming.

"Hold on, Patches. I'm on my way," Leo called. He grinned as he skipped down the hall, a carrot in each hand. I bet he'll call me like this every day when I get home from school, Leo thought. A pet who says hello, now that's something special.

Reader's Response ～ Did you share Leo's disappointment about the chameleon? Why or why not?

Library Link ～ *This story is from the book* Toad Food & Measle Soup *by Christine McDonnell. If you enjoyed this story, you might like to read the entire book.*

Camouflage Quiz

1. Which animal is see-through?
   a. jellyfish   b. moth   c. mosquito

2. Which animal turns white in winter?
   a. hare   b. sheep dog   c. brown bear

3. Which animal loses its spots as it grows up?
   a. baby black panther
   b. baby giraffe
   c. baby lion

4. Which animal plays dead to avoid attack?
   a. male beaver
   b. grass snake
   c. sea turtle

5. Which animal is considered
   the Master of Disguise?
   a. arctic polar bear
   b. chameleon
   c. leopard

Quick Fact
In nature, red, yellow, and black are used as warning colors. They tell other animals to keep well away.

Answers: 1. a 2. a 3. c 4. b 5. b

413

A Zookeeper's Challenge

from *Andy Bear: A Polar Cub Grows Up at the Zoo*
by Ginny Johnston and Judy Cutchins
photographs by Constance Noble

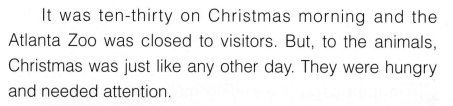
A zookeeper faces many challenges at work. The zookeeper in this story, Constance Noble, rescues a new-born polar bear cub. In order to keep it alive, she must take the cub home and care for it twenty-four hours a day. Constance faces many challenges as the cub grows old enough to live on its own in the zoo.

It was ten-thirty on Christmas morning and the Atlanta Zoo was closed to visitors. But, to the animals, Christmas was just like any other day. They were hungry and needed attention.

Most of the zookeepers had finished their work and gone home for the day. Only Constance Noble and one other keeper were still working. Constance loved her work at the zoo. She had cared for lions, bobcats, monkeys, sea lions, and bears for more than ten years. The animals seemed to know she was their friend.

"What a warm morning for December," Constance thought as she walked along the zookeeper's pathway behind the bear cages.

Grizzlies, Asiatic black bears, Malayan sun bears, Kodiaks, and polar bears all lived at the zoo. Each kind of bear had a cage with both indoor and outdoor areas. Inside each cage were two small "dens." These cavelike rooms allowed the bears some peace and quiet away from crowds of visitors. One of the dens in each cage opened into an outside yard with a swimming pool. In the yard the bears could exercise or sleep in the sunshine while visitors watched.

Climbing the ladder behind the polar bears' cage, Constance looked over the high rock wall into the yard below. She saw only Thor, the 1200-pound male bear, sleeping comfortably in the yard. Linda, the female polar bear, was inside the den. The two Siberian polar bears had shared a cage at the zoo for almost twenty years. Zookeepers had placed them together as playmates when they were very young. In the wild, male bears are loners, rarely having any contact with females. At the zoo, Thor and Linda have developed an unusual polar bear relationship because they are constant companions.

In their cage, the sliding metal door between the inside dens and the outside yard was open so the bears could go in or out as they pleased. Constance tossed two pounds of chunky, dry food called "bear chow" into the yard. Seeing nothing unusual, she climbed down and went next door to feed the grizzlies, then the Kodiaks.

Just as she was finishing her work at the Kodiaks' cage, the quiet of the Christmas morning was shattered by ear-splitting screams and frightening howls. These terrifying sounds were coming from the polar bears!

Constance rushed behind the cages and looked through a small back door into the polar bears' den. She could see Thor. His head was lowered and he was snorting fiercely as he tried to come into the den. Inside, Linda was moaning and howling as she blocked the doorway with her 700-pound body. The screams were coming from a corner inside the dark den.

Constance knew immediately what was happening. During the night Linda had given birth to a cub and was protecting it from the powerful Thor. Now that he was awake, the father bear, with his extraordinary sense of smell, had discovered the new cub inside the den. If Thor got to the baby he would kill it.

A male polar bear will kill any newcomer, even his own cub. In the Arctic, polar bear mothers and newborn cubs live beneath the snow in large dens safely hidden from the male bears for several months. But, here at the zoo it was different. Zookeepers were afraid to move Thor away from Linda. She might be so lonely and upset she would not take care of her cub.

The only way the baby bear could survive was for Constance to rescue it quickly. For the past few years, all of Linda's cubs had been killed before the zookeepers could get to them.

Constance knew how dangerous polar bears could be, especially at a time like this. These enormous white bears have more strength than gorillas. Constance would be killed if she went inside the den now. Somehow, she had to drive both bears out into the yard. Then she could close the sliding den door, lock them out, and go safely into the den. But how could she force them out?

Grabbing a bucket of bear chow, she rushed up the ladder and threw the food over the wall, hoping to attract Thor and Linda into the yard. It didn't work.

Hurrying down the ladder, she snatched up the hose and sprayed water through an opening in the door. But the bears didn't budge. They stood face to face, Thor growling, Linda moaning, and from deep inside the den, the newborn cub screaming.

Constance, a quiet and gentle zookeeper, was becoming desperate. She knew she was running out of time. Although Linda snapped and growled at Thor, she could not keep him away from the cub much longer. Constance tried the last thing she could think of—she threw a screaming fit! She yelled at the bears, waved her arms, and banged on the door of the cage.

Thor was so surprised he backed out of the doorway. The startled Linda followed him into the yard. Constance couldn't believe her eyes. Quickly she ran to pull the handle that closed the den's sliding door. Both adult polar bears were locked out. At last, the cub would be safe.

Constance unlocked the zookeeper's doorway and crawled into the den. She stood up slowly and squinted in the darkness. At first she couldn't see anything. The cub was quiet now, making it even harder to find. Constance shuffled her feet along the floor hoping not to step on the baby. When her foot bumped into the cub, it began to scream again. As her eyes adjusted to the dimness of the den, Constance could just about see the shape of the cub. It was no bigger than a guinea pig. She picked it up, gently snuggling its warm body to her chest, and headed for the zoo clinic.

By the time she arrived at the clinic, the cub was quiet. Constance examined the baby. It was a perfectly healthy boy!

The zookeepers had decided to name the next male cub born at the zoo Andrew, in honor of the city's mayor, Andrew Young. Later they gave the tiny cub a middle name, Nicholas, because he was born on

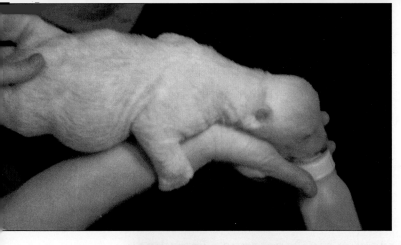

Andy is one-week old.

Andy opened his eyes when he was four weeks old.

Christmas morning. Andrew Nicholas Polar Bear was called Andy for short.

Andy weighed just under 1 1/2 pounds. He had a pink nose and his tiny ears were flat against his head. His eyes were closed and his wrinkled, pink body was covered with fine, white fur. Although Andy could already hold his head up, it would be weeks before he could walk.

Constance placed Andy in an incubator where he would be safe and warm. She made a formula of evaporated milk and water. Every hour and a half, she squirted a little of the mixture into Andy's mouth.

While the other zookeeper watched Andy, Constance left the clinic just long enough to check on Thor and Linda.

Thor was resting quietly now on a large rock in the yard. But Linda was moaning and pacing around. She didn't understand why her cub was gone. Constance wished she could explain to the lonely mother bear that this was the only way her cub could survive at the zoo.

Zoo officials were excited about the birth of Andy and the miraculous rescue by Constance. They knew this rare baby polar bear would need attention twenty-four hours a day. Constance was placed in charge of the new cub. Since she could not live at the small zoo clinic, Constance took Andy home with her. While Constance cared for Andy at her apartment, another zookeeper would do her zoo chores until she returned.

For the next few months, Constance would have to become a mother polar bear—comforting, warming, and feeding the baby bear night and day. Constance knew that

Healthy and curious, Andy is eager to explore.

Andy Bear thinks he's found a new playmate in the mirror.

Andy has fun playing in
Constance's flower garden.

What do you think Andy is looking for?

the biggest problem would be mixing a formula identical to real polar bear milk. The milk of the mother polar bear is very different from any milk Constance could buy. It is much thicker and creamier.

Constance watched Andy closely and kept a diary of each change in the little bear as he grew. When Andy was just three days old, Constance noticed that his soft pink nose and pink foot pads were starting to turn black. This was good news; it meant the cub was growing normally. She was still feeding him every hour and a half. After the first week, Andy had gained one pound. Now, he weighed 2 1/2 pounds!

One stormy evening, Constance sat in her bedroom jotting notes in her diary about Andy's tenth day. Nearby, Andy was crawling around in his playpen. He couldn't walk yet, because his little legs would not hold him up.

421

Suddenly, a flash of lightning and a crash of thunder startled the bear cub, and he began to cry.

Over the next few days, Constance noticed that Andy was very sensitive to loud noises. The ring of the telephone scared him and caused him to whimper. Constance asked her friends not to call. She stopped using her noisy dishwasher. Even the television and radio had to be turned down so low they could hardly be heard.

Andy was changing in other ways, too. When he was twenty-eight days old, his shiny, dark eyes opened for the first time. Thicker fur was beginning to cover his body. Constance had been working so hard, she had not had time to notice what a beautiful animal little Andrew Nicholas was becoming. He was less like a furry ball and more like a polar bear. He was developing the long muscular neck that makes polar bears look so different from other bears.

Although the first four weeks had not been easy, the next four were even harder. By the end of January, Andy was becoming very sick. Just as Constance had feared, the milk formula was the cause of his problems. His delicate digestive system was not working properly. Constance knew if Andy got any sicker, he could die. Polar cubs are so rare in captivity that neither Constance nor the zoo veterinarian knew exactly what to do for Andy. They tried several "people" medicines, hoping to find the one that would save Andy's life.

To make matters worse, Andy was cutting his baby teeth, and his gums were very sore. The doctor gave him mild painkillers to make the teething easier. Constance wondered how this tiny bear that weighed just 5 pounds could possibly survive. It seemed hopeless, but she would not give up.

Hour after hour, day after day, Constance sat with the sick little bear until the medicines finally began to work. Andy at last rested more comfortably. Constance was using a different formula consisting of cream and water, and Andy was feeling much better. His digestive problems were finally over and his baby teeth were all in place. By the last week in February, Constance could relax a little. Now two months old, Andy was gaining weight again, and his eyes were shining brightly.

Constance watched one morning as Andy stretched, yawned, and rolled onto his stomach after a long nap. On unsteady but determined legs, he took his first steps. Nine-week-old Andy was walking! Now Constance would have to watch him even more closely.

Andy began to suck on everything he came near. He sucked on his blanket and on Constance's arm. His sharp little teeth caused a painful bite, but when she pulled away, Andy screamed. Constance solved the problem by giving Andy a baby bottle nipple to use as a pacifier.

One afternoon in late March, Constance sat relaxing by her window watching a rare southern snowfall gently cover the ground. She decided to give Andy a taste of what "real" Arctic polar bear life might be like.

She bundled herself up with a coat and gloves and opened the back door. Andy stepped uncertainly onto the soft white blanket of snow. Suddenly, out he went! He looked like a running, sliding snowball of fur. A squirrel scurried to the warmth of its nearby nest.

Do you think polar bears grow much faster than people? Why?

Constance knew Andy wouldn't be cold because polar bears have thick fur and layers of fat to keep them warm. Even the bottoms of their feet are covered with fur. In the Arctic, temperatures drop to forty degrees below zero.

Constance and her friends enjoyed romping with Andy Bear, but they were always careful of the frisky cub's teeth. Constance had already lost a fingernail because of his powerful bite. Even three-month-old polar bears have very strong jaws. Constance knew that although she had rescued Andy and raised him from a tiny cub, he was not a pet. In just a few months he would weigh over 100 pounds and be a strong and unpredictable polar bear.

By spring, Andy was becoming more curious and playful. He climbed on the kitchen counters and chewed on the furniture. Andy was wrecking Constance's apartment. Outdoors, he splashed in the water, dug in the garden, and explored in the yard. At 25 pounds, Andy was becoming a problem around the house. His claws were over an inch long and his teeth were very sharp. It was time for Andy to return to the zoo.

Reader's Response ∾ How would you feel about doing what Constance does?

Zoos of the FUTURE

Zoos with barred cages may soon be out of date. Today there are a number of new zoos where animals live in open areas that look like their natural habitats. Often moats or ditches separate animals from visitors. Some people prefer to call these new zoos "habitat exhibits."

At the National Bison Range, between 300 and 400 bison, or buffalo as they are sometimes called, roam over 19,000 acres of Montana grass and timberland. In addition to buffalo, visitors may also spot elk, deer, and bighorn sheep as they drive through the range.

The Arizona-Sonora Desert Museum only displays animals that live in the Sonora Desert. Careful attention is also given to plant life, rock formations, soil, and the importance of water in a desert environment.

Can you guess what a hippoquarium is? Visitors to the Toledo Zoo in Ohio watch hippos in their underwater home, a re-creation of an African river, which is the hippos' natural habitat. People view the hippos through glass panels in a tunnel that runs along one side of the river.

The Mouse at the Seashore

written and illustrated by
Arnold Lobel

A Mouse told his mother and father that he was going on a trip to the seashore.

"We are very alarmed!" they cried. "The world is full of terrors. You must not go!"

"I have made my decision," said the Mouse firmly. "I have never seen the ocean, and it is high time that I did. Nothing can make me change my mind."

"Then we cannot stop you," said Mother and Father Mouse, "but do be careful!"

The next day, in the first light of dawn, the Mouse began his journey. Even before the morning had ended, the Mouse came to know trouble and fear.

A Cat jumped out from behind a tree.

"I will eat you for lunch," he said.

It was a narrow escape for the Mouse. He ran for his life, but he left a part of his tail in the mouth of the Cat.

By afternoon the Mouse had been attacked by birds and dogs. He had lost his way several times. He was bruised and bloodied. He was tired and frightened.

At evening the Mouse slowly climbed the last hill and saw the seashore spreading out before him. He watched the waves rolling onto the beach, one after another. All the colors of the sunset filled the sky.

"How beautiful!" cried the Mouse. "I wish that Mother and Father were here to see this with me."

The moon and the stars began to appear over the ocean. The Mouse sat silently on the top of the hill. He was overwhelmed by a feeling of deep peace and contentment.

All the miles of a hard road are worth
a moment of true happiness.

GUASUITA
and the GIFT
of
FIRE

an Uruguayan Folk Tale
by Elena Pesce
retold by Martha Daniel

CHARACTERS: NARRATOR   WISEMAN
               GUASUITA   OWL
               CROW   FIREFATHER
               WEASEL   FIRE (TWO ACTORS)

ACT I

SETTING: *Long ago, under a locust tree in Uruguay*

As the curtain rises GUASUITA *and a* WISEMAN
are sitting on the ground bundled in blankets. OWL
and CROW *sit nearby perched by the tree.*

429

NARRATOR: A long time ago, in Uruguay, the Charrúas, Bohanes, and Chaná tribes lived in the regions around the river known as Paraná Guazú. They lived without fire and were very cold—until one brave Indian girl decided to get the gift of fire for her people. This is the story of that girl.

GUASUITA: Oh, Wiseman, it is so very cold today. Everyone in the tribe is cold. Like the tribes of the Bohanes and the Chaná Indians, I have learned to live with the cold. But, Wiseman, I have heard that some people do have this gift of fire. They are never cold and even cook their food. How can this be?

WISEMAN: Yes, you have heard correctly. Other people do have the gift of fire. They cook their meat over the fire. They keep warm. They even sit in the evenings and gaze at the beautiful, curling reddish ribbons of fire.

GUASUITA: And they and their children are never cold?

WISEMAN: Never.

GUASUITA: I want *my* people and their children to be warm. Where can I get this gift of fire?

WISEMAN: Some people say fire can be found in the mountains. Other people say it can be found in trees. Still other people say you can only get fire from lightning.

GUASUITA: But, Wiseman, what do *you* say? My mother and father say that wisemen know such things.

NARRATOR: When Owl and Crow overhear Guasuita and the Wiseman talking about fire, they lean in closer. They too are very cold, and want to hear what the Wiseman says. (CROW *squawks.*)

OWL: Be quiet, Crow! I want to find out how to get the gift of fire.

CROW: Not so fast, Owl! You'll share it with me! And if that girl gets it, we will snatch it from her and keep it for ourselves.

OWL: Perhaps we don't need to be quite so selfish. Maybe we won't need all of the fire. We could share a little spark with our relatives and friends—if there is enough!

CROW: You said the right words, my friend—"If there is enough." Now let us listen to the Wiseman speak. (OWL *and* CROW *fade into the background as the* WISEMAN *begins to speak.*)

WISEMAN: Guasuita, I do not know how to answer you. Perhaps you should go talk to the Firefather. If you wish, I can tell you where you can find the Firefather.

GUASUITA: Oh, please tell me, Wiseman. I wish to search for this gift of fire for my people.

WISEMAN: Then I will try to help you. You are a generous and brave young girl, but you must remember: it will take more than generosity and bravery to get the gift of fire. The Firefather is the wisest of all men. You may not understand why the Firefather does what he does or says what he says, but you must remain polite and patient at all times. The Firefather can be rude and moody, or he can be generous and gracious. You can never tell. But still you must be respectful at all times. Can you remember that, Guasuita?

GUASUITA: I think so, Wiseman. But tell me, Wiseman, where can I find the Firefather?

NARRATOR: At the mention of this question, Crow and Owl fly down closer to the Wiseman and Guasuita. Owl brushes Crow, and Crow squawks.

WISEMAN: Ah, it is Crow and Owl. Come closer, Guasuita, and I will tell only you where to find the Firefather.

(*The* WISEMAN *begins to whisper.* CROW *and* OWL *try to listen.*)

OWL: What are they saying?

CROW: Quiet! I can't hear a thing because you are making so much noise. (*They try to listen. The* WISEMAN *finishes whispering to* GUASUITA. *She walks away.*)

OWL: I couldn't hear either. Let's see if Guasuita will help us. (OWL *and* CROW *fly down from the tree and follow* GUASUITA.)

CROW: Guasuita, we couldn't help but overhear that you are going in search of fire. May we come with you?

GUASUITA: Yes, I would be glad to have you come along. (WEASEL *now enters.*) Hello, Weasel. I am very glad to see you. Crow, Owl, and I are going in search of fire. I would be very grateful if you would come along.

WEASEL: I would be pleased and honored to come with you on such a quest.

GUASUITA: Then come along, and our journey will begin.

ACT II

SETTING: *Some weeks later, very far away from home*

NARRATOR: Guasuita, uplifted by her generous thoughts and ideas, left her tribe and traveled with the three animals in search of fire. Since the Wiseman had told her that the Firefather lived at the top of the most colorful hill in the region, she and her friends looked for that hill. After walking for a few weeks, Guasuita found a colorful hill surrounded by a magnificent glow. The glow was as beautiful as the sun's.

GUASUITA: Now, Weasel, Crow, and Owl, listen carefully. You must be polite to the man who guards the fire. He must see that our intentions are good. He must understand that we do not want the fire only for ourselves but also for the cold children we have left behind.

OWL: (OWL *looks at* CROW *and smiles.*) Yes, of course, Guasuita.

NARRATOR: When they got to the top of the hill they saw the little old man. For the first time, they all saw fire. (*The* FIREFATHER *is feeding small branches to* FIRE. FIRE *is represented by two actors with red and yellow streamers tied to their arms and legs. They make the sizzling and crackling noises of fire as they wave their arms and dance around each other.*)

434

GUASUITA: For years I have heard about fire, but seeing it is like nothing I have heard described! See how its beauty reaches for the sky and disappears, only to reappear and reach up again. Let us all approach the Firefather. And everyone, please remember to be polite. (*They approach the fire.*)

GUASUITA: Good evening, Firefather.

FIREFATHER: I'm not saying hello to you.

WEASEL: A most pleasant evening, Firefather.

FIREFATHER: I'm not saying hello to you, either. You've come to steal my fire, haven't you?

CROW: You're quite right about that! (*To* OWL) Now, Owl, let's go! (CROW *and* OWL *fly around* FIRE *trying to pick it up.*) This is our fire now! Fire for us! And only for us!

GUASUITA: No! No! You mustn't do that!

FIREFATHER: Keep away! Keep away! (*CROW and OWL reach for the fire, but instead of carrying fire away, they are burned. They both cry out in pain and fly away.*) HA! HA! HA! Fire is not so easily stolen, you see! (*Seeing GUASUITA still standing there*) Now what do *you* want?

GUASUITA: Firefather, Weasel and I have come to ask for fire. We are not like Owl and Crow who wished to steal fire for themselves. We come from the land around the Paraná Guazú River. Our fields are damp and cold and our children shiver and eat uncooked food.

FIREFATHER: I don't give fire.

GUASUITA: Firefather, I beg of you. Please tell me why you will not give me and my people the gift of fire.

FIREFATHER: Just because.

GUASUITA: Firefather, please! Give me ten good reasons why you will not give us a little fire.

FIREFATHER: Because I don't feel like it. Ten times!

GUASUITA: Are you angry because Owl and Crow tried to steal fire from you?

FIREFATHER: Oh, no! That made me laugh. I'm just in a bad mood, that's all. Today I'm not giving out fire. If you had come yesterday, I would have given you a huge amount. Why don't you come yesterday?

GUASUITA: I can't come yesterday. Yesterday is over and done with.

FIREFATHER: Well then, you'll just have to go without fire.

GUASUITA: Firefather, can't you give me just a little bit of fire?

FIREFATHER: I'm not answering you.

GUASUITA: Firefather, what if I tell you a story and make your bad mood go away?

FIREFATHER: (Crossing his arms and sitting down to listen, he glares at WEASEL and GUASUITA.) All right, you two, tell me a story. But it had better be a good one! (Thirty seconds pass. Neither GUASUITA nor WEASEL speak. FIREFATHER stares at WEASEL.) I don't hear anything, Weasel! Can't you talk?

WEASEL: I'm sorry, sir! I can't concentrate on a story when someone is staring at me.

FIREFATHER: So now we have a dishonest Crow and Owl and a simple Weasel. I am not impressed with your friends, Guasuita.

NARRATOR: *(The two FIRE actors sit facing each other with their heads on their knees.)* Believing she had failed in her quest, Guasuita looked at the fire, which was now drawn together and was sleeping peacefully. Guasuita remembered the cold, dark fields around the Paraná Guazú River.

GUASUITA: Firefather, if you only knew. . . . In my own country where the river Paraná Guazú runs, the fields are very damp. Children shiver and hug their mothers close, but they're cold just the same. When the moon takes her place in the night sky, the children sleep hugging one another, because they do not have bonfires to keep them warm. Won't you please show me how to get fire, for the sake of the children?

FIREFATHER: *(Stroking his chin and thinking)* Well, I don't know what to do. I'm in such a bad mood that I can't give you fire. I simply never do that when I'm angry. But what you tell me is very sad. I think I will sleep on it for a while. (FIREFATHER *sits on a rock with his head in his hands and closes his eyes. He begins to snore.)*

GUASUITA: *(Disappointed)* He's asleep. Oh, I have failed! Now I must return to the tribe without a single spark of fire!

WEASEL: You haven't failed yet. Let's wake him up.

GUASUITA: No! We can't wake him up. That will only make him angrier.

WEASEL: Perhaps after a nap, he will change his mind. It's worth a try. (WEASEL *goes and taps* FIREFATHER *on the shoulder.*) Wake up, Firefather. (GUASUITA *cowers with fear.*)

FIREFATHER: (*Wakes up, stretches, and yawns*) Ah, that was a good sleep, but I have to get going now. Maybe I'll find someone who needs a few bright, red-hot embers. . . .

GUASUITA: (*Surprised*) Are you in a good mood?

FIREFATHER: Yes, I'm in a very good mood.

GUASUITA: (*Cautiously*) Will you give away fire now?

FIREFATHER: Of course. I'm the guardian of fire, and my job is to maintain and distribute fire to those in need.

GUASUITA: (*Excitedly*) Well, I and my people are in need of fire.

FIREFATHER: Well, all right! I will give you fire. I will give you a few stones.

GUASUITA: (*Confused*) Stones? Does fire come from stones?

FIREFATHER: Yes. Fire can be obtained from stones, and from wood, and it can even be seen in some metals such as gold and silver. (*He hands her two stones.*) Well, that's it. I'm going back to sleep now.

GUASUITA: But, wait! How do I get fire from these stones?

FIREFATHER: You'll get it by friction.

GUASUITA: (*Asking* WEASEL *quietly*) What is friction? I'm afraid to ask.

WEASEL: Honorable Firefather, what is friction?

FIREFATHER: (*Amused by* WEASEL's *curiosity*) Friction. (*He pats* WEASEL *on the head.*) You are very wise to ask about things you don't understand. It's the only way you learn. (*He takes the stones from* GUASUITA.) Friction is what you get when you rub two things together. (*He rubs the stones together.*) This is how you get fire. Then you feed the flames with small branches and dry leaves to make bonfires, large or small. (*He tosses some small branches into* FIRE. FIRE *jumps and makes crackling noises.*) Now I must sleep.

GUASUITA: Thank you very much, Firefather. You are wise and just.

WEASEL: Thank you, Firefather.

FIREFATHER: You're welcome. Goodbye, goodbye, see you *not* so soon.

GUASUITA: (*to* WEASEL) That must be his special way of saying goodbye. And I must thank you, Weasel, for asking a question. I was afraid a question like that would put him into a bad mood again.

WEASEL: It was a risk, but since Firefather thought I was not very smart anyway, I had nothing to lose.

GUASUITA: And it all worked out very well. Now we can return to Paraná Guazú with fire for all our people!

NARRATOR: From that time on, there was fire in the lands of the Charrúa Indians, and in the lands of the Bohanes and Chanás. All peoples had fire, thanks to Guasuita's courage—and Weasel's good question.

Reader's Response ∾ "Guasuita and the Gift of Fire" has many characters. If you could be one of the characters, which one would you choose? What do you especially like about that character?

FIRE STORIES

Fire was so important to civilization that people made up stories to explain where it came from.

According to the ancient Greeks, the god Prometheus gave fire to people after Zeus, the king of the gods, had deprived them of it in anger. Zeus thought fire would make humans too powerful. He punished Prometheus, but it was too late. Prometheus had already given people the gift of fire.

In an old Mexican story, the Fire Lady owned all the fire. She refused to share it. A clever possum promised to bring fire to the people. He went to see the Fire Lady. "May I warm myself by your fire?" he asked. He got so close to the flames that his tail began to burn. Quickly he ran from house to house, leaving some fire at each one. That's how the people got fire—and the possum got a bald tail.

In the United States, a spider in Cherokee myth captured fire and gave it to the other animals for warmth.

Where do *you* think fire came from?

PELÉ

THE KING OF SOCCER

by Clare and Frank Gault

A small boy danced barefoot out into the street and began kicking at the air as if he were kicking a soccer ball. But there was no ball. Nearby, a group of men and boys huddled around a radio, listening to a local soccer game: Bauru against São Carlos, a neighboring town in southeastern Brazil. The year was 1948.

One of the men smiled as he watched the boy acting like a real soccer player. The boy was eight years old. His name was Edson Arantes do Nascimento, but his friends called him Pelé (pronounced *peh-LAY*).

Pelé kept kicking at the air. He could imagine himself out on the soccer field, dribbling the ball downfield with his feet, passing it to a teammate, then taking a pass in return and kicking a goal.

Suddenly, the radio announcer became excited. Bauru had the ball near the São Carlos goal. Pelé stopped to listen. A player nicknamed Dondinho was moving in to take a shot, and it looked as if he would score.

Dondinho kicked, but he missed. Everybody groaned.

Dondinho was one of the policemen in town, but he played soccer part-time for the local club to earn a little extra money for his family. He was also Pelé's father. Pelé ran home. Soon his father arrived, too, looking very sad.

Pelé's mother said, "See what that game does to you. You missed a goal, and now you'll be sad for days. I pray Pelé never plays soccer." But that night, when Pelé's father, mother, grandmother, younger brother, and sister gathered for prayers, Pelé prayed he *would* become a great soccer player.

The next morning, Pelé dressed to go to school. He put his lunch in a paper bag. He put in his soccer ball, too: one of his father's old socks stuffed hard with newspapers and laced shut with string. It was no bigger than a large orange and not very round, but it was the only soccer ball Pelé had. He had no money to buy a real one.

Pelé took his soccer ball everywhere. He would practice kicking it as he walked down the street. He would dribble it. Or aim it at a telephone pole. He could do almost anything with it.

That morning Pelé didn't plan on going to school. Instead he went to the field behind the town's soccer stadium. He could often get in on a game there.

Pelé played soccer most of the day with his friends. When he got home, he quickly hid his ball, but he couldn't hide all the dirt on his white shirt. His mother knew right away what he had been doing. She grabbed him by the ear and dragged him over her knee to spank him. "Playing hooky from school to play soccer; I'll teach you."

Pelé was spanked often, but it didn't stop him from playing soccer. The games were too much fun. But after a while, Pelé felt he was missing something. He wanted his own team that could play other teams on a regular soccer field with a real ball.

"If we had uniforms," he told his friends, "other teams

would play us as a team. We could call ourselves the 'Seventh of September.'" (The seventh of September is Brazil's Independence Day.) To get money for uniforms, the boys collected old bottles and anything else they could find. They went up and down the streets and alleys. They poked into trash cans. They raked the city dump. When they had a big pile of old bottles, scrap metal, pieces of pipe, and old pieces of furniture, they took it all to a junk man to sell. Finally they had scraped together enough money to buy shirts and pants, but not enough for shoes and socks.

"We'll just have to be known as Seventh of September, the barefoot team," said Pelé.

The Seventh of September played every other team they could, and in time they became famous in the area. When Pelé was about eleven years old, the mayor of Bauru decided to hold a big tournament for all the younger teams. It was to be held in the city stadium with professional referees, just like big league soccer.

Pelé and his friends wanted to enter the tournament, but they needed new uniforms. This time, a traveling salesman helped them. He was a soccer fan and had heard of the barefoot team. He put up the money for uniforms, socks, and shoes. However, he asked that the team be called "Little America" after his favorite big league team, "America," in Rio de Janeiro.

That seemed to be a small price to pay. As soon as their equipment came, the boys started to practice. But after only a few minutes they were unhappy. They had never played in shoes before.

"I can't feel the ball," Pelé said. "I kick it, but it won't go where I want it to."

So they all took off their shoes and went back to playing barefoot. One of the tournament officials saw them. "Boys, you have to wear shoes in the games, so you might as well get used to them. Without shoes you can't play."

The boys had no choice but to put their shoes back on. They got blisters the first day, but after a few days, the shoes became more comfortable. And Pelé began to get the "feel" of the ball. He found he could kick with his toes as well as with the sides of his feet. The ball traveled farther with less effort. Wearing shoes is better, he finally decided.

Sixteen teams entered the tournament. Little America won their first game; then they won their second game and their third.

Suddenly they were in the finals, playing for the championship before a huge crowd.

It was a hard, close game, but years of playing together paid off. Pelé was especially good that day, dribbling, passing, and shooting all over the field.

Late in the game, Pelé got the ball and dribbled it quickly toward the goal. An opposing player moved in to take the ball away. Suddenly, Pelé stopped cold and changed direction, still controlling the ball with his feet. The other player tried to change direction, too, but he slipped and fell to the ground.

In a flash, Pelé was racing for the goal. Only the goalkeeper was in his way now. Out from the net came the goalie to try to smother the ball. Pelé faked a kick. The goalie dove, but the ball wasn't where he thought it would be. Pelé angled a soft shot for the corner of the net. Bounce. Bounce. The goalie raced for it. But it went into the net.

It was a goal.

The crowd stood and cheered. Little America had won. The crowd started to chant, "Pelé, Pelé, Pelé." Pelé heard his name and ran around the field, his arms raised in victory. The people threw coins out onto the field. They added up to $3.50, more money than he had ever seen before.

A few days later, Pelé's father found him sitting behind the fence in back of the house, thinking about the victory and smoking a cigarette.

His father looked at him for a minute and then said, "How long have you been smoking?"

"Not long," answered Pelé. "Only a few days."

"Do you enjoy it?" his father asked.

"Not really. I just thought I'd try it," Pelé said.

"Well," said his father, "cigarettes will cut down on your wind, and nobody needs wind like a soccer player. If you want to be a great player, you'll protect your body." He turned and went back into the house.

Pelé put the cigarette out and threw the others into the trash can. He never smoked again.

When Pelé was fifteen years old, a big league team named after a large port city in Brazil, Santos, signed him to a contract.

In 1957, Pelé was chosen to be on Brazil's national soccer team.

For the first time, he was to be paid for playing soccer. Pelé started with the junior Santos team. He practiced and played with them for three months before he got his chance to play with the Santos' first team. He entered an exhibition game as center forward in the second half and scored his first goal in big league competition.

449

Pelé has no trouble keeping the ball away from an opponent.

By spring of the following year, Pelé was a regular starter with the Santos. And after only two months of play, he became so well known around the big leagues that he was chosen to be on Brazil's national team. He was still only sixteen years old.

In his first game for the national team, Pelé went in during the second half. He scored the only goal for Brazil as they lost to Argentina, 2 to 1. But just a few days later, they played Argentina again. Pelé was a starter and scored another goal.

This time Brazil won, 2 to 0. The next year, 1958, was a World Cup year. Every four years the major soccer-playing countries hold a series of games ending in a finals to decide the victor. The World Cup is given to the best national team in the world.

Pelé was only seventeen years old, but he was chosen for Brazil's World Cup team. In the quarter-finals against Wales, Pelé scored what he feels is one of the most important goals of his career. Brazil won, 1 to 0, and went into the semi-finals, beating France as Pelé scored three times. And in the finals, Pelé scored twice more as Brazil beat Sweden, 5 to 2.

It was Brazil's first World Cup title. Pelé had scored six goals in the three games he played.

Pelé was famous. His feats in the World Cup, with the national team, and with the Santos were the talk of the soccer world. Every team wanted him. Every country wanted him. Then the government of Brazil acted. Pelé was declared a "national treasure." Brazil had passed a law to stop people from taking national treasures out of the country. The law was meant to protect works of art and important relics. But this time the law was used to keep a human being in the country.

Brazil won the World Cup again four years later and then again eight years after that. And over this span of years, Pelé's team, the Santos, won state and international team titles time

after time. Pelé proved that he truly was a "national treasure."

Pelé scored 1,220 goals, including 95 for the Brazilian national team. That is a fantastic total for soccer, as many games are low-scoring, often decided by one or two goals.

How could you measure Pelé's feats in soccer in terms of other sports? In baseball, it would be like hitting a home run in every game. Or in basketball, like averaging 50 points per game.

Why has Pelé been such an outstanding player? Speed, of course, is one reason. Pelé can run. And he can change direction and speed quickly. That makes it hard to cover him. Other players can't seem to block him out. But his supreme skill is in ball control. Sometimes it almost seems as if the ball were tied to his foot.

Other times he seems to have magical control over it. The ball does exactly what he wants it to do.

Most teams try to stop Pelé by putting two or three players to guard him. Of course, when they do that, Pelé's teammates are in a good spot to score. So Pelé's value to his team is much greater than just the goals he scores. He sets up as many goals for his teammates as he scores himself. It's no wonder that Pelé has been acclaimed all over the world as "the greatest soccer player who ever lived."

In 1974, Pelé said he would retire. Giant crowds shouted *"Pelé, Pelé, Pelé,"* and *"Stay, stay, stay."* But Pelé felt it was time to quit. He was thirty-three years old, and he wanted to relax and spend more time with his wife and two young children. But in 1975, with the permission of the Brazilian government, Pelé signed a contract to play for the New York Cosmos Soccer Team. He couldn't resist trying to beat the last challenge—making soccer a major sport in the United States. Right from his first appearance, crowds doubled and tripled. Pelé excited more interest and enthusiasm in soccer than there had ever been before.

Three weeks after arriving in New York, Pelé was seen playing soccer with a bunch of boys in Central Park. When Pelé saw the boys playing, he couldn't stay away, just as he couldn't stay away from the games when he was a barefoot kid kicking an old sock stuffed with newspapers.

Reader's Response ～ Pelé was best in the world at what he did. What would you like to become best at?

Q. Who Hit 18 World Series Home Runs, the Most in Baseball World Series History?

(To find out: Match each of the 12 clues below with the name of a place from the slugger's suitcase. Using the first letter of each place named, spell out the answer.)

1. This city is the capital of Russia and was the site of the 1980 Summer Olympics.

2. On a map, this country looks like a boot, and its soccer team won the 1982 World Cup.

3. This country is the United States' northern neighbor, and it is the home of eight National Hockey League Teams.

4. This state, known as the Bluegrass State, is the site of a very famous horse race.

5. This nation across the Atlantic Ocean is part of the United Kingdom and is the place where the game of cricket developed.

6. This country in southeastern Europe hosted the 1984 Winter Olympics.

7. This country is the United States' neighbor to the south, and it is a place where bullfighting is a popular sport.

8. This U. S. state has the largest area of any in the union, and the Iditarod dogsled race is held here every year.

9. Known as the Tar Heel State, this is the state where Michael Jordan grew up.

10. This city is the capital of Japan and was the site of the Summer Olympics in 1964.

11. This is the largest city in California, and the home of the 1988 World Series Champs.

12. Wayne Gretzky led this Canadian city's hockey team to four championships.

Rufus M.

by ELEANOR ESTES

Rufus M. That's the way Rufus wrote his name on his heavy arithmetic paper and on his blue-lined spelling paper. Rufus M. went on one side of the paper. His age, seven, went on the other. Rufus had not learned to write his name in school, though that is one place for learning to write. He had not learned to write his name at home either, though that is another place for learning to write. The place where he had learned to write his name was the library, long ago before he ever went to school at all. This is the way it happened.

One day when Rufus had been riding his scooter up and down the street, being the motorman, the conductor, the passengers, the steam, and the whistle of a locomotive, he came home and found Joey, Jane, and Sylvie, all reading in the front yard. Joey and Jane were sitting on the steps of the porch and Sylvie was sprawled in the hammock, a book in one hand, a chocolate-covered peppermint in the other.

Rufus stood with one bare foot on his scooter and one on the grass and watched them. Sylvie read the fastest. This was natural since she was the oldest. But Joey turned the pages almost as fast and Jane went lickety-cut on the good parts. They were all reading books and he couldn't even read yet. These books they were reading were library books. The library must be open today. It wasn't open every day, just a few days a week.

"I want to go to the library," said Rufus. "And get a book," he added.

"We all just came home from there," said Jane, while Joey and Sylvie merely went on reading as though Rufus had said nothing. "Besides," she added, "why do you want a book anyway? You can't even read yet."

This was true and it made Rufus mad. He liked to do everything that they did. He even liked to sew if they were sewing. He never thought whether sewing was for girls only or not. When he saw Jane sewing, he asked Mama to let him sew too. So Mama tied a thread to the head of a pin and Rufus poked that in and out of a piece of goods. That's the way he sewed. It looked like what Jane was doing and Rufus was convinced that he was sewing too, though he could not see much sense in it.

Now here were the other Moffats, all with books from the library. And there were three more books stacked up on the porch that looked like big people's books without pictures. They were for Mama no doubt. This meant that he was the only one here who did not have a book.

"I want a book from the library," said Rufus. A flick of the page as Sylvie turned it over was all the answer he got. It seemed to Rufus as though even Catherine-the-cat gave him a scornful glance because he could not read yet and did not have a book.

Rufus turned his scooter around and went out of the yard. Just wait! Read? Why, soon he'd read as fast if not faster than they did. Reading looked easy. It was just flipping pages. Who couldn't do that?

Rufus thought that it was not hard to get a book out of the library. All you did was go in, look for a book that you liked, give it to the lady to punch, and come home with it. He knew where the library was for he had often gone there with Jane and some of the others. While Jane went off to the shelves to find a book, he and Joey played the game of Find the Duke in the Palmer Cox Brownie books. This was a game that the two boys had made up. They would turn the pages of one of the Brownie books, any of them, and try to be the first to spot the duke, the brownie in the tall hat. The library lady thought that this was a noisy game, and said she wished they would not play it there. Rufus hoped to bring a Brownie book home now.

"Toot-toot!" he sang to clear the way. Straight down Elm Street was the way to the library; the same way that led to Sunday School, and Rufus knew it well. He liked sidewalks that were white the best for he could go the fastest on these.

"Toot-toot!" Rufus hurried down the street. When he arrived at the library, he hid his scooter in the pine trees that grew under the windows beside the steps. Christmas trees, Rufus called them. The ground was covered with brown pine needles and they were soft to walk upon. Rufus always went into the library the same way. He climbed the stairs, encircled the light on the granite arm of the steps, and marched into the library.

Rufus stepped carefully on the strips of rubber matting that led to the desk. This matting looked like dirty licorice. But it wasn't licorice. He knew because once when Sylvie had brought him here when he was scarcely more than three he had tasted a torn corner of it. It was not good to eat.

The library lady was sitting at the desk playing with some cards. Rufus stepped off the matting. The cool, shiny floor felt good to his bare feet. He went over to the shelves and luckily did find one of the big Palmer Cox Brownie books there. It would be fun to play the game of Find the Duke at home. Until now he had played it only in the library. Maybe Jane or Joey would play it with him right now. He laughed out loud at the thought.

"Sh-sh-sh, quiet," said the lady at the desk.

Rufus clapped his chubby fist over his mouth. Goodness! He had forgotten where he was. Do not laugh or talk out loud in the library. He knew these rules. Well, he didn't want to stay here any longer today anyway. He wanted to read at home with the others. He took the book to the lady to punch.

She didn't punch it though. She took it and she put it on the table behind her and then she started to play cards again.

"That's my book," said Rufus.

"Do you have a card?" the lady asked.

Rufus felt in his pockets. Sometimes he carried around an old playing card or two. Today he didn't have one.

"No," he said.

"You'll have to have a card to get a book."

"I'll go and get one," said Rufus.

The lady put down her cards. "I mean a library card," she explained kindly. "It looks to me as though you are too little to have a library card. Do you have one?"

"No," said Rufus. "I'd like to though."

"I'm afraid you're too little," said the lady. "You have to write your name to get one. Can you do that?"

Rufus nodded his head confidently. Writing. Lines up and down. He'd seen that done. And the letters that Mama had tied in bundles in the closet under the stairs were covered with writing. Of course he could write.

"Well, let's see your hands," said the lady.

Rufus obligingly showed this lady his hands, but she did not like the look of them. She cringed and clasped her head as though the sight hurt her.

"Oh," she gasped. "You'll just have to go home and wash them before we can even think about joining the library and borrowing books."

This was a complication upon which Rufus had not reckoned. However, all it meant was a slight delay. He'd wash his hands and then he'd get the book. He turned and went out of the library, found his scooter safe among the Christmas trees, and pushed it home. He surprised Mama by asking to have his hands washed. When this was done, he mounted his scooter again and returned all the long way to the library. It was not just a little trip to the library. It was a long one. A long one and a hot one on a day like this. But he didn't notice that. All he was bent on was getting his book and taking it home and reading with the others on the front porch. They were all still there, brushing flies away and reading.

Again Rufus hid his scooter in the pine trees, encircled the light, and went in.

"Hello," he said.

"Well," said the lady. "How are they now?"

Rufus had forgotten he had had to wash his hands. He thought she was referring to the other Moffats. "Fine," he said.

"Let me see them," she said, and she held up her hands.

Oh! His hands! Well, they were all right, thought Rufus, for Mama had just washed them. He showed them to the lady. There was silence while she studied them. Then she shook her head. She still did not like them.

"Ts,ts,ts!" she said. "They'll have to be cleaner than that."

Rufus looked at his hands. Supposing he went all the way home and washed them again, she still might not like them. However, if that is what she wanted, he would have to do that before he could get the Brownie book . . . and he started for the door.

"Well now, let's see what we can do," said the lady. "I know what," she said. "It's against the rules but perhaps we can wash them in here." And she led Rufus into a little room that smelled of paste where lots of new books and old books were stacked up. In one corner was a little round sink and Rufus washed his hands again. Then they returned to the desk. The lady got a chair and put a newspaper on it. She made Rufus stand on this because he was not big enough to write at the desk otherwise.

Then the lady put a piece of paper covered with a lot of printing in front of Rufus, dipped a pen in the ink well and gave it to him.

"All right," she said. "Here's your application. Write your name here."

All the writing Rufus had ever done before had been on big pieces of brown wrapping paper with lots of room on them.

461

Rufus had often covered those great sheets of paper with his own kind of writing at home. Lines up and down.

But on this paper there wasn't much space. It was already covered with writing. However, there was a tiny little empty space and that was where Rufus must write his name, the lady said. So, little space or not, Rufus confidently grasped the pen with his left hand and dug it into the paper. He was not accustomed to pens, having always worked with pencils until now, and he made a great many holes and blots and scratches.

"Gracious," said the lady. "Don't bear down so hard! And why don't you hold it in your right hand?" she asked, moving the pen back into his right hand.

Rufus started again scraping his lines up and down and all over the page, this time using his right hand. Wherever there was an empty space he wrote. He even wrote over some of the print for good measure. Then he waited for the lady, who had gone off to get a book for some man, to come back and look.

"Oh," she said as she settled herself in her swivel chair, "is that the way you write? Well . . . it's nice, but what does it say?"

"Says Rufus Moffat. My name."

Apparently these lines up and down did not spell Rufus Moffat to this lady. She shook her head.

"It's nice," she repeated. "Very nice. But nobody but you knows what it says. You have to learn to write your name better than that before you can join the library."

Rufus was silent. He had come to the library all by himself, gone back home to wash his hands, and come back because he wanted to take books home and read them the way the others did. He had worked hard. He did not like to think he might have to go home without a book.

The library lady looked at him a moment and then she said quickly before he could get himself all the way off the big chair, "Maybe you can *print* your name."

Rufus looked at her hopefully. He thought he could write better than he could print, for his writing certainly looked to him exactly like all grown people's writing. Still he'd try to print if that was what she wanted.

The lady printed some letters on the top of a piece of paper. "There," she said. "That's your name. Copy it ten times and then we'll try it on another application."

Rufus worked hard. He worked so hard the knuckles showed white on his brown fist. He worked for a long, long time, now with his right hand and now with his left. Sometimes a boy or a girl came in, looked over his shoulder and watched, but he paid no attention. From time to time the lady studied his work and she said, "That's fine. That's fine." At last she said, "Well, maybe now we can try." And she gave him another application.

All Rufus could get, with his large generous letters, in that tiny little space where he was supposed to print his name, was R-U-F. The other letters he scattered here and there on the card. The lady did not like this either. She gave him still another blank. Rufus tried to print smaller and this time he got RUFUS in the space, and also he crowded an M at the end. Since he was doing so well now the lady herself printed the *offat* part of Moffat on the next line.

"This will have to do," she said. "Now take this home and ask your mother to sign it on the other side. Bring it back on Thursday and you'll get your card."

Rufus's face was shiny and streaked with dirt where he had rubbed it. He never knew there was all this work to getting a book. The other Moffats just came in and got books. Well maybe they had had to do this once too.

Rufus held his hard-earned application in one hand and steered his scooter with the other. When he reached home Joey, Jane and Sylvie were not around any longer. Mama signed his card for him, saying, "My! So you've learned how to write!"

"Print," corrected Rufus.

Mama kissed Rufus and he went back out. The lady had said to come back on Thursday, but he wanted a book today. When the other Moffats came home, he'd be sitting on the top step of the porch, reading. That would surprise them. He smiled to himself as he made his way to the library for the third time.

Once his application blew away. Fortunately it landed in a thistle bush and did not get very torn. The rest of the way Rufus clutched it carefully. He climbed the granite steps to the library again only to find that the big round dark brown doors were closed. Rufus tried to open them but he couldn't. He knocked at the door, even kicked it with his foot, but there was no answer. He pounded on the door but nobody came.

A big boy strode past with his newspapers. "Hey, kid," he said to Rufus. "Library's closed!" And off he went, whistling.

Rufus looked after him. The fellow said the library was closed. How could it have closed so fast? He had been here such a little while ago. The lady must still be here. He did want his Brownie book. If only he could see in, he might see the lady and get his book. The windows were high up but they had very wide sills. Rufus was a wonderful climber. He could shinny up trees and poles faster than anybody on the block. Faster than Joey. Now, helping himself up by means of one of the pine trees that grew close to the building, and by sticking his toes in the ivy and rough places in the bricks, he scrambled up the wall. He hoisted himself up on one of the sills and sat there. He peered in. It was dark inside, for the shades had been drawn almost all the way down.

"Library lady!" he called, and he knocked on the window-pane. There was no answer. He put his hands on each side of his face to shield his eyes, and he looked in for a long, long time. He could not believe that she had left. Rufus was resolved to get a book. He had lost track of the number of times he had been back and forth from home to the library, and the library home. Maybe the lady was in the cellar. He climbed down, stubbing his big toe on the bricks as he did so. He stooped down beside one of the low dirt-spattered cellar windows. He couldn't see in. He lay flat on the ground, wiped one spot clean on the window, picked up a few pieces of coal from the sill and put them in his pocket for Mama.

"Hey, lady," he called.

He gave the cellar window a little push. It wasn't locked so he opened it a little and looked in. All he could see was a high pile of coal reaching up to this window. Of course he didn't put any of that coal in his pocket for that would be stealing.

"Hey, lady," he yelled again. His voice echoed in the

cellar but the library lady did not answer.
He called out, "Hey, lady," every few
seconds, but all that answered him was an
echo. He pushed the window open a little wider.
All of a sudden it swung wide open and Rufus slid
in, right on top of the coal pile, and crash, clatter,
bang! He slid to the bottom, making a great racket.

bang!

A little light shone through the dusty windows, but
on the whole it was very dark and spooky down here and
Rufus really wished that he was back on the outside looking
in. However, since he was in the library, why not go upstairs
quick, get the Brownie book, and go home? The window had
banged shut, but he thought he could climb up the coal pile, pull
the window up and get out. He certainly hoped he could anyway. Supposing he couldn't and he had to stay in this cellar!
Well, that he would not think about. He looked around in the
dusky light and saw a staircase across the cellar. Luckily
his application was still good. It was torn and dirty but it still had
his name on it, RUFUS M, and that was the important part.
He'd leave this on the desk in exchange for the Brownie book.

Rufus cautiously made his way over to the steps but he
stopped halfway across the cellar. Somebody had opened the
door at the top of the stairs. He couldn't see who it was, but
he did see the light reflected and that's how he knew that
somebody had opened the door. It must be the lady. He was
just going to say, "Hey, lady," when he thought, "Gee, maybe
it isn't the lady. Maybe it's a spooky thing."

Then the light went away, the door was closed, and Rufus
was left in the dark again. He didn't like it down here. He
started to go back to the coal pile to get out of this place. Then
he felt of his application. What a lot of work he had done to
get a book and now that he was this near to getting one, should
he give up? No. Anyway, if it was the lady up there, he knew

her and she knew him and neither one of them was scared of the other. And Mama always said there's no such thing as a spooky thing.

So Rufus bravely made his way again to the stairs. He tiptoed up them. The door at the head was not closed tightly. He pushed it open and found himself right in the library. But goodness! There in the little sink room right opposite him was the library lady!

Rufus stared at her in silence. The library lady was eating. Rufus had never seen her do anything before but play cards, punch books, and carry great piles of them around. Now she was eating. Mama said not to stare at anybody while they were eating. Still Rufus didn't know the library lady ate, so it was hard for him not to look at her.

She had a little gas stove in there. She could cook there. She was reading a book at the same time that she was eating. Sylvie could do that too. This lady did not see him. "Hey, lady," said Rufus.

The librarian jumped up out of her seat. "Was that you in the cellar? I thought I heard somebody. Goodness, young man! I thought you had gone home long ago."

Rufus didn't say anything. He just stood there. He had gone home and he had come back lots of times. He had the whole thing in his mind; the coming and going, and going and coming, and sliding down the coal pile, but he did not know where to begin, how to tell it.

"Didn't you know the library is closed now?" she demanded, coming across the floor with firm steps.

Rufus remained silent. No, he hadn't known it. The fellow had told him but he hadn't believed him. Now he could see for himself that the library was closed so the library lady could eat. If the lady would let him take his book, he'd go home and stay there. He'd play the game of Find the Duke with Jane. He hopefully held out his card with his name on it.

"Here this is," he said.

But the lady acted as though she didn't even see it. She led Rufus over to the door.

"All right now," she said. "Out with you!" But just as she opened the door the sound of water boiling over on the stove struck their ears, and back she raced to her little room.

"Gracious!" she exclaimed. "What a day!"

Before the door could close on him, Rufus followed her in and sat down on the edge of a chair. The lady thought he had gone and started to sip her tea. Rufus watched her quietly, waiting for her to finish.

After a while the lady brushed the crumbs off her lap. And then she washed her hands and the dishes in the little sink where Rufus had washed his hands. In a library a lady could eat and could wash. Maybe she slept here too. Maybe she lived here.

"Do you live here?" Rufus asked her.

"Mercy on us!" exclaimed the lady. "Where'd you come from? Didn't I send you home? No, I don't live here and neither do you. Come now, out with you, young man. I mean it." The lady called all boys "young man" and all girls "Susie." She came out of the little room and she opened the big brown door again. "There," she said. "Come back on Thursday."

Rufus's eyes filled up with tears.

"Here's this," he said again, holding up his application in a last desperate attempt. But the lady shook her head. Rufus went slowly down the steps, felt around in the bushes for his scooter, and with drooping spirits he mounted it. Then for the second time that day, the library lady changed her mind.

"Oh, well," she said, "come back here, young man. I'm not supposed to do business when the library's closed, but I see we'll have to make an exception."

So Rufus rubbed his sooty hands over his face, hid his scooter in the bushes again, climbed the granite steps and, without circling the light, he went back in and gave the lady his application.

The lady took it gingerly. "My, it's dirty," she said. "You really ought to sign another one."

"And go home with it?" asked Rufus. He really didn't believe this was possible. He wiped his hot face on his sleeve and looked up at the lady in exhaustion. What he was thinking was: All right. If he had to sign another one, all right. But would she just please stay open until he got back?

However, this was not necessary. The lady said, "Well now, I'll try to clean this old one up. But remember, young man, always have everything clean—your hands, your book, everything, when you come to the library."

Rufus nodded solemnly. "My feet too," he assured her.

Then the lady made Rufus wash his hands again. They really were very bad this time, for he had been in a coal pile, and now at last she gave Rufus the book he wanted—one of the Palmer Cox Brownie books. This one was "The Brownies in the Philippines."

And Rufus went home.

When he reached home, he showed Mama his book. She smiled at him, and gave his cheek a pat. She thought it was fine that he had gone to the library and joined all by himself and taken out a book. And she thought it was fine when Rufus sat down at the kitchen table, was busy and quiet for a long, long time, and then showed her what he had done.

He had printed RUFUS M. That was what he had done.

And that's the way he learned to sign his name. And that's the way he always did sign his name for a long, long time.

But, of course, that was before he ever went to school at all, when the Moffats still lived in the old house, the yellow house on New Dollar Street; before this country had gone into the war; and before Mr. Abbot, the curate, started leaving his overshoes on the Moffats' front porch.

Reader's Response ∿ Try to remember the day you received your first library card. How was your day the same or different from Rufus's adventure?

Library Link ∿ *If you enjoyed this story by Eleanor Estes, you might also like to read* The Moffat Museum.

BROWSING FOR BOOKS

A Great Place to Shop

Of course you've been to a library, in your school or your town. You may even go there regularly to take out books. Libraries are great places to borrow books, but if you want a book to keep, or to give to someone else, a bookstore is the place to go. Have you ever been to a bookstore? If you have, you know that bookstores, like libraries, are wonderful places to browse in, whether you want to buy a book or just see what's new.

Most bookstores have a young reader's section, where you'll find books stacked on tables and shelves just like in the library. Are you looking for a new Einstein Anderson, or a Great Brain adventure for yourself or to give to a friend? You'll find all the books by each author together in one place.

There are books about pets, cookbooks, books of jokes and riddles, and books of games. They're all at your bookstore.

If you need a gift for a little person you know, check the shelves of picture books and easy readers. One of your old favorites might make a perfect present. A bookstore is also a great place to shop for Mom and Dad. Are they interested in cameras, gardening, sports, traveling, or music? You'll find books on all those topics and many more besides. Look for the special tables of books on sale. They often have wonderful picture books that cost only a small part of their original price.

Bookstores are like libraries. They have something for everyone. And they're just as much fun.

TWO PIANO
TUNERS

written and illustrated by
M. B. GOFFSTEIN

Every morning Reuben Weinstock, the piano tuner, got stiffly out of bed, and washed and shaved in hot water at the kitchen sink. Then he went into his bedroom and brushed his thick gray hair, got dressed in a clean shirt and trousers, put his beautiful old maroon wool robe over them, and tying the silky tasseled cord around his waist, went back into the kitchen to start breakfast cooking.

He put water on the stove in a blue and white enameled saucepan and an old yellow coffee pot. Then he opened the cupboard and set the table with a blue plate and an orange plate, a navy-blue bowl and a green bowl, plaster salt and pepper shakers that had seashells stuck into them and bright red plastic tops, two white paper napkins, two knives and two spoons with yellow plastic handles, and two big white cups.

Almost everything in the cupboard had been given to Reuben Weinstock two years ago by the ladies whose pianos he tuned, when they heard that his son and daughter-in-law had died in another town and left him their little girl.

"But how can you take her?" Mrs. Perlman had asked him kindly. "You are a widower, Mr. Weinstock, and you are not a young man any more, either. What can you give her?"

"Well, I know music," he had said. "I know music. I have tuned pianos for all the great pianists, and I used to travel with Isaac Lipman. I can teach the little girl to play the piano and she might become a great concert artist!"

"Or a piano teacher," agreed Mrs. Perlman.

Almost all the ladies had given him something— dishes, little dresses, a small bed and dresser. "And if you need any advice, please feel free to ask me," every one of them said.

By the time he finished setting the table, the water on the stove was boiling. Reuben Weinstock gently dropped three brown eggs into the blue and white saucepan, measured coffee into the yellow pot, took out a bottle of milk and a dish of butter, and put four slices of bread on the toast rack. Then he slowly went upstairs, holding on to the rail.

There was only one room upstairs, a big low-ceilinged room. When Reuben Weinstock climbed the top step, he was standing right in the middle of it, looking down at a long little bump under a fuzzy blue blanket.

"Debbie," he whispered. "It's morning, Debbie."

The long bump curled into a round ball under the blanket.

"Wake up, little Debbie!"

"Hm-m-m-m-m," sang the bump. "Hm-m-m-m-m."

"Hm-m-m-m-m," sang Mr. Weinstock, a little bit lower. "Hm-m-m-m-m. I'm afraid you are sharp again this morning, Debbie."

She jumped out of bed in her long pink pajamas and ran downstairs to play middle C on the piano: C! C! "You are right, Grandpa Reuben," she called, and went into the kitchen to wash her face and brush her teeth at the sink.

475

When she came back upstairs, her bed was made and Mr. Weinstock, whose back ached from bending over, was laying out her clean clothes on it.

"Oh no, Grandpa!" cried Debbie. "Not my jumper! Don't you remember that I don't have school today, so I don't have to wear my jumper?"

"I thought you wanted to come with me to the Auditorium, to tune the grand piano."

"Of course I do!"

"Would you like to wear a prettier dress?"

"I want to wear pants."

"Not to go with me," said Mr. Weinstock.

"Oh, Grandpa Reuben," stormed Debbie. "I want to *help* you."

"Then put on your jumper," he said, stroking her bushy hair kindly, "and if you can play your piano lesson well this morning, you may carry my black bag into the Auditorium."

"Will the pianist be there?"

"I think so."

"And won't he be amazed to see a little girl coming to tune that piano?"

"He certainly will be," agreed Mr. Weinstock as he began to make his way carefully downstairs.

"If he thinks I tuned the piano, he won't show up for the concert," chuckled Debbie, who had dressed and gotten downstairs at his heels. "He'll be too scared!"

After breakfast, while Mr. Weinstock cleared the kitchen table, washed the dishes, and swept up the crumbs, Debbie played her piano lesson for him. It was *Reverie*, by Felix Mendelssohn, and she had been playing it for the past three weeks.

Now Mr. Weinstock came in, drying the last dish. "It is still not so good," he said sadly.

Debbie jumped down from the piano stool. "I know it," she said. "We have to tune this old piano again."

She started to raise the lid, but Mr. Weinstock went back into the kitchen to hang up his dishtowel, saying, "We must leave for the Auditorium. Get your coat and hat, Debbie—and brush your hair."

Then he went into his bedroom and changed from his robe to the jacket that matched his dark blue pants. He tucked a clean handkerchief into his pocket and helped Debbie on with her coat.

"I'm sorry you played so badly," he said as he tied her hat strings under her chin.

But when they got to the Auditorium, he handed her his black bag anyway, and Debbie proudly carried it inside.

The pianist was already there, but he did not even see her. "Reuben!" he cried, and hurried up the aisle, past rows of empty seats, to hug Mr. Weinstock.

"Isaac!" Mr. Weinstock hugged him back.

They kept their hands on each other's shoulders and beamed at each other. "You look well! You look well!" they said.

"But what are you doing here?" asked Mr. Weinstock.

"You were expecting Walter Bernheimer?"

"Yes!"

"I heard from my manager that he couldn't get here, and I decided to surprise you. I have been on the train since yesterday morning, in order to play here this afternoon."

479

"You! Oh, that's wonderful. Oh, now we'll hear some real music!"

"And I, once again, after all these years, will play on a piano that is perfectly tuned," said the great concert pianist.

He looked down, as if to make sure that Reuben Weinstock had his bag of tuning instruments with him, and he saw Debbie, still holding on to it.

"Who is this?" he asked.

"This is the piano tuner," joked Mr. Weinstock. He put his hand on Debbie's shoulder. "This is my granddaughter, Deborah Weinstock, who came to live with me two years ago."

"And I really *could* tune that piano."

"You could?"

Debbie nodded uncertainly.

"I want her to play the piano and she always wants to tune or make repairs."

"That kind of work isn't good for a pianist's hands," Isaac Lipman warned her.

Debbie tucked her hand into her grandfather's hand. "Well, I'm going to be a piano tuner," she said.

"Your grandfather is the best piano tuner in the world, you know, so I hope you are taking good care of him."

"I'm going to," said Debbie.

Isaac Lipman put his arm around Mr. Weinstock for a moment. "Now I must go back to the dressing room and rest," he said. "Please come back when you have finished your work and we'll have a good visit."

They all walked down the aisle together. Isaac Lipman went up onto the stage and disappeared, while Mr. Weinstock and Debbie took off their coats and hats and laid them on two chairs in the front row. Then they took off their overshoes and went up the stairs to the stage.

Mr. Lipman had been practicing before they came, so the grand piano was already open and the top was up. Mr. Weinstock slid out the music rack and carried it to the back of the stage and leaned it up against the wall.

Then he went back to the piano, sat down, adjusted the bench, and played a few notes. He got up again to take off his jacket and hang it over the back of a wooden chair that was standing near the piano, and he rolled up his shirt sleeves.

Debbie had set his bag down on the floor beside the piano bench. Mr. Weinstock knelt down and opened it and took out his tuning hammer and screwdriver, a strip of red felt, and two little gray felt wedges. He took his tuning fork out of its case and put the case back into his bag.

He stood up and laid the red felt strip inside the piano and began to poke it between the strings with his screwdriver. Then he fitted the tuning hammer onto a pin, hit the tuning fork against his knee and touched it to the metal frame, listened, sat down again, and began to tune the grand piano.

C! C! C! he played. C! C! C! And he pushed the hammer a little to the left. C AND C! F AND C! G AND C! G AND D! F AND D! A AND D! He played each interval over and over again, turning the tuning pins one at a time with the tuning hammer, winding the piano strings more tightly or loosening them a little, until each note was pure and beautiful.

F AND A! F AND A! Debbie stood looking into the piano, at the long line of strings, the heavy iron frame, the yellow wood sounding board, and the flat black dampers, and hummed the notes that were being tuned. She was enjoying the feeling she had of being able to sing two notes at a time.

She always knew which notes would come next; she knew the whole tuning pattern by heart. She thought it was beautiful and exciting, and she liked it better than any music she had ever heard.

"Please stop that, Debbie," said Mr. Weinstock. "I can't hear anything when you hum."

Debbie put her hand over her mouth and Mr. Weinstock went on tuning: A AND E! A AND E! G AND E! E AND B! Then Debbie forgot and started humming again.

"Debbie!"

"I'm sorry, Grandpa."

G AND B! B AND D! G AND B AND D! G AND B AND D! B AND F-SHARP! F-SHARP AND A! "Debbie?" said Mr. Weinstock.

She looked at him in amazement. "I wasn't humming!"

"No, I just remembered that I'm supposed to tune Mrs. Perlman's piano too, this morning."

"Oh," said Debbie.

"Would you go over to her house now, and ask her if I may do it tomorrow instead?"

"Do I have to go now, before you're through working on this piano?"

"I would like you to, so you'll be back in time to visit with Mr. Lipman."

"But are you going to take out the action?"

Debbie loved to see the long row of hammers, with their thin shanks and workmanlike red and gray and white felt tops, flip up when Mr. Weinstock hit the keys. She liked the files, the grease, the needles, and all of the good little tools her grandfather might use if he took the action out of the piano.

"No," said Mr. Weinstock. "Mr. Lipman didn't say that there was anything wrong, and everything seems fine to me."

"But you might have to change a string."

"I hope not. Anyway, you've seen me do that a hundred times."

"I like it when they break," said Debbie.

"Well, you'll be back long before I'm done!"

So Debbie walked across the front of the stage, down the steps, and over to the seat that held her coat and hat. She put them on, then sat down to buckle her overshoes.

"Can you do everything by yourself?" Mr. Weinstock called from the stage.

"Yuh," said Debbie, holding her hat strings down with her chin while she tried to make a bow.

But Mr. Weinstock came down to help her. "Now, you be sure to tell Mrs. Perlman that Isaac Lipman is here, so she won't miss the concert this afternoon. And ask her if it's all right to tune her piano tomorrow."

"I will."

"Be very careful."

Debbie nodded seriously. She walked up the dim, empty aisle alone, opened the door, and went into the lobby. She took a drink from the drinking fountain, then she pushed open one of the heavy front doors and went outside. It had been snowing just a little, not enough to stick.

She went down the wide, gray stone steps to the sidewalk. Two big dogs, one black and one tan, and a little spotted dog stood talking together on the corner. "Hello," thought Debbie. "Hello, dogs, here comes the piano tuner!"

She crossed the street and started up the long block, looking at each house as she passed it: the white one with red shutters, the dark green one with yellow trimming, the pretty little gray house with soft brown bushes in front and a baby looking out the window. "There goes the piano tuner," she thought for the baby.

And she went past Mrs. Perlman's brown house with white lace curtains in the windows. She was going home first!

Their house was painted yellow, with a dark red roof. It was at the end of the block behind a grassy, empty lot. Debbie cut through the lot and went in the back door and through the kitchen.

In the living room, next to the piano, was a bureau with a lot of old tuning instruments in its bottom drawer. Debbie sat down on the carpet and pulled the drawer out. She took out the tuning hammer that Reuben Weinstock never used because its handle was too long. It was a little bit rusty, but so was the only tuning fork Debbie could find that said C on it. She found one gray felt wedge and one black rubber one.

Debbie brought them upstairs to her room and put them on the bed while she took off her coat, got out of her jumper, stepped into her pants, and put the coat back on.

The pants had an elasticized waistband which was perfect for holding the tuning hammer up inside them, and she put the tuning fork and wedges into her back pocket. She buttoned her coat on the way downstairs and went out the door, back through the vacant lot, and down the block to Mrs. Perlman's house.

She climbed the front steps and pressed the doorbell, and waited for a long time. Finally she pressed the bell again.

"Why, Debbie," said Mrs. Perlman, opening the door. "I looked out the window before, but I couldn't see anyone!"

"That's all right," said Debbie.

"Won't you come in?"

"My grandpa says, he hopes you don't mind if I tune your piano."

"What?"

"Well, his friend Isaac Lipman came to give a concert, and he says you should come."

"Isaac Lipman came here?"

"He's at the Auditorium, and Grandpa Reuben is tuning the piano for *him* instead of for Walter Bernheimer," Debbie explained.

"Do you mean to say that Isaac Lipman is giving a concert here, this afternoon?"

"Yes, and I have to help my grandpa. He asked me to come and tune your piano."

"Oh, how thrilling!" exclaimed Mrs. Perlman.

"I'll do a good job," said Debbie, taking off her coat on her way over to Mrs. Perlman's little upright piano in the living room.

"But—" said Mrs. Perlman. "Oh, what does it matter?" she thought. "She's too little to hurt anything, and Mr. Weinstock will certainly do it over again, anyway." So she followed Debbie into the living room and began to take the little round lace doilies and candy dishes and china figurines away from the top of the piano.

Debbie put her coat and hat down on a slippery satin chair, and took off her overshoes and put them in the hall. Then, when Mrs. Perlman had finished clearing the piano top, she helped Debbie raise the lid and pull off the front panel. They set it carefully down on the carpet and leaned it against the wall.

Debbie pulled the tuning hammer out of her waistband, the tuning fork and wedges out of her pocket, and sat down at the piano, looking at the strings. There were two strings for each note.

She hit the tuning fork against her knee, held it to a part of the metal frame, listened to it carefully, and then tried the piano: C! C! C! C!

"Would you like to have some cookies and a glass of milk, Debbie?"

"Maybe later," Debbie said. She fitted her tuning hammer onto the pin that held the first string for middle C, and put a wedge between the other C string and the first C-sharp string.

She hit the tuning fork against her knee again, and held it to the metal frame, and listened very, very closely. C! C! she played, and pushed the hammer. C! C! C! C! C! The gray felt wedge fell out, and Debbie put it back. C! C! C! C! C! C! C! She wished that Mrs. Perlman wouldn't keep standing right beside her.

Luckily, Mrs. Perlman, who had always been a great admirer of Isaac Lipman, felt that she could not wait another minute to decide what to wear to his concert. She patted Debbie on the shoulder and ran upstairs.

As Reuben Weinstock finished tuning the bass notes on the grand piano in the Auditorium, he thought to himself that Debbie should be back any moment. He moved his tuning hammer and screwdriver up to the top of the piano, pushed wedges between the strings, and started tuning the treble notes.

He kept looking at the door while he worked, and by the time he had finished tuning the treble and testing the whole keyboard up and down, and Debbie still had not come, he felt very, very worried. He put his tools back into his black bag, shut it, and sat back down on the piano bench, with his eyes on the door.

"Reuben," said Isaac Lipman, coming onto the stage behind him, "if only I had known what a comfortable couch there is in the dressing room in this Auditorium, I would have come here before. I had a wonderful sleep!"

Mr. Weinstock turned to look at him but did not smile.

"What's the matter?" asked Isaac Lipman.

"Where did that little granddaughter of yours go? I want to hear her play."

Mr. Weinstock stood up. "I sent her to ask one of our neighbors, who lives only a block away from here, if I may tune her piano tomorrow instead of today, because you are here. She should have been back an hour ago."

"She probably stayed there to tune it herself," said Mr. Lipman. "Let me try the piano while we are waiting for her. Then I want to take you both out to lunch."

He sat down and began to play. "Bravo!" he said.
"Bravo, Reuben. There are few enough good piano tuners
in the world, but there is only one Reuben Weinstock."

But Mr. Weinstock had left the stage and was
standing in front of the first row of seats, putting on his
coat and hat. "Thank you," he said. His hands were
shaking and he could hardly button his overcoat.

"Are you going out to find the little girl? Just wait a
minute and I'll come with you. I think a little walk would
be good for me after that nap." And Isaac Lipman went
backstage to get his things from the dressing room.

"She hasn't come back yet? All right, let's go," he
said, coming down from the stage wearing his coat and
scarf and a black fur hat.

"I'm so sorry this had to happen today, while you are
here—and before your concert," Mr. Weinstock said to
as they walked up the aisle. They went through the
 outdoors.

 sorry because of you," said Isaac Lipman.
 ell, Reuben. You seem very tired. I'm
 on you, taking care of that

 d Mr. Weinstock. "He and

 Weinstock. "But

489

 in silence, looking
 who might have seen
 of them for a while,
 with the baby.

A minute later they came to Mrs. Perlman's house and Reuben Weinstock stopped. "This is where she was supposed to come," he said.

A AND E! A AND E! A AND E! they heard in the damp air. A AND E! A AND E! A AND E!

"Ah," said Isaac Lipman. "You see, I was right!"

"But how—" began Mr. Weinstock. "But she will ruin the piano!" he said. "She doesn't know how to tune a piano. She has never tuned one before."

"If she has been living with you for two years, then I'm sure she knows how. But Reuben, she is very naughty!"

Mr. Weinstock put his hand on his friend's arm. "Don't say that. Thank God, she is safe. Whatever she has done to the piano, I can fix. She probably meant to help me. She always wants to help me!"

"She *should* help you, Reuben."

"She is only a little girl. I don't want her to help me; I have to help her. I am giving her piano lessons—that is all I can give her. But I have been hoping that she will be a concert artist someday."

"When I was her age, I had already played for the Empress of Russia," said Isaac Lipman. "Reuben, your little granddaughter may be as talented as I am. But if she doesn't want to be a pianist more than anything else in the world, she will certainly never be one. She says she wants to be a piano tuner, so let's see how well she is tuning that piano." And taking Mr. Weinstock's arm, he marched up the walk to the front door and pressed the bell.

They stood on the top step and listened to Debbie's

tuning until Mrs. Perlman opened the door. "Oh!" she gasped.

"Mrs. Perlman, may I present Mr. Isaac Lipman?" said Mr. Weinstock.

"How do you do. I'm so thrilled to meet you! I recognized you from your picture. Do you know, I have your autograph? I've kept it for twenty years. Debbie said you were here. She's in the living room, tuning my piano. Come in, come in!"

They wiped their feet on the mat and took off their boots. Then they followed Mrs. Perlman into the living room, wearing their coats and holding their hats.

Debbie was standing between the piano bench and the keyboard, looking impatient and unhappy. "I've only done two octaves," she said.

"You shouldn't have done any," said her grandfather. "You should have come right back to the Auditorium. I was very worried about you."

"Won't you take off your coats and sit down?" Mrs. Perlman was asking.

"Mr. Lipman can't—" began Mr. Weinstock.

But Isaac Lipman took off his coat and scarf and handed them to Mrs. Perlman. "Thank you very much," he said. "I am sorry to trouble you."

"It's not any trouble. It's an honor!" said Mrs. Perlman. "Let me take your coat, Mr. Weinstock."

"Get out of there for a minute," Mr. Lipman said to Debbie, "and let me see if you are doing a good job."

"I've only done two octaves," Debbie repeated, but she took the wedges out of the strings, picked up the tuning hammer, and slid out.

Mr. Lipman sat down and began to play.

"On my piano!" marveled Mrs. Perlman, coming back from hanging up the coats in her hall closet. "Isaac Lipman, playing on my piano!"

Mr. Lipman smiled. "Now, Debbie," he said. "I have traveled all over the world giving concerts, and I have played on pianos tuned by hundreds of different piano tuners—"

"And Grandpa Reuben was the best?" asked Debbie.

"That's right."

"Well, it's very, very hard to get every note dead on, the way he does," she told him.

"It would be almost impossible with that kind of tuning hammer," said Mr. Weinstock. "It's no good. The handle is too long. I'm surprised you didn't break any strings."

"Then I think she did pretty well!" said Mr. Lipman.

"And what tuning fork did you use?" her grandfather asked her. "This? It's all rusted." He hit it against his shoe and held it to his ear. "It doesn't play a true C any more, Debbie."

Debbie's eyes filled with tears.

"Come," said Mr. Lipman, getting up from the piano. "I want to take you all out to lunch."

"My husband will be coming home for lunch soon," said Mrs. Perlman. "I've got a big meal ready, so please stay and eat with us."

"Ah," said Isaac Lipman. "A home-cooked meal. . ."

"It would be a great honor to have you."

"Thank you."

"It is very kind of you, Mrs. Perlman," said Reuben

Weinstock, "and I am sorry about your piano. I'll come and tune it first thing tomorrow."

Mrs. Perlman put her arm around Debbie. "Please don't say anything more about it," she said.

"And now," said Isaac Lipman, "I would like to hear Debbie play."

"Play the Mendelssohn *Reverie*, Debbie," said Mr. Weinstock. "We will all remember that the piano is out of tune."

Mrs. Perlman and the two men sat down, and Debbie went to the piano.

"Is there anything you would rather play?" Isaac Lipman asked her when she was done. "Is there any other piece that you like to play better than this one?"

"No," said Debbie.

Mr. Lipman shook his head sadly, smiling at Mr. Weinstock.

"I think she will be a very lovely piano teacher someday," Mrs. Perlman said kindly, getting up to go to the kitchen.

"The world would be a better place if people who did not like to play the piano did not teach the piano," said Mr. Lipman. "Everybody should take the responsibility for finding out what it is he really wants to do."

"I want to be a piano tuner," said Debbie. "And I want to be as good as my grandpa."

"Right now, you had better go home and put on a dress," Mr. Weinstock told her. "And don't stop to tune any more pianos on the way. Come straight back here, because we must have lunch in plenty of time before the concert."

"Wait until she hears you play!" he said to Isaac Lipman, after he had helped Debbie on with her coat and hat and opened the front door for her. "And if that doesn't inspire her. . ."

"I think it *will* inspire her," chuckled Mr. Lipman. "I think it will inspire her to want to tune grand pianos for concert pianists."

Mr. Weinstock laughed. "If that's the case," he said, "then maybe I had better teach her how."

"Well, I think you should, Reuben. It seems to me she has a real talent for it."

"Yes, I was amazed at how well she was doing! But, you know, I wanted something better for her."

"What could be better than doing what you love?" asked Mr. Lipman.

At the concert, Debbie and Mr. Weinstock and Mr. and Mrs. Perlman sat in the first row of seats, a little bit over to the left, so they could watch Isaac Lipman's hands.

Everybody in town seemed to have heard that he had come, and all the seats in the Auditorium quickly filled with dressed-up and excited people, who rose to their feet clapping and shouting "Bravo!" when the lights went down and the famous pianist walked out onto the stage.

He bowed to the audience and, sweeping back his long coattails, sat down at the piano. Everyone in the audience held his breath while Mr. Lipman sat with his head bowed and his hands in his lap. After he had raised them to the keyboard and begun to play the first piece on the program, a long fantasy and fugue by Bach, everyone began to breathe again.

They clapped loudly when it was over, and Mr. Lipman stood beside the grand piano and bowed. Then he swept back his coattails and sat down again, looking at his hands in his lap. The audience waited quietly, and he began to play a sonata in three movements by Beethoven.

At the end of the first movement, Mr. Perlman and Debbie clapped, but Mrs. Perlman and Mr. Weinstock did not. Debbie was amazed. "Didn't you think it was good?" she asked her grandfather.

"It isn't over yet," he said.

After the second movement no one clapped, but after the third, which was really the end of the piece, everyone clapped and shouted "Bravo! Bravo!" Mr. Lipman bowed and left the stage, but the clapping and calling continued until he came back to bow two more times. Then the lights came on and everybody got up to walk around.

"That was good," said Debbie.

"You liked it!"

"Yes. No matter how hard he played, the piano stayed in tune. You did such a good job," said Debbie.

"It sounds as if you've got an assistant there, Mr. Weinstock," said Mr. Perlman.

"Sh-h," whispered Mrs. Perlman. "He doesn't want her to be a piano tuner! He wants her to be a pianist."

"What's wrong with being a—" began Mr. Perlman, but the lights started to dim and everyone went back to their seats.

On the second half of the program, Isaac Lipman played two rhapsodies by Brahms, and *Carnaval*, by Schumann. At the end of the concert the audience clapped and clapped and called "Encore! Encore!" until he came out on the stage again and sat back down at the piano. He looked out at the audience and said, "A waltz by Chopin."

"Ah-h-h," said the audience.

They clapped and clapped when it was over. Mr. Lipman bowed and left the stage. The audience kept clapping, and he came back, bowed, and left the stage again. The audience kept on clapping until he came back and sat down at the piano again: "*Reverie*, by Mendelssohn."

"Oh-h-h," murmured the audience, and Isaac Lipman played the same piece Debbie had played that morning. After he finished, bowed, and left the stage, Mr. Weinstock, still clapping, said to Debbie, "Wouldn't you like to be able to play it like that?"

"No," said Debbie. "Grandpa Reuben—"

Mr. Lipman came back onto the center of the stage, bowed again and again, and went out. Then the lights came on in the Auditorium, and the concert was over.

"Grandpa Reuben, please let me be a piano tuner," said Debbie.

"We must go backstage and say goodbye to Mr. Lipman now," said Mr. Weinstock. "He will be leaving right away."

The whole audience was pushing backstage to shake hands with the great pianist. "Please, Grandpa Reuben," said Debbie. "Please teach me how to be a good piano tuner!"

"What's wrong with being a piano tuner?" asked Mr. Perlman. "Especially a good one!"

"Nothing," said Mr. Weinstock. "Debbie—"

They had come near Mr. Lipman by this time, and even though he was talking to some other people, he reached out and took Debbie by the hand. "You must come to the City and tune my piano sometime," he said.

"Yes, but first I am going to teach her how to do it," said Mr. Weinstock. "I was just about to say so."

Isaac Lipman was as delighted as Debbie. "So even after hearing one of my concerts, you would rather tune pianos than play them," he said. "Well, I was just like that at your age. I could only think of one thing. For me, of course, it was playing! When I get back to the City, Debbie, I am going to send you a leather bag of your own, filled with good tuning instruments."

"Thank you very much!" said Debbie. "And—"

"Yes?"

"And regulating tools too, Mr. Lipman? Key pliers and bending pliers and a key spacer and parallel pliers and a capstan screw regulator and a capstan wrench and a spring adjusting hook and a spoon bending iron and—"

Some of the people who were standing near them were laughing.

"Everything!" cried Mr. Lipman. "I will ask the head of the piano factory for one of everything."

"Except the tools that I invented," put in Mr. Weinstock. "But I am going to make those for her, and she will be the only other piano tuner to have them."

Debbie put her hand into his. "I'll be just like you," she said.

Now early every morning Debbie Weinstock jumps quickly out of bed and runs downstairs to wash her face and brush her teeth at the kitchen sink. She puts water on to boil in the blue and white enameled saucepan and the old yellow coffee pot, and sets the table with the blue plate and the orange plate, the navy-blue bowl and the green bowl, the plaster salt and pepper shakers with seashells stuck into them and bright red plastic tops, the knives and spoons with yellow plastic handles, two white paper napkins, and two big white cups.

Then she goes out into the hall to wake up her grandfather. "Hm-m-m-m-m," she sings in front of his closed bedroom door. "Hm-m-m-m-m."

"Hm-m-m-m-m," comes Mr. Weinstock's voice on the exact same note. "Hm-m-m-m-m. I think we are both right this morning, Debbie."

She takes her shining new tuning fork out of its case, hits it against her knee, and holds it, singing, to her ear. "We *are* right, Grandpa Reuben!" she says, and goes upstairs to get dressed and make her bed while Mr. Weinstock is getting up.

Selected illustrations from Two Piano Tuners by M. B. Goffstein.

GLOSSARY

Full pronunciation key* The pronunciation of each word is shown just after the word, in this way: **abbreviate** (ə brē′vē āt).

The letters and signs used are pronounced as in the words below.

The mark ′ is placed after a syllable with a primary or heavy accent as in the example above.

The mark ′ after a syllable shows a secondary or lighter accent, as in **abbreviation** (ə brē′vē ā′shən).

SYMBOL	KEY WORDS	SYMBOL	KEY WORDS	SYMBOL	KEY WORDS
a	ask, fat	ə	a in ago	ch	chin, arch
ā	ape, date		e in agent	ŋ	ring, singer
ä	car, father		e in father	sh	she, dash
			i in unity	th	thin, truth
e	elf, ten		o in collect	*th*	then, father
er	berry, care		u in focus	zh	s in pleasure
ē	even, meet				
		b	bed, dub	′	as in (ā′b′l)
i	is, hit	d	did, had		
ir	mirror, here	f	fall, off		
ī	ice, fire	g	get, dog		
		h	he, ahead		
		j	joy, jump		
o	lot, pond	k	kill, bake		
ō	open, go	l	let, ball		
ô	law, horn	m	met, trim		
oi	oil, point	n	not, ton		
ၯ	look, pull	p	put, tap		
o͞o	ooze, tool	r	red, dear		
yၯ	unite, cure	s	sell, pass		
yo͞o	cute, few	t	top, hat		
ou	out, crowd	v	vat, have		
		w	will, always		
u	up, cut	y	yet, yard		
ur	fur, fern	z	zebra, haze		

*Pronunciation key and respellings adapted from *Webster's New World Dictionary, Basic School Edition,* Copyright © 1983 by Simon & Schuster, Inc. Reprinted by permission.

A

a·bom·i·na·ble (ə bom′ə nə b'l) *adjective.* disgusting; unpleasant; very bad: The smell coming from the garbage dump was *abominable.*

ac·cuse (ə kyo͞oz′) *verb.* **1.** to charge a person with breaking the law. **2.** to blame.

ac·cus·tomed (ə kus′təmd) *adjective.* usual. **accustomed to** —*verb.* to have become familiar.

ad·just (ə just′) *verb.* **1.** to change or rearrange to fit. **2.** to grow used to: He *adjusted* to his new school. **adjusted, adjusting.**

ad·mire (əd mīr′) *verb.* to think of with delight or wonder. **admired, admiring.**

ad·mit (əd mit′) *verb.* **1.** to allow to enter. **2.** to accept as true; to confess. **admitted, admitting.**

ad·ver·tise (ad′vər tīz) *verb.* **1.** to tell about a product so as to make people want to buy it. **2.** to put a notice in a newspaper or other public place: He *advertised* his car and sold it. **advertised, advertising.**

ad·vice (əd vīs′) *noun.* opinion as to what to do or how to do something: I asked his *advice* about what car to buy.

af·ford (ə fôrd′) *verb.* to have enough money to be able to buy.

a·ground (ə ground′) *adverb, adjective.* onto the shore, ocean bottom, and so on: The ship went *aground* on the sandy shore.

al·ien (āl′yən) *noun.* **1.** a foreigner. **2.** an imaginary being from another planet that comes to earth: The *aliens* climbed down from the spaceship. **aliens.**

al·low·ance (ə lou′əns) *noun.* an amount of money given to a child at a regular time.

al·pha·bet·i·cal (al′fə bet′i k'l) *adjective.* **1.** having to do with the alphabet. **2.** arranged in order by letter of the alphabet.

a·maze (ə māz′) *verb.* to cause feelings of surprise. **amazed, amazing.**

a·mount (ə mount′) *verb.* to add up; total: The bill will *amount* to $7.25. —*noun.* a quantity.

a·muse (ə myo͞oz′) *verb.* **1.** to keep busy or interested with something pleasant: We *amused* ourselves with a game. **2.** to make laugh or smile. **amused, amusing.**

an·cient (ān′shənt) *adjective.* **1.** occurring a long time ago, especially existing before about A.D. 500. **2.** very old: We discovered some *ancient* pottery in the cave.

an·i·mate (an′ə māt) *verb.* **1.** to give life to: Pulling the strings *animated* the puppet. **2.** to create as an animated cartoon. **animated, animating.**

a·non·y·mous (ə non′ə məs) *adjective.* made or done by someone whose name is unknown: The poem was written by an *anonymous* poet.

Advertise did not always have to do with selling something. It once meant "to catch people's attention." The word comes from the French word *avertir,* "to warn." In fact, an **advertisement** was originally a warning.

aground

animated

astonishment

bannister

barefoot

an·tic·i·pa·tion (an tis′ə pā′shən) *noun*. the act of looking forward to; waiting.

a·pol·o·gize (ə pol′ə jīz) *verb*. to say that you are sorry. *British spelling: apologise.*

ap·pe·tite (ap′ə tīt) *noun*. a desire for food.

ap·point·ment (ə point′mənt) *noun*. an arrangement to meet someone at a certain time.

ar·ti·cle (är′ti k'l) *noun*. **1.** one of a group of things. **2.** a piece of writing, as in a magazine. **3.** any of the words *the, an*, or *a*. **articles.**

as·sem·ble (ə sem′b'l) *verb*. **1.** to gather. **2.** to put the parts of something together: I like *assembling* model planes. **assembled, assembling.**

as·ton·ish·ment (ə ston′ish mənt) *noun*. the state of being surprised.

as·tound (ə stound′) *verb*. to surprise so much as to confuse someone. —**astounded** *adjective*. greatly surprised, unable to speak. **astounding.**

a·sy·lum (ə sī′ləm) *noun*. a place where helpless people, such as the poor, sick, or insane, were cared for: In the past, a person who was mentally ill was put into an *asylum*.

at·tract (ə trakt′) *verb*. to pull toward.

a·ve·nue (av′ə noo *or* av′ə nyoo) *noun*. a street.

av·er·age (av′rij *or* av′ər ij) *noun*. **1.** the number gotten by dividing the sum of several numbers by the number of things added.

2. the usual kind or amount. —*verb*. **1.** to figure the average. **2.** to do or be something regularly: Jane *averages* three miles a day running. **averages.**

a·wait (ə wāt′) *verb*. **1.** to wait for. **2.** to be ready for: A special treat *awaits* you. **awaits, awaited, awaiting.**

awk·ward (ôk′wərd) *adjective*. **1.** clumsy. **2.** hard to use; not convenient: The handle is in an *awkward* place. **3.** not comfortable. **4.** embarrassing.

B

back·ground (bak′ground) *noun*. the part of a picture that is toward the back: The *background* in my painting is blue like the sky.

bail (bāl) *noun*. money given to a court as a promise that a person will show up for a trial.

ban·nis·ter (ban′əs tər) *noun*. a rail along a set of stairs for people to hold on to.

bare (ber) *adjective*. **1.** uncovered: The branches of the tree were *bare* in winter. **2.** empty. **3.** plain.

bare·foot (ber′foot) *adjective*. with bare feet. —*adverb*. without shoes and socks.

bar·gain (bär′g'n) *noun*. **1.** an arrangement to give or do something in return for something else. **2.** something gotten for a lower price than usual: That shirt was a *bargain* at $5.00. —*verb*. to try to get the best price: She had to *bargain* to get the bike at a lower price.

barn·yard (bärn′yärd) *noun*. the area outside a barn that is often fenced in.

bee·tle (bēt″l) *noun*. an insect with a pair of hard front wings and a pair of thin back wings.

be·long·ings (bi lông′iṅgz) *plural noun*. things that belong to a person.

be·tray (bi trā′) *verb*. **1.** to help your country's enemy. **2.** to fail to keep a promise: They *betrayed* us by not returning the money they borrowed. —**betrayed** *adjective*. disappointed because a promise was not kept.

black·ness (blak′nis) *noun*. the quality of being black.

blos·som (blos′əm) *noun*. a flower. **blossoms.**

blotched (bloċhd) *adjective*. spotted, patched, or stained.

blunt (blunt) *adjective*. **1.** not sharp. **2.** speaking very honestly. —*verb*. to make dull: He *blunted* the knife when he cut the wood. **blunted, blunting.**

bon·fire (bon′fīr) *noun*. an outdoor fire. **bonfires.**

bra·zier (brā′zhər) *noun*. a metal pan that holds burning coals or charcoal.

break·through (brāk′thrōō) *noun*. an important discovery or idea: The telephone was a *breakthrough* in the way we communicate.

bun·dle (bun′d′l) *noun*. **1.** things wrapped up together. **2.** any package.

C

---

cal·i·co (kal′ə kō) *noun*. a cotton cloth printed with a colored pattern.

cam·ou·flage (kam′ə fläzh) *noun*. **1.** the act of hiding things by making them look like the background. **2.** a disguise in nature where something looks like its background: The insects in the grass turned green as a *camouflage.*

cap·tured (kap′chərd) *adjective*. caught and held by force: The *captured* lion is in the cage.

ca·reer (kə rir′) *noun*. the way someone earns a living; one's life work.

cau·tion (kô′shən) *verb*. to tell to be careful; to warn of danger.

cel·e·brate (sel′ə brāt) *verb*. to honor a day or event in a special way: We will *celebrate* my birthday on Wednesday. **celebrated, celebrating.** —**celebration** *noun*. a special party in honor of an event: We have many special *celebrations*. **celebrations.**

cham·pi·on·ship (ċham′pē ən ship′) *noun*. first place: Their team won the *championship* in the spelling contest.

a fat	ɔi oil	ch chin
ā ape	ͻͻ look	sh she
ä car, father	ōͻ tool	th thin
e ten	ͻu out	*th* then
er care	u up	zh leisure
ē even	ur fur	ṅg ring
i hit		
ir here	ə = a *in* ago	
ī bite, fire	e *in* agent	
o lot	i *in* unity	
ō go	o *in* collect	
ô law, horn	u *in* focus	

barnyard

blossoms

---◇---

Calico cloth got its name from Calicut, a city in southwest India. This brightly colored, printed cloth made in Calicut was introduced to Europe during the Age of Exploration in the 1500s.

505

chisel

coasting

chat (chat) *verb.* to talk in a relaxed way. **chatted, chatting.**

chill (chil) *verb.* to make or become cool: We *chilled* the lemonade. **chilled, chilling.**

chis·el (chiz″l) *noun.* a tool with a strong blade used for cutting stone.

chore (chôr) *noun.* **1.** a job that has to be done regularly: He helps by doing *chores* around the house. **2.** a hard or boring task. **chores.**

cir·cuit (sur′kit) *noun.* **1.** the act of going around something. **2.** the path of an electric current; any wiring connected into this path: The repair person checked the electric *circuits* in the radio. **circuits.**

cir·cu·la·tion (sur′kyə lā′shən) *noun.* **1.** the average number of copies of a newspaper or magazine sold every week or month. **2.** movement from place to place.

cit·i·zen (sit′ə zən) *noun.* a person who is a member of a country or state because of being born there or having been made a member by law: Only a *citizen* can vote. **citizens.**

clat·ter (klat′ər) *noun.* sharp, clashing sounds.

clear (klir) *adjective.* **1.** without clouds. **2.** can be seen through. **3.** easy to understand. **4.** without anything in the way. —*verb.* **1.** to make something easy to see or understand. **2.** to remove: They were *clearing* brush from the garden. **cleared, clearing.**

clench (klench) *verb.* **1.** to close tightly together. **2.** to hold firmly: He *clenched* the prize tightly in his hand. —**clenched** *adjective.* tightly closed: The dog's *clenched* teeth would not release the stick.

cli·mate (klī′mət) *noun.* **1.** the average weather in a place over a period of time. **2.** an area with certain weather conditions: The birds fly south to a warm *climate* in the winter.

coast (kōst) *noun.* land along the sea. —*verb.* **1.** to sail along a coast. **2.** to slide downhill. **coasted, coasting.**

col·o·nize (kol′ə nīz) *verb.* **1.** to start a colony. **2.** to settle in a new place: The Pilgrims set out to *colonize* North America.

col·or·ful (kul′ər fəl) *adjective.* full of color; bright.

com·bi·na·tion (kom′bə nā′shən) *noun.* **1.** a joining: The party was fun because of a *combination* of good food and games. **2.** the series of numbers that must be turned in the right order to open a lock.

com·mit (kə mit′) *verb.* **1.** to give in charge; place as a trust. **2.** to do something wrong. **committed, committing.**

com·pe·ti·tion (kom′pə tish′ən) *noun.* a contest.

com·plain (kəm plān′) *verb*. **1.** to find fault with something: He *complained* about the bad weather. **2.** to report something bad. **complained, complaining.**

com·pli·cat·ed (kom′plə kāt′id) *adjective*. not simple.

com·posed (kəm pōzd′) *adjective*. calm; not excited: She appeared *composed* as she spoke.

con·cen·trate (kon′sən trāt) *verb*. to gather your thoughts: You need to *concentrate* on what the teacher says.

con·duc·tor (kən duk′tər) *noun*. **1.** a person who directs. **2.** a person who works on a train, subway, and so on.

con·sole (kən sōl′) *verb*. to cheer up; comfort.

con·so·nant (kon′sə nənt) *noun*. all the letters of the alphabet except *a, e, i, o,* and *u*. **consonants.**

con·tent·ed (kən ten′tid) *adjective*. pleased with what you have. —**contentedly** *adverb*.

con·test (kon′test) *noun*. **1.** an argument or struggle. **2.** a race or game that people try to win: Who will win the jumping *contest*?

con·tract (kon′trakt) *noun*. an agreement, especially one that is written: He signed a *contract* to play baseball for the team.

con·trol·ler (kən trōl′ər) *noun*. **1.** a person in charge of spending for a company or the government.

2. person or thing that controls: The *controller* on the toy train is broken, so you can't make it move.

co·op·er·ate (kō op′ə rāt) *verb*. to work together on something to get it done. **cooperated, cooperating.**

cor·rect (kə rekt′) *adjective*. **1.** without mistakes. **2.** proper. —**correctly** *adverb*.

coy·o·te (kī ōt′ē *or* kī′ōt) *noun*. a small wolf that lives in the western part of North America.

co·zy (kō′zē) *adjective*. warm and comfortable; snug.

cre·ate (krē āt′) *verb*. to make; bring about: We tried to *create* a beautiful mural.

cul·ture (kul′chər) *noun*. **1.** the use of soil for crops. **2.** improvement by study of the mind or manners. **3.** the ideas, skills, arts, and tools of a certain people; way of life: We studied the *culture* of the Iroquois Indians.

cup·board (kub′ərd) *noun*. a cabinet with shelves used to store dishes, food, and so on.

cu·ri·os·i·ty (kyoor′ē os′ə tē) *noun*. a strong feeling of wanting to know or learn.

cur·i·ous (kyoor′ē əs) *adjective*. **1.** eager to learn more about something. **2.** odd or unusual: We did not understand the *curious* language they used.

a fat	ɔi oil	ch chin
ā ape	oo look	sh she
ä car, father	ōō tool	th thin
e ten	ou out	*th* then
er care	u up	zh leisure
ē even	ur fur	ng ring
i hit		
ir here	ə = a *in* ago	
ī bite, fire	e *in* agent	
o lot	i *in* unity	
ō go	o *in* collect	
ô law, horn	u *in* focus	

coyote

Coyote came into English in two steps. First, the Spanish colonists in Mexico borrowed the word *coyotl* from the Aztec language, changing it to *coyote*. American English then borrowed the word from the Spanish.

507

D

lion's **den**

dar·ing (der′iṅg) *adjective*. bold enough to take risks; fearless: The *daring* pilot flew the new plane.

day·dream (dā′drēm) *noun*. pleasant thinking or wishing: I have *daydreams* about being a dancer. —*verb*. to have pleasant thoughts and wishful dreams while awake. **daydreams.**

de·clare (di kler′) *verb*. to say or announce: I *declare!* I am surprised.

de·fense (di fens′ *or* dē′fens) *noun*. protecting against attack or danger: Our only *defense* against the cold was our warm goose-down jackets.

den (den) *noun*. **1.** a cave where a wild animal lives. **2.** a room where one works or reads. **dens.**

de·ny (di nī′) *verb*. **1.** to say that something is not true: A small child may *deny* taking a cookie. **2.** to refuse to give or allow. **denied, denies, denying.**

de·pend·a·ble (di pen′də b′l) *adjective*. that can be counted on: The bus is *dependable* in all kinds of weather.

de·ri·sive (di rī′siv) *adjective*. making fun of.

des·per·ate (des′pər it) *adjective*. **1.** reckless because you have lost hope: He took the chance because he was *desperate*. **2.** very much in need.

dim

de·ter·mi·na·tion (di tʉr′mə nā′shən) *noun*. firmness of purpose; fixed intention: His *determination* to succeed made him a winner.

de·vel·op (di vel′əp) *verb*. **1.** to make or become better or larger; grow. **2.** to make the picture show on a photographic film: We got our pictures *developed*. **developed, developing.**

de·vel·op·ment (di vel′əp mənt) *noun*. **1.** the act of growing or improving. **2.** a happening; an event: We waited to see how the *developments* affected the mystery. **developments.**

di·ges·tive (di jes′tiv *or* dī jes′tiv) *adjective*. having to do with the process of using food in the body: *Digestive* juices help your stomach change food so that your body can use it.

dig·ni·ty (dig′nə tē) *noun*. **1.** the quality of being worthy. **2.** a grand appearance. **3.** pride; self-respect.

dim (dim) *adjective*. **1.** not bright; somewhat dark. **2.** not clearly heard or understood. —**dimness** *noun*. the quality of not being clear or bright: It was hard to see her in the *dimness* of the room.

dis·ap·point (dis ə point′) *verb*. to fail to give or do what is expected: We *disappointed* our teacher with our poor test scores. —**disappointed.** *adjective*. defeated in expectation or hope: The *disappointed* teacher read the test scores to the class. —**disappointment** *noun*. the state of being dissatisfied.

dis·be·lief (dis bə lēf′) *noun*. not believing: The crowd listened in *disbelief*.

dis·in·te·grate (dis in′tə grāt) *verb*. to break up into pieces: My clay statue *disintegrated* when it fell. **disintegrated, disintegrating.**

dis·tant (dis′tənt) *adjective*. **1.** far apart in space or time: The rocket sped to a *distant* planet. **2.** unfriendly. **3.** not closely related.

dis·tinc·tive (dis tiṅgk′tiv) *adjective*. making different from others: The fox has a *distinctive* red coat.

dis·tress (dis tres′) *verb*. to cause pain, sadness, or worry. **distressed.** —**distressing** *adjective*. painful; worrisome.

dis·trib·ute (dis trib′yo͞ot) *verb*. **1.** to give out: The teacher began to *distribute* paper to the students. **2.** to spread out.

dis·turb (dis turb′) *verb*. **1.** to break up the quiet of a place. **2.** to make worried. **3.** to bother or interrupt: We *disturbed* mother as she rested. **disturbed, disturbing.**

doubt·ful (dout′fəl) *adjective*. feeling not sure; questioning. —**doubtfully** *adverb*. in a doubtful way.

down·cast (do͞un′kast) *adjective*. **1.** looking downward. **2.** very unhappy.

dread·ful (dred′fəl) *adjective*. **1.** causing fear. **2.** very bad; unpleasant.

drib·ble (drib′′l) *verb*. **1.** to flow in drops. **2.** to let drip from the mouth. **3.** to bounce a ball with your hands in basketball or kick it along lightly with your feet in soccer. **dribbled, dribbling.**

driz·zle (driz′′l) *noun*. light rain.

E

ea·ger (ē′gər) *adjective*. wanting very much. —**eagerly** *adverb*. in an eager way.

earn·ings (ur′niṅgz) *plural noun*. money received for work done: I bought a bike with my *earnings* from raking leaves.

ed·i·to·ri·al (ed′ə tôr′ē əl) *noun*. an article that gives the opinion of the editor or owner of a newspaper or magazine: An *editorial* in our school newspaper said that teachers should assign more homework.

ef·fect (ə fekt′) *noun*. **1.** a result. **2.** an impression made on the mind: The special *effects* in this movie made the monster look real. **effects.**

e·lec·tron·ics (i lek′tron′iks) *plural noun*. the science of electricity and electrical devices: Studying *electronics* helped us understand how a computer works.

em·bar·rass (im ber′əs) *verb*. to make uncomfortable: I *embarrassed* him when I said how I felt. **embarrassed, embarrassing.**

e·merge (i murj′) *verb*. **1.** to appear: The bear *emerged* from his hiding place. **2.** to become known. **emerged, emerging.**

a fat	ȯi oil	ch chin
ā ape	o͝o look	sh she
ä car, father	o͞o tool	th thin
e ten	ou out	*th* then
er care	u up	zh leisure
ē even	ur fur	ṅg ring
i hit		
ir here	ə = a *in* ago	
ī bite, fire	e *in* agent	
o lot	i *in* unity	
ō go	o *in* collect	
ô law, horn	u *in* focus	

distinctive stripes

Doubt came into English from French. The original Latin, *dubitare*, meant "to hesitate or be undecided." When *doubt* was first used in English, it meant "fear." Over time, its original Latin meaning took over again.

dribble

509

equipment

exhibition

e·mer·gen·cy (i mʉr′jən sē) *noun.* a problem that needs action right away.

e·mo·tion (i mō′shən) *noun.* **1.** a strong feeling. **2.** any feeling such as love, hate, joy, or fear.

en·coun·ter (in koun′tər) *verb.* to meet someone without planning it. —*noun.* a meeting by chance.

e·nor·mous (i nôr′məs) *adjective.* huge; larger than normal.

en·ter·tain (en tər tān′) *verb.* **1.** to give pleasure to: They *entertained* us by singing. **2.** to have as a guest. **entertained.**

en·thu·si·asm (in thōō′zē az′m) *noun.* strong liking or interest.

e·quip·ment (i kwip′mənt) *noun.* special things needed for an activity: Do you have your football *equipment* with you?

er·rand (er′ənd) *noun.* **1.** a short trip to do something. **2.** the task to be done.

e·vent (i vent′) *noun.* **1.** a happening. **2.** any of the contests in a sports program: The best *event* of the field day was the sack race.

ev·i·dence (ev′ə dəns) *noun.* something that shows or proves: The footprints were *evidence* that the children had been there.

ev·i·dent (ev′ə dənt) *adjective.* easy to see; plain. —**evidently** *adverb.*

ex·act (ig zakt′) *adjective.* not having any mistakes. —**exactly** *adverb.* accurately: He made sure the rules were *exactly* followed.

ex·hi·bi·tion (ek sə bish′ən) *noun.* **1.** the act of showing. **2.** a public show: We saw an art *exhibition.*

ex·per·i·ment (ik sper′ə mənt) *noun.* a test to find out whether an idea is correct. —*verb.* to test an idea to see if it is correct: The scientist will *experiment* with a new way to make electricity.

ex·pert (ek′spərt *or* ik spʉrt′) *adjective.* having special knowledge or experience; very skillful: She is an *expert* house painter.

ex·traor·di·nar·y (ik strôr′d′n er′ē) *adjective.* very unusual.

F

fare (fer) *noun.* money paid for a trip on a bus, plane, train, and so on: The *fare* is 50 cents.

far·thest (fär′*th*ist) *adjective.* most distant: Pluto is the *farthest* planet from the Earth. —*adverb.* at the greatest distance.

fate (fāt) *noun.* **1.** a power that is supposed to decide ahead of time what will happen. **2.** the way things turn out in the end: What will my *fate* be on this test? **fates.**

fear·ful (fir′fəl) *adjective.* **1.** causing terror. **2.** feeling frightened. **3.** caused by being afraid. —**fearfully** *adverb.* in a scary or scared way.

fear·some (fir'səm) *adjective.* frightening.

fes·ti·val (fes'tə v'l) *noun.* **1.** a happy holiday. **2.** a time of special celebration.

film (film) *noun.* **1.** a thin coating. **2.** a roll of material that is used for taking photographs. **3.** a movie. —*verb.* to make a movie: The director will *film* the story.

firm (furm) *noun.* a business company: This *firm* builds trucks.

fit (fit) *verb.* **1.** to be the correct size for. **2.** to be suitable for. — **fitting** *adjective.* correct or satisfactory for something or someone; suitable: It seemed *fitting* to name our new puppy Splash, since he loves to swim.

fling (fliñg) *verb.* to throw; to move suddenly and hard: She *flung* herself over the fence. **flung, flinging.**

floun·der (flɑun'dər) *verb.* **1.** to walk in a clumsy way through mud, snow, and so on: He was *floundering* as he walked in the wet sand near the ocean. **2.** to speak or act in a confused way. **floundered, floundering.**

flus·ter (flus'tər) *verb.* to confuse. **flustered, flustering.**

for·bid (fər bid') *verb.* to refuse permission for something. —**forbidden** *adjective.* not allowed: Sitting on the stairs is a *forbidden* activity. **forbidding.**

form·u·la (fôr'myə lə) *noun.* **1.** a phrase used over and over.

2. a set of directions for doing something. **3.** a special mixture of milk and other things fed to a baby: The *formula* is in the baby's bottle.

fric·tion (frik'shən) *noun.* the rubbing of one thing against another: The *friction* of the bike wheel against the frame caused a squeak.

func·tion (fuñgk'shən) *noun.* the purpose of a thing. —*verb.* to do its proper work. —**functional** *adjective.* working correctly.

fun·gus (fuñg'gəs) *noun.* a plant with no leaves: Molds, mushrooms, and mildew are forms of *fungi.* —**fungi** (fun'jī *or* fuñg'gī) *plural noun.*

fu·ri·ous (fyʊr'ē əs) *adjective.* **1.** full of anger: He was *furious* at the mistake. **2.** very strong or fierce.

a fat	oi oil	ch chin
ā ape	͟oo look	sh she
ä car, father	͞oo tool	th thin
e ten	ou out	*th* then
er care	u up	zh leisure
ē even	ur fur	ñg ring
i hit		
ir here	ə = a *in* ago	
ī bite, fire	e *in* agent	
o lot	i *in* unity	
ō go	o *in* collect	
ô law, horn	u *in* focus	

Flounder, as a *verb,* is probably the result of a mistake! It seems to have come about as a combination of *founder* ("to fall or stumble") and *blunder* ("to move in a clumsy way"). Its word history has nothing to do with a fish named flounder flopping about.

G

gait (gāt) *noun.* a way of walking or running: The horse had a bouncing *gait.*

gear (gir) *noun.* a wheel with metal teeth that fit into the teeth of another wheel, making the two move together. **gears.**

gen·er·ous (jen'ər əs) *adjective.* willing to share; not selfish.

gears

guard

ges·ture (jes'chər) *noun*. **1.** a motion made with hands or arms to show an idea or feeling. **2.** anything said or done to show one's feelings. —**gesturing** *verb*. making a gesture: She was *gesturing* to us to hurry. **gestured.**

glare (gler) *noun*. **1.** a blinding light. **2.** an angry stare. —*verb* **1.** to shine so brightly that it hurts the eyes. **2.** to stare in anger: I *glared* at the puppy when it ate my sneaker. —**glared.**

gloom·y (gloom'ē) *adjective*. **1.** dark or dim. **2.** very sad. —**gloomily** *adverb*. in a sad way.

goal (gōl) *noun*. **1.** the place where a race ends. **2.** a purpose. **3.** the net into which a ball must go in some games; a score made by getting the ball into this net: She kicked the ball toward the *goal*.

grace (grās) *noun*. **1.** beauty of form. **2.** pleasing manner. **3.** a short prayer said before meals.

gra·cious (grā'shəs) *adjective*. **1.** kind and polite. **2.** full of comfort.

grasp (grasp) *verb*. to grip firmly with the hand. —*noun*. a grip by the hand: She had the book firmly in her *grasp*.

griz·zled (griz"ld) *adjective*. gray or streaked with gray.

grove (grōv) *noun*. a small group of trees.

guard (gärd) *verb*. **1.** to watch over. **2.** to keep from escaping. —*noun*. **1.** the act of guarding. **2.** a

gush

person who protects something or someone.

guard·i·an (gär'dē ən) *noun*. **1.** a person who takes care of a child. **2.** a person who protects: The *guardian* watched over the jewels.

gush (gush) *verb*. **1.** to flow out with force: The water *gushed* from the faucet. **2.** to talk with too much feeling in a silly way. **gushed, gushing.**

H

halt (hôlt) *verb*. to stop or hold back. —**halting** *adjective*. slow and uneven: At the end of the tiring day, he walked with *halting* steps. —**haltingly** *adverb*. in a slow, careful way.

harm (härm) *noun*. damage or hurt: Our cat can do a lot of *harm* to the furniture. —*verb*. to damage or hurt.

hatch (hach) *verb*. **1.** to sit on eggs until the young come out. **2.** to come out from an egg: Baby robins *hatch* from blue eggs. **3.** to bring forth baby animals.

haugh·ty (hôt'ē) *adjective*. showing too much pride in yourself. —**haughtily** *adverb*. in a prideful way: She spoke *haughtily* of her famous family.

heart·i·ly (härt"l ē) *adverb*. **1.** in a friendly way. **2.** with eagerness: They greeted us *heartily*.

hedge (hej) *noun*. a row of bushes planted close together.

heed·less (hēd′lis) *adjective*. careless. —**heedlessly** *adverb*. in a careless way: They walked into the street *heedlessly*.

hes·i·tate (hez′ə tāt) *verb*. **1.** to stop because you don't feel sure: I *hesitated* to ask to borrow money. **2.** to feel unwilling. **hesitated, hesitating.**

his·to·ri·an (his tôr′ē ən) *noun*. a person who is an expert in history or writes about history.

hobble (hob″l) *verb*. **1.** to walk in a lame or clumsy way. **2.** to keep from moving by tying the legs together: It took four of us to *hobble* the herd of sheep. **3.** to get in the way of; hinder. —*noun*. **1.** a limping walk. **2.** a rope used to hobble a horse.

hold (hōld) *verb*. **1.** to keep in the hands or arms. **2.** to keep in a certain place. **3.** to have room for. **held, holding.** —*noun*. **1.** the act of grasping. **2.** the inside of a ship: The crates are in the *hold* of the ship.

home·land (hōm′land) *noun*. the country where you were born or where you live.

home·stead (hōm′sted) *noun*. **1.** a family's home, including the house and land around it. **2.** a piece of land given to a settler to farm by the U.S. government: They were given a *homestead* in the Dakota Territory.

hon·or·a·ble (on′ər ə b′l) *adjective*. **1.** worthy of being respected. **2.** honest.

hos·tile (hos′t′l) *adjective*. **1.** like an enemy. **2.** showing hate; unfriendly: She gave me a *hostile* look before the race.

hut (hut) *noun*. a plain, little house: Their cabin was only a *hut* in the woods.

I

i·den·ti·cal (ī den′ti k′l) *adjective*. exactly alike: The two dresses are *identical*.

il·lus·trate (il′ə strāt *or* i lus′trāt) *verb*. **1.** to make clear with examples. **2.** to draw pictures or paintings to explain or decorate: The artist is *illustrating* a new story. **illustrated, illustrating.**

i·mag·i·na·tion (i maj′ə nā′shən) *noun*. making up pictures or ideas in your mind: In my *imagination* I can travel anywhere.

im·mi·grate (im′ə grāt) *verb*. to move to another country to live. **immigrated, immigrating.** —**immigration** *noun*. the act of coming to live in a new country: There was much *immigration* in the early 1900s.

im·per·ti·nent (im pʉr′t′n ənt) *adjective*. outwardly disrespectful; rude: The teacher thought the students were being *impertinent*.

a fat	oi oil	ch chin
ā ape	oo look	sh she
ä car, father	ōo tool	th thin
e ten	ou out	th then
er care	u up	zh leisure
ē even	ur fur	ng ring
i hit		
ir here	ə = a *in* ago	
ī bite, fire	e *in* agent	
o lot	i *in* unity	
ō go	o *in* collect	
ô law, horn	u *in* focus	

hut

◇

Illustrate used to mean "to throw light on." A picture or drawing that explains something does, in a sense, throw light on what is being explained. It makes it easier to understand.

im·press (im pres′) *verb*. to affect someone's feelings. **impressing, impressed.**

in·ac·cur·ate (in ak′yər it) *adjective*. wrong.

in·dig·nant (in dig′nənt) *adjective*. angry about something that is unfair or mean. —**indignantly** *adverb*. in an angry way: She spoke *indignantly* when she wasn't allowed to race.

in·fec·tious (in fek′shəs) *adjective*. **1.** something caused by infection. **2.** something that spreads to others: Colds are *infectious*.

in·i·tial (i nish′əl) *adjective*. at the beginning; first. —*noun*. the first letter of a name: His name is Charles John King, so his last *initial* is K. **initials.**

in·no·cent (in′ə sənt) *adjective*. not guilty of a crime.

in·sane (in sān′) *adjective*. mentally ill; not sane (now seldom used): Mentally ill people used to be called *insane*.

in·spi·ra·tion (in′spə rā′shən) *noun*. something that brings about a thought or an action: Their courage was an *inspiration* to us.

in·te·grate (in′tə grāt) *verb*. to bring together; unite. —**integrated** *adjective*. a bringing together of people of different races: Many people wanted schools *integrated*.

in·ten·tion (in ten′shən) *noun*. a purpose for doing something: Her *intentions* were good, but she didn't solve the problem. **intentions.**

in·tro·duce (in trə do͞os′ *or* in trə dyo͞os′) *verb*. to make known; present: He is *introducing* his friends to his family at the party. **introduced, introducing.**

in·vent (in vent′) *verb*. to make something that did not exist before: Who *invented* the airplane? **invented, inventing.**

in·vest·ment (in vest′mənt) *noun*. **1.** spending of money or time in order to get something in return: Buying that stock was a good *investment*. **2.** the amount of money invested.

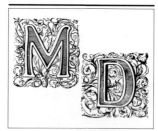

Matt Dowd's **initials**

knee **joint**

J

joint (joint) *noun*. **1.** a place where two things or parts are joined: The two pieces of wood that are my desk top came apart at the *joint*. **2.** a place or part where two bones are joined: Mario's *joints* were stiff after he ran five miles. **joints.**

jour·ney (jur′nē) *noun*. a trip from one place to another.

L

lane (lān) *noun*. **1.** a narrow path; a narrow country road: The *lane* wound through the woods. **2.** any narrow way through something. **3.** a path for ships, cars, and so on.

lan·tern (lan'tərn) *noun*. a glass or paper case that holds a light and protects it from wind and rain.

league (lēg) *noun*. people or groups joined together for a common purpose: The ten teams formed a *league* to play against one another.

lean-to (lēn'tōō) *noun*. a shed with a roof that slants up and rests against a building.

ledge (lej) *noun*. a flat, narrow part of a cliff or wall that looks like a shelf: The bird perched on the rocky *ledge*.

limp (limp) *verb*. to walk in an uneven way because of a lame leg. —*noun*. a lameness in walking. —*adjective*. not stiff or firm; flexible: The new tree was *limp* after the storm.

lone·ly (lōn'lē) *adjective*. **1.** unhappy because you are alone: I was *lonely* without my brother. **2.** without others nearby.

lu·na·tic (lōō'nə tik) *adjective*. **1.** mentally ill; insane. **2.** very foolish. —*noun*. a person who is mentally ill (now seldom used).

lurch (lurch) *verb*. to lean or roll suddenly to one side: The boat was *lurching* back and forth on the waves. **lurched, lurching.**

M

man·ag·er (man'ij ər) *noun*. a person who controls a business, sports team, and so on.

mar·vel (mär'v'l) *verb*. to wonder or be amazed by: We *marvel* at the way she skates. **marveled.**

match·mak·er (mach'māk ər) *noun*. a person who arranges for two people to marry.

min·i·a·ture (min'ē ə chər *or* min'i chər) *adjective*. very tiny. —*noun*. a very small copy or model.

mi·rac·u·lous (mi rak'yōō ləs) *adjective*. **1.** having to do with something remarkable. **2.** amazing: The rescue from the fire was *miraculous*.

mis·cal·cu·late (mis kal'kyə lāt) *verb*. to make a mistake in figuring or planning: We *miscalculated* the distance we had to drive. **miscalculated, miscalculating.**

moist (moist) *adjective*. slightly wet: The ground was *moist* after the light rain.

a fat	oi oil	ch chin
ā ape	oo look	sh she
ä car, father	ōō tool	th thin
e ten	ou out	*th* then
er care	u up	zh leisure
ē even	ur fur	ng ring
i hit		
ir here	ə = a *in* ago	
ī bite, fire	e *in* agent	
o lot	i *in* unity	
ō go	o *in* collect	
ô law, horn	u *in* focus	

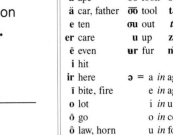
lantern

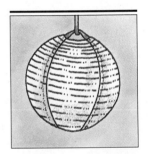
ledge

miniatures

515

mon·o·logue (mon′ə lôg) *noun*. **1.** a long speech by one person during a conversation: Her *monologue* kept us listening for a long time. **2.** a part of a play in which one person speaks alone.

mur·mur (mʉr′mər) *verb*. **1.** to make a low, steady sound. **2.** to speak softly. **murmured, murmuring.**

mut·ter (mut′ər) *verb*. **1.** to speak in low tones with your mouth almost closed: She *muttered* to herself about the high prices. **2.** to complain. **muttered, muttering.**

necklace

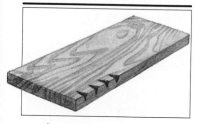

notches

N

na·tion·al (nash′ə n′l) *adjective*. having to do with a whole country: We sang the *national* anthem.

na·tive (nā′tiv) *adjective*. **1.** having to do with the place where you were born. **2.** born in a certain country or state: She is a *native* Californian.

nat·u·ral·ize (nach′ər ə līz) *verb*. to make someone a citizen of a country. **naturalized, naturalizing.** —**naturalization** *noun*. process of becoming a citizen.

neck·lace (nek′lis) *noun*. jewelry like a string of beads or a chain worn around the neck.

nerv·ous (nʉr′vəs) *adjective*. **1.** easily upset. **2.** feeling fearful. —**nervously** *adverb*. in a nervous way.

nes·tle (nes″l) *verb*. to lie down in a snug way: The puppy *nestled* in my arms. **nestled, nestling.**

news·stand (no͞oz′stand *or* nyo͞oz′stand) *noun*. place where newspapers are sold.

night·mare (nīt′mer) *noun*. a frightening dream.

noose (no͞os) *noun*. **1.** a loop of rope with a slipknot that tightens as the rope is pulled. **2.** anything that traps or binds: His arms felt like a *noose* as he tackled my legs in the football game.

notch (noch) *noun*. a cut shaped like a *V* on an edge or surface: We cut a *notch* in the tree. **notches.**

no·tion (nō′shən) *noun*. a general idea about something. —**notions** *plural noun*. small useful things such as needles and thread sold in a store: The counter that sells *notions* will have buttons.

nui·sance (no͞o′s′ns *or* nyo͞o′s′ns) *noun*. a thing or person who bothers you: My baby brother is a *nuisance* when he cries.

numb (num) *adjective*. able to feel very little or nothing at all: Our fingers were *numb* from the cold.

O

of·fend (ə fend′) *verb*. **1.** to hurt someone's feelings. **2.** to be unpleasant. **offended.**

o·gre (ō′gər) *noun*. **1.** in fairy tales, a cruel giant. **2.** an evil person. **ogres.**

op·er·a·tive (op′ə rā tiv *or* op′ər ə tiv) *adjective*. working: He repaired the machine, so it is *operative*.

or·di·nar·y (ôr′d′n er′ē) *adjective*. **1.** usual, normal. **2.** not special.

or·i·gin (ôr′ə jin) *noun*. the place where something began; beginning: The alphabet has its *origin* in ancient Phoenicia. **origins.**

o·rig·i·nal (ə rij′ə n′l) *adjective*. **1.** first: The *original* building stood over there. **2.** not copied. **—originally** *adverb*. in the first place.

out·raged (out′rājd) *adjective*. very offended: They were *outraged* at the criminal's behavior.

o·ver·lap (ō vər lap′) *verb*. to touch and lie partly on top of something: The shingles on the roof have to *overlap* to keep rain out.

ox cart (oks′ kärt′) *noun*. a wagon pulled by one or more oxen.

P

pam·phlet (pam′flit) *noun*. a thin booklet with paper covers.

pant (pant) *verb*. to breathe hard and quickly: The dog was *panting* after the race. **panted, panting.**

par·a·keet (par′ə kēt) *noun*. a small parrot with a long tail.

par·tic·i·pate (pär tis′ə pāt) *verb*. take part in: We want to *participate* in the game.

part·ner (pärt′nər) *noun*. **1.** one of the owners of a business. **2.** one of two players on a team. **3.** one of two people who dance together.

patch·work (pach′wurk) *adjective*. made from pieces of colored cloth; having patchy colors.

pa·tience (pā′shəns) *noun*. the ability to put up with things without complaining: My teacher showed *patience* when my work was late.

pause (pôz) *noun*. a short stop. —*verb*. to stop for a short time: We *paused* to rest after running to the store. **paused.**

peace·ful·ly (pēs′fəl ē) *adverb*. **1.** quietly and calmly: The lake seemed to glow *peacefully* in the sun. **2.** not in a fighting manner.

pe·cul·iar (pi kyool′yər) *adjective*. strange; odd: The purple horse looked quite *peculiar*.

per·ish (per′ish) *verb*. to die: We could *perish* from the cold.

per·mis·si·ble (pər mis′ə b′l) *adjective*. allowed: It is not *permissible* to talk loudly in the library.

a fat	oi oil	ch chin
ā ape	oo look	sh she
ä car, father	ōo tool	th thin
e ten	ou out	*th* then
er care	u up	zh leisure
ē even	ur fur	n͡g ring
i hit		
ir here	ə = a *in* ago	
ī bite, fire	e *in* agent	
o lot	i *in* unity	
ō go	o *in* collect	
ô law, horn	u *in* focus	

Ogre is a monster of a word. It was first used by the French writer Charles Perrault in 1697. Where he got it is not known. Perhaps it came from the Italian *orco*, or "demon," which might also have been spelled *orgo*.

parakeet

517

per·mis·sion (pər mish'ən) *noun*. approval; consent: I need my parent's *permission* to go on the class trip.

phrase (frāz) *noun*. **1.** a group of words that express an idea—not a complete sentence. **2.** a short, catchy expression: "All's well that ends well" is a well-known *phrase*. —*verb*. to say or write something in a particular way.

pick·le (pik"l) *noun*. **1.** a cucumber or other food flavored in a spicy liquid solution. **2.** an unpleasant or difficult situation; trouble; used in everyday talk. —*adjective*. preserved in a pickle liquid: We made our own *pickled* spaghetti sauce. **pickled.**

Pig Latin (pig lat"n) *noun*. a secret language.

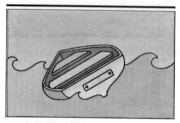

pitched

pitch (pich) *verb*. **1.** to throw or toss. **2.** to throw a ball to the batter in baseball. **3.** to set up a tent. **4.** to fall forward. **5.** to be tossed up and down on the water: The boat *pitched* on the waves. **pitched, pitching.**

plum·age (plōō'mij) *noun*. a bird's feathers: My canary has bright yellow *plumage*.

pod (pod) *noun*. the shell that holds seeds of a plant. **pods.**

poul·try (pōl'trē) *noun*. birds such as chickens and turkeys that are raised for food.

prowl

pray (prā) *verb*. **1.** to talk to God in worship or to ask for something. **2.** to beg for something.

prey (prā) *noun*. an animal that is hunted: A mouse can be the *prey* of a cat.

prism (priz'm) *noun*. a piece of glass that breaks light rays into colors of the rainbow.

proj·ect (prə jekt') *verb*. **1.** to throw forward. **2.** to cause an image to be seen on a surface: Our teacher *projects* slides on the screen while he speaks. **projects, projected, projecting.**

pro·jec·tion (prə jek'shən) *noun*. **1.** an image shown on a surface: That picture on the wall is a *projection* from the slide. **2.** something that sticks out.

pro·pel (prə pel') *verb*. to push forward: A bicycle is *propelled* by the pedals. **propelled, propelling.**

pro·tect (prə tekt') *verb*. to defend against danger or harm: The police officer was *protecting* us from the cars as we crossed the street. **protected, protecting.**

pro·vid·ing (prə vīd'iñg) . *conjunction*. on the condition that; if: You may go, *providing* you finish your work first.

prowl (proul) *verb*. to walk in a quiet, secret way: The tiger is *prowling* in the forest. **prowled, prowling.**

pub·lish (pub'lish) *verb*. to prepare a book, magazine, or newspaper for sale: They have been *publishing* that newspaper for more than fifty years. **published, publishing.**

pun·ish·ment (pun'ish mənt) *noun.* what is done to someone as a penalty for doing something wrong: The little boy's *punishment* was to stay in his room.

pup·pet (pup'it) *noun.* a small doll moved by strings or by hand.

pur·suit (pər sōot' *or* pər syōot') *noun.* **1.** following in order to catch up to something: We set out in *pursuit* of the runaway dog. **2.** a hobby or job.

Q

quiv·er (kwiv'ər) *verb.* to shake or tremble: The leaves *quivered* in the breeze. **quivered.** —**quivering** *adjective.* shaking, trembling.

R

ra·di·ant (rā'dē ənt) *adjective.* **1.** shining brightly. **2.** showing joy: Her face was *radiant* with happiness.

rare·ly (rer'lē) *adverb.* not often: I *rarely* think about her.

re·al·is·tic (rē ə lis'tik) *adjective.* **1.** facing facts; practical. **2.** showing things as they really are in art and literature.

re·cite (ri sīt') *verb.* to say out loud something that you have memorized: I will *recite* the poem "Fog" to the class.

re·flec·tion (ri flek'shən) *noun.* something thrown back; an image: Look at your *reflection* in the mirror.

re·form (ri fôrm') *noun.* improvement of what is bad, as in government: The new mayor sees the need for many *reforms*. **reforms.**

re·fund (ri fund') *verb.* to give back money —(rē'fund) *noun.* the money given back: We asked for *refunds* for the broken toys. **refunds.**

reg·is·ter (rej'is tər) *noun.* a machine for counting and keeping a record of: He put my money in the cash *register* and gave me my change.

re·mark·a·ble (ri märk'ə b'l) *adjective.* worth noticing because it is very unusual: That is a *remarkable* achievement.

re·port·er (ri pôrt'ər) *noun.* a person who writes about the news for a newspaper, radio, or TV station: Nick is a *reporter* for our school paper.

res·cue (res'kyōo) *verb.* to save from danger: Firefighters *rescue* people from burning buildings.

re·serve (ri zurv') *verb.* to set aside for use later: I *reserved* a seat on the plane. **reserved, reserving.**

res·i·dence (rez'i dəns) *noun.* **1.** the place where you live; home. **2.** the act of living in a place.

a fat	oi oil	ch chin
ā ape	ŏŏ look	sh she
ä car, father	ōō tool	th thin
e ten	ou out	*th* then
er care	u up	zh leisure
ē even	ur fur	ŋ ring
i hit		
ir here	ə = a *in* ago	
ī bite, fire	e *in* agent	
o lot	i *in* unity	
ō go	o *in* collect	
ô law, horn	u *in* focus	

puppets

Quiver, "to shake," comes from the Middle English word *cwyver,* which meant "nimble or quick." When a leaf quivers, it moves quickly.

leaf **ribs**

Robot, a machine doing human work, was first used in Karel Capek's play *R. U. R.* (Rossum's Universal Robots). The word comes from the Czech *robota,* which means "compulsory service."

seed head

re·solve (ri zolv′) *verb.* to make up your mind: I *resolved* to do better in school. **resolved, resolving.**

re·verse (ri vurs′) *verb.* **1.** to turn backward, inside out, or upside down. **2.** to move in an opposite way: She *reversed* directions. **reversed, reversing.**

re·vis·it (ri viz′it) *verb.* to go back again: I enjoy *revisiting* the park every spring. **revisited, revisiting.**

re·ward·ing (ri wôrd′ing) *adjective.* giving a sense of satisfaction: I find helping my neighbors very *rewarding.*

re·wind (rē wīnd′) *verb.* to wind again: We *rewound* the videotape after we watched it. **rewound, rewinding.**

rhyme (rīm) *noun.* **1.** sounds at the ends of words that are alike. **2.** a word that ends with the same sound as another: The words ''cat'' and ''bat'' and ''make'' and ''cake'' are *rhymes.* **rhymes.**

rib (rib) *noun.* **1.** one of the curved bones that go from the backbone around to form the chest. **2.** a large vein in a leaf: Each *rib* in a leaf is raised.

rid·dle (rid″l) *noun.* a puzzle in the form of a question with a tricky answer that is hard to guess. **riddles.**

ro·bot (rō′bət) *noun.* **1.** a machine made to look and work like a human being. **2.** a person who acts like a machine: He moves just like a *robot.*

S

scarce (skers) *adjective.* **1.** not common: Really good ideas are *scarce.* **2.** hard to get.

scene (sēn) *noun.* **1.** the place where something happens. **2.** part of a play: The *scene* begins when the first actor enters the room. **3.** a view; landscape.

sculp·ture (skulp′chər) *noun.* **1.** the art of carving wood, chiseling stone, or working with metal to make statues: We studied *sculpture* in art class. **2.** a statue or figure made this way.

se·cret ser·vice (sē′krit sur′vis) *noun.* group of people in government who do detective work in secret.

seed head (sēd hed) *noun.* the blossom part of a flower that is full of seeds: Dandelion *seed heads* are fun to blow on. **seed heads.**

seethe (sē*th*) *verb.* **1.** to bubble or foam: All the ideas *seethed* in his head. **2.** to be very upset. **seethed, seething.**

se·lec·tion (sə lek′shən) *noun.* **1.** a choice. **2.** the thing or things chosen: We have a large *selection* of books.

sel·fish (sel′fish) *adjective.* thinking only of yourself, instead of caring about others: It was *selfish* to keep all the fruit to yourself.

se·ri·ous (sir'ē əs) *adjective*. not joking or fooling.

ses·sion (sesh'ən) *noun*. the meeting of a court, class, and so on, to do its work.

set·tle·ment (set"l mənt) *noun*. **1.** a place where people have gone to make their homes in a new land; colony: The first *settlement* in Massachusetts was at Plymouth. **2.** a small village: There was a *settlement* on the shore of the lake. **3.** an agreement or understanding.

sew·er (sōō'ər *or* syōō'ər) *noun*. a pipe that is placed underground to carry away water and waste.

shaft (shaft) *noun*. **1.** the long handle of an arrow. **2.** a long part or handle of an object. **3.** one of the two poles from a wagon to which an animal may be harnessed.

shape·less (shāp'lis) *adjective*. without a clear form: The *shapeless* pile of clothing in the dark room looked like a monster to the child.

shel·ter (shel'tər) *noun*. a thing that covers and protects. —**sheltered** *verb*. provided protection from weather or danger: We were *sheltered* from the rain under the trees. **sheltering.**

shiv·er (shiv'ər) *verb*. to shake from fear or cold: We *shivered* as we waited in the cold. **shivered, shivering.**

shore (shôr) *noun*. **1.** land at the edge of a sea or lake: The cabins were built along the *shores* of the

lake. **2.** land, not water. **shores.**

siz·zle (siz"l) *verb*. to make a hissing sound like something frying. —**sizzling** *adjective*. hissing: The water in the hot pan made a *sizzling* sound.

skin·flint (skin'flint) *noun*. a person who is not willing to spend money: A *skinflint* won't give money to charity.

slang (slang) *noun*. words and phrases that are popular in everyday speech but are not accepted in formal writing: We are not supposed to use *slang* in our papers at school.

slope (slōp) *noun*. land that slants up or down: We slid down the *slopes* of the snowy hills on our sleds. **slopes.**

slum (slum) *noun*. a poor, dirty, crowded part of a city: Jan works to help people who live in the *slums*. **slums.**

snatch (snach) *verb*. to grab or grasp suddenly. **snatched, snatching.**

soc·cer (sok'ər) *noun*. a game in which a round ball is moved by kicking or by using any part of the body except the hands.

sof·ten (sôf"n) *verb*. to make or become less hard or easy to bend or crush. —**softening** *adjective*. becoming less and less hard: The *softening* butter was left out.

sor·row (sär'ō) *noun*. **1.** sad feeling: I felt *sorrow* at the bad news. **2.** trouble that causes sad feelings: The accident was a great *sorrow* to them.

a fat	oi oil	ch chin
ā ape	oo look	sh she
ä car, father	ōō tool	th thin
e ten	ou out	th then
er care	u up	zh leisure
ē even	ur fur	ng ring
i hit		
ir here	ə = a *in* ago
ī bite, fire	e *in* agent
o lot	i *in* unity
ō go	o *in* collect
ô law, horn	u *in* focus

settlement

Shiver comes from a Middle English word, *chivere*. Chivere most likely was used to refer to the chattering of the teeth with cold. After the word's spelling changed to what it is now, it changed to mean "a shaking of the whole body."

soccer

521

source (sôrs) *noun.* **1.** the beginning of a river or stream, such as a lake or glacier. **2.** a thing or place from which something comes: We had to list our *sources* for the book report. **sources.**

spe·cial·ty (spesh′əl tē) *noun.* **1.** a special interest or study: Her *specialty* is the Egyptians. **2.** a special product.

spe·cies (spē′shēz) *noun.* a group of plants or animals that are alike in certain ways.

spec·ta·tor (spek′tāt′ər) *noun.* a person who watches something. **spectators.**

sports·man·ship (spôrts′mən ship) *noun.* fair play in sports, including not complaining about losing or bragging about winning: Good *sportsmanship* is important in any game.

sprout (sprout) *verb.* to begin to grow: The seeds I planted have *sprouted.* **sprouted, sprouting.**

star·va·tion (stär vā′shən) *noun.* dying or suffering from lack of food.

stat·ic (stat′ik) *noun.* crackling sounds heard on the radio: The *static* was so loud it drowned out the music.

stern (sturn) *adjective.* very strict or harsh: The police officer looked very *stern* as she spoke to the robber.

strand (strand) *noun.* **1.** a thread or wire twisted together to make a rope or cable. **2.** something that

is like a string or rope: She twisted *strands* of her hair as she talked. **strands.** —*verb.* to put in a helpless situation. **stranded.**

stran·ger (strān′jər) *noun.* **1.** a person new to a place. **2.** a person you don't know: Never talk to a *stranger.*

strap (strap) *noun.* a narrow piece of leather or other material that is used to tie or hold things together. —*verb.* to fasten with a strap: We *strapped* the suitcases to the top of the car. **strapped, strapping.**

string·y (string′ē) *adjective.* **1.** looking like a string: My dog's hair looked *stringy* when he came out of the water. **2.** having long, tough fibers, like celery.

stump (stump) *noun.* the part of a tree left after the rest of the tree has been cut down.

suc·tion (suk′shən) *noun.* the act of drawing air out of an object. —**suction cup** *noun.* a circular object, often made of rubber, that sticks to a surface when pressed against it.

sup·ply (sə plī′) *verb.* to give what is needed. —*noun.* the amount of something that you have available: Our *supply* of paper is running low.

surge (surj) *noun.* **1.** a wave of water coming in a sudden rush. **2.** any sudden, strong rush: There was a *surge* of interest in the new club.

strands

stump

sur·vive (sər vīv′) *verb.* **1.** to live or last longer than something else; outlive. **2.** to continue to live in spite of a serious problem: Many people *survived* the airplane crash. **survived, surviving.**

sus·pect (sə spekt′) *verb.* **1.** to think someone is guilty. **2.** to guess: I *suspected* that they would be late again. **suspected.**

syl·la·ble (sil′ə b'l) *noun.* part of a word that you say as a single sound: "Newspaper" has three *syllables.* **syllables.**

sym·pa·thet·ic (sim′pə thet′ik) *adjective.* feeling or showing that you feel sorry for someone. —**sympathetically** *adverb.* in a sympathetic way: He spoke *sympathetically* to the sick man.

T

tame (tām) *adjective.* **1.** trained not to be wild, like a pet. **2.** gentle and easy to control. —**tamely** *adverb.* in a tame way: The lion sat *tamely* on its stool.

tech·nique (tek nēk′) *noun.* a way of using tools or materials: We have to learn many *techniques* to make a mosaic. **techniques.**

ten·ta·tive (ten′tə tiv) *adjective.* not definite or final. —**tentatively**

adverb. in a tentative way: They planned the party *tentatively* for December 1.

thatch (thach) *noun.* a roof made of straw. —*verb.* to make a roof with straw. —**thatched** *adjective.* having a straw roof.

thaw (thô) *verb.* to melt; to become unfrozen: The frozen ground will *thaw* in the spring.

the·a·ter (thē′ə tər) *noun.* a place where a play or movie is shown: We found good seats in the movie *theater.*

the·o·ry (thē′ə rē) *noun.* **1.** an explanation of how or why something happens. **2.** an idea or guess: My *theory* is that my cat broke the vase.

toad·stool (tōd′stool) *noun.* a poisonous mushroom. **toadstools.**

tol·er·ate (tol′ə rāt) *verb.* **1.** to let something go on without trying to stop it: He *tolerated* our silliness. **2.** to put up with something; endure. **tolerated, tolerating.**

tour·na·ment (toor′nə mənt) *noun.* **1.** a contest in which knights on horseback use lances to try to knock one another off their horses. **2.** in sports, a group of games in which one team will win a championship: We came in first in the basketball *tournament.*

trag·e·dy (traj′ə dē) *noun.* a very sad happening.

a fat	ȯi oil	ch chin
ā ape	o͝o look	sh she
ä car, father	o͞o tool	th thin
e ten	ou out	*th* then
er care	u up	zh leisure
ē even	ur fur	ŋ ring
i hit		
ir here	ə = a *in* ago	
ī bite, fire	e *in* agent	
o lot	i *in* unity	
ō go	o *in* collect	
ô law, horn	u *in* focus	

————◇————

Suspect comes from the Latin word *suspectus.* When the Ancient Romans said *suspectus,* they did not mean that they thought a person was guilty. They meant that the person was admired or looked up to. Meanings do change over time!

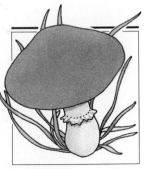

toadstool

523

Triumphant comes from the Latin *triumphus*. A Roman triumph was a ceremony when a victorious general came home to Rome. The Latin word probably came from the Greek word *thriambos*, a song to Dionysus, the god of festivals.

twilight

trans·form (trans fôrm′) *verb*. to change from one form to another or to change the way something looks. **transformed, transforming.** —**transformation** *noun*. a changing of the form or look of something: In the fairy tale, the frog went through a *transformation* and became a prince.

trans·late (trans lāt′ *or* trans′lāt) *verb*. to put into the words of a different language: I am *translating* this story into Spanish. **translated, translating.**

trem·ble (trem′b′l) *verb*. to shake from cold or fear: I was *trembling* with fear at the scary movie. **trembled, trembling.**

tre·men·dous (tri men′dəs) adjective. **1.** very large; huge: That dog looked *tremendous* to the little boy. **2.** wonderful.

tribe (trīb) *noun*. a group of people who live together and are led by a chief: There were many American Indian *tribes*. **tribes.**

trib·ute (trib′yo͞ot) *noun*. something given or done to show thanks or respect: She was given a medal as a *tribute* to her bravery.

trick·le (trik′′l) *verb*. to flow slowly or in drops: Water *trickled* out of the faucet one drop at a time. **trickled, trickling.**

tri·ple (trip′′l) *adjective*. **1.** made up of three: I made *triple* copies of my report. **2.** three times as much.

tri·um·phant (trī um′fənt) *adjective*. **1.** having won a victory. **2.** happy about a victory. —**triumphantly** *adverb*. in a joyous and victorious way.

trou·ble·some (trub′′l səm) *adjective*. giving trouble; causing worry: My dog has become very *troublesome* with his barking.

tuft (tuft) *noun*. a bunch of hairs, feathers, grass, and so on, growing together or tied together.

tur·ret (tur′it) *noun*. **1.** a small tower, usually at the end of a building or castle. **2.** a low tower or dome, often one that revolves: The merry-go-round looked like a *turret*.

tun·dra (tun′drə *or* to͞on′drə) *noun*. a large, flat, treeless area in arctic regions.

twi·light (twī′līt) *noun*. **1.** the dim light just after sunset. **2.** the time just after sunset and before it becomes dark: All the kids in the neighborhood played games in the long summer *twilight*.

U

un·der·cov·er (un′dər kuv′ər) *adverb*. acting in secret or done in secret: She is working *undercover* as a police officer.

un·dig·ni·fied (un dig'nə fīd) *adjective.* appearing not worthy; without self-respect: He looked *undignified* in that silly costume.

un·ex·pect·ed (un'ik spek'tid) *adjective.* surprising; sudden: His arrival was *unexpected.*

un·grate·ful (un grāt'fəl) *adjective.* not feeling thankful: He seemed *ungrateful* when we gave him the gift.

u·ni·form (yo͞o'nə fôrm) *noun.* special clothes worn by the members of a certain group. **uniforms.**

un·mesh (un mesh') *verb.* to come apart, for example, as gears do when pulled apart. **unmeshing.** —**unmeshed** *adjective.* no longer fitting together closely: The bicycle wouldn't operate because the gear and chain became *unmeshed.*

un·u·su·al (un yo͞o'zho͞o wəl) *adjective.* not usual; not common: We saw some *unusual* birds at the zoo.

up·end (up end') *verb.* to stand on end. **upended, upending.**

V

veg·e·ta·tion (vej ə tā'shən) *noun.* things growing from the ground; plants: The rain forest was filled with lush *vegetation.*

ven·ture (ven'chər) *verb.* to go somewhere even though there is some danger: I *ventured* into the dark forest. **ventured, venturing.**

verse (vʉrs) *noun.* **1.** poems. **2.** a group of lines that make up one section of a poem: We took turns reading the *verses* of the poem. **verses.**

vic·tor (vik'tər) *noun.* the winner in a battle or contest.

vig·il (vij'əl) *noun.* the act of staying awake at night to keep watch.

W

wan·der (won'dər *or* wôn'dər) *verb.* to go from place to place without reason; ramble. **wandered, wandering.**

wea·ry (wir'ē) *adjective.* tired. —**wearily** *adverb.* in a tired way.

weep (wēp) *verb.* to cry. **wept, weeping.**

wol·ver·ine (wo͞ol və rēn') *noun.* a strong, stocky animal found in northern North America, Europe, and Asia.

work·house (wʉrk'hous) *noun.* a place where people who broke the law were forced to live and work for a certain length of time (*no longer used*). **workhouses.**

wor·thy (wʉr'thē) *adjective.* **1.** having merit. **2.** good enough for: Her bravery is *worthy* of our gratitude.

a fat	oi oil	ch chin
ā ape	o͝o look	sh she
ä car, father	o͞o tool	th thin
e ten	ou out	*th* then
er care	u up	zh leisure
ē even	ur fur	n̑g ring
i hit		
ir here	ə = a *in* ago
ī bite, fire	e *in* agent
o lot	i *in* unity
ō go	o *in* collect
ô law, horn	u *in* focus

uniform

wolverine

525

ABOUT THE
Authors & Illustrators

BYRD BAYLOR

❋ Byrd Baylor was born in Texas. She grew up in the deserts of the Southwest and spent many summers in Mexico. Many of her stories and poems are set in the desert. *Before You Came This Way* describes what life might have been like in the southwestern canyons in the prehistoric ages. Several of Byrd Baylor's books have been named Caldecott Honor Books, and she also has received the Catlin Peace Pipe Award. Sometimes she writes under the name of Byrd Baylor Schweitzer. *(Born 1924)*

MARGARET WISE BROWN

■ When Margaret Wise Brown was growing up, she liked to play outdoors. The woods and beaches near her home were her favorite places to play. She lived in the country and had "thirty rabbits, ten squirrels, a bowl of goldfish, a collie of her own and six other 'borrowed' dogs, but only three children to play with her. . . ." She took a course in writing when she was in college, but she did not write her first book until she was twenty-eight years old. She wrote books under other names, including Golden MacDonald and Timothy Hay. Many of her books have won awards. *(1910–1952)*

CLYDE ROBERT BULLA

▲ Clyde Robert Bulla wanted to be a writer from the time he was young. Although he never had any formal training in writing, he read lots of books. When he was in the first grade he thought words were wonderful. "By writing them and putting them together, I could make them say whatever I wanted them to say. It was a kind of magic. Reading was a kind of magic, too." Bulla says that by the time he was ready for the third grade, he had read most of the books in the school library. When he was in the fourth grade, he won a prize for a story he wrote. As a grown-up, he has continued to win prizes and awards for his writing. *(Born 1914)*

LORNA DEE CERVANTES

✳ Lorna Dee Cervantes was born in San Francisco and is a descendant of *Californios* — Spanish families who settled California in the seventeenth and eighteenth centuries. She began to write at age eight, composing simple verses that formed the basis of her first poetry book, *Emplumada,* which she compiled many years later. After graduating from high school, Lorna began college and founded the Chicano literary magazine *Mango.* Several of Lorna Dee Cervantes' poems have received wide recognition. She enjoys writing about her Hispanic roots and expresses her feelings openly about living and working in two cultures. She wrote "This Morning There Were Rainbows in the Sprinklers" when she was fourteen years old. *(Born 1954)*

SCOTT CORBETT

■ Scott Corbett has written many books for young readers. His nonfiction works include a series of "What Makes It Work" books. One of these, *What Makes a Car Go?* was translated into Arabic. It was used to teach adult Arabs about how cars work. Many of his fiction books are based on real-life settings. He says, "Settings often give me a starting point for a story. A visit to the country place of a friend who raises prize geese was the beginning of *The Case of the Gone Goose.* The whole series of 'Trick' books began with Kerby Maxwell playing in a small public park modeled on one that was part of my boyhood." *(Born 1913)*

ELEANOR ESTES

▲ Eleanor Estes wrote many award-winning books and magazine articles. The setting for many of her stories was her hometown of West Haven, Connecticut. She once said, "My first four years at school were spent in the small wooden school that is the scene for a chapter in *The Moffats.* The remaining years were spent in a pretty, ivy-covered brick school. In one of those classrooms, the hero dog of *Ginger Pye,* the book which won the Newbery Medal, appeared in the window with a pencil in his mouth, earning the nickname of 'intellectual dog.' " *(1906–1988)*

SID FLEISCHMAN

✳ Sid Fleischman has won many awards for his writing, including the Boston Globe-Horn Book Award. He has written many books and stories for young people. Sid Fleischman says that he writes very slowly and he thinks out his ideas before he writes. "On some days I will get only one page of work finished; on other days, five or six. While this method of working might drive other writers out of their minds, it has taught me to write it right—the first time." One of the novels he wrote was *Mr. Mysterious*. He says that writing that book was a treat. "As I finished each chapter, I read it to my children. When I couldn't figure out what was to happen next, I asked them for ideas." *(Born 1920)*

KARAMA FUFUKA

◼ Karama Fufuka was born in Chicago as Sharon Morgan. She is a member of the League of Black Women and has worked for several community programs. One of her books is entitled *My Daddy Is a Cool Dude, and Other Poems*. In addition to her writing, her interests include sewing, painting, and reading. *(Born 1951)*

CLARE AND FRANK GAULT

▲ Clare Gault was a schoolteacher when she and her husband Frank got the idea for writing sports books. At that time, their sons were just learning to read, and there were not enough books to satisfy their interest in sports. Since the children she taught in school had the same problem, they decided to try to do something about it. Some of their books are nonfiction, such as *Pelé: The King of Soccer*. Other books are fiction, but they also have a sports theme. Frank and Clare Gault wrote books about subjects that they thought would interest young people. He said, "Our books encourage youngsters to read." *(Clare Gault, born 1925; Frank Gault, 1926–1982)*

JAN SPIVEY GILCHRIST

✳ A native of Chicago, Jan Spivey Gilchrist can't remember a time when she didn't want to be an artist. After earning a Bachelor of Science degree in art education from Eastern Illinois University, Jan went on to receive her master's degree in painting from the University of Northern Iowa. She has taught art in the public schools of Illinois and Massachusetts, but now devotes her time solely to illustrating. The artist says she always wanted to tell stories in pictures. She got that chance when author Eloise Greenfield recommended her to illustrate *Children of Long Ago*, a book of poems that Eloise Greenfield's mother had written. Jan Spivey Gilchrist also illustrated *Nathaniel Talking*, a collection of poems by Eloise Greenfield. "Nathaniel's Rap" is from this collection.

M. B. GOFFSTEIN

■ When Marilyn Brooke Goffstein Schaaf writes and illustrates books, she uses the name M. B. Goffstein. She says, "One of the main things I have tried to show in my books is the beauty and dignity of a life of hard work to make something good, that you believe in." She has won awards for several of her books. *Fish for Supper* was an American Library Association Notable Book and a Caldecott Honor Book. *My Noah's Ark*, which also won a Notable Book award, is about a wooden toy that endured through ninety years of a family's history. *(Born 1940)*

ELOISE GREENFIELD

▲ Eloise Greenfield's biographies, fiction, and poetry have received many awards for excellence, including the first Carter G. Woodson Award and the Jane Addams Children's Book Award. Ms. Greenfield has taught creative writing in the Washington, D. C. schools and says her major goal is "to provide nourishing literature for children." *(Born 1929)*

WOODY GUTHRIE

✽ Woodrow Wilson Guthrie was born in Oklahoma. He was a folk singer, a songwriter, and an author. He wrote nearly one thousand songs, and believed that people who liked to hear folk music should be able to do so, even if they didn't have much money. During World War II, he performed for soldiers who were stationed overseas. Other folk singers, including Bob Dylan, have said that Woody Guthrie had a great influence on them. *(1912–1967)*

531

LANGSTON HUGHES

■ Langston Hughes won many awards for his poems, short stories, and novels. He began to write poetry when he was elected class poet in grammar school. "The day I was elected, I went home and wondered what I should write. Since we had eight teachers in our school, I thought there should be one verse for each teacher. . . . And since the teachers were to have eight verses, I felt the class should have eight, too. I said our class was the greatest class ever graduated. So at graduation, when I read the poem, naturally everybody applauded loudly. That was the way I began to write poetry." *(1902–1967)*

ARNOLD LOBEL

▲ Arnold Lobel wrote and illustrated books for young people. Many of his books won awards. *Frog and Toad Are Friends* was a Caldecott Honor Book, and *Frog and Toad Together* was a Newbery Honor Book. In 1981, Arnold Lobel won the Caldecott Medal for his book *Fables*, which includes the story "The Mouse at the Seashore." *(1933–1978)*

MARGARET MAHY

✳ Margaret Mahy lives in New Zealand. She has written many stories for young people. She says, "I have been interested in writing children's stories for many years. All stories, even the simplest ones, seem to be little pieces of biography, even if what one is recounting is only one's childhood games and dreams." Among the awards Margaret Mahy has won are the Kate Greenaway Medal and the Carnegie Medal Award. *(Born 1936)*

PEGGY MANN

■ Peggy Mann has written stories for young people and for adults. Some of her children's books were adapted for television, including *The Street of the Flower Boxes*, which won a Peabody Award, and *My Dad Lives in a Downtown Hotel*, which was nominated for an Emmy. Peggy Mann likes to travel. She has been around the world and has made many trips to Europe and Israel. She says that Easter Island in the Southeastern Pacific Ocean and Nepal in Asia are two of the most fascinating places to visit.

CHRISTINE MCDONNELL

▲ Christine McDonnell is a teacher and a writer. Many of the stories she writes are about a girl named Ivy. Christine McDonnell says some of the things that happen to Ivy are based on her own childhood. Another made-up character she writes about is Leo. Look for Leo in the book *Toad Food & Measle Soup*. *(Born 1949)*

ALICE MCLERRAN

✳ Alice McLerran writes books for young people. She is also an archaeologist. She says that her love for mountains began when she was 18 years old and spent a year in the Andes. She wrote the story *The Mountain That Loved a Bird* when she and her family were on a camping trip to Mount Rainier in Washington state. Alice McLerran says, "One of the pleasures of writing is being able to ensure that endings are as they should be."

533

MARVIN MILLER

■ Marvin Miller was born in a small town in Pennsylvania. He says, "I always had a special curiosity about things, and I became interested in magic at an early age." He worked his way through college by being a stage magician. In addition to writing the T*A*C*K* books with his co-author, Nancy Robinson, he writes puzzles for a national magazine and invents magic tricks for magicians.

MARY O'NEILL

▲ Mary O'Neill was born in New York City. She once worked for the Peace Corps as a teacher in Ghana. One of her most popular books, *Hailstones and Halibut Bones*, has been published in several different editions. Her books have been recognized by the *New York Times Book Review* as among the best books for children. *(1908–1990)*

JACK PRELUTSKY

✳ Jack Prelutsky is a singer, actor, translator, and poet. A friend persuaded him to get his drawings of imaginary animals and funny verse published. Since then he has written many books of poetry. He says that all of his characters contain parts of people he knows and parts of himself. Some of his books have been chosen as Junior Literary Guild selections and American Library Association Notable Books.

ROBERT QUACKENBUSH

■ Robert Quackenbush was born in Hollywood, California. His last name is Dutch and means "duck in the bush." Robert Quackenbush writes and illustrates books for young people. He is also an art teacher. Several of his books have been chosen as Junior Literary Guild selections. *(Born 1929)*

ROBERT H. REDDING

▲ Robert H. Redding was born in Los Angeles, California. He grew up in Alaska, where he still lives. One of his books, *North to the Wilderness*, tells about his boyhood in Alaska. He also writes books about animals. Robert Redding worked full-time for the highway department, so he wrote early in the morning. He says, "As any writer can tell you, inspiration counts for about five percent of his work; the remaining ninety-five percent is accomplished by keeping the seat of the pants glued to the seat of the chair." *(Born 1919)*

LAURA E. RICHARDS

✳ Laura Richards loved to read from the time she was a young child. When she was four years old, her mother found her lying on the floor turning the pages of a book and reciting a poem she had learned. "On being interrogated, I said I was reading. I have been reading ever since. . . . I would rather read poetry than eat my dinner any day. It has been so all my life." Laura Richards' book *Captain January* was made into a movie starring Shirley Temple. *(1850–1943)*

NANCY K. ROBINSON

✳ Nancy K. Robinson is the author of a number of books and articles. She is married and has two children. She received the Four Leaf Clover Award for her contribution to the reading pleasure of children. She also received the United States Customs Award for an article about a coast guard cutter. She and Marvin Miller are the co-authors of the *Can You Solve It?* series. Nancy Robinson has also written "Men of Bronze," a TV show for public television. *(Born 1942)*

ALVIN SCHWARTZ

■ Alvin Schwartz once said, "I write books because it provides me with a rather remarkable opportunity to explore in depth what interests me." During his career, he wrote more than fifty books for young people and for adults. He was well-known for his collections of folklore, tall tales, and scary stories. *(Born 1927)*

GEORGE SELDEN

▲ George Selden was born in Hartford, Connecticut, and lived much of his life in New York City. People often asked him how he got the idea for *The Cricket in Times Square*. He said, "One night I was coming home on the subway, and I did hear a cricket chirp in the Times Square subway station. The story formed in my mind within minutes." He also wrote a series of "Cricket" books, and the stories have been made into plays, films, and television programs. *(1929–1989)*

ISAAC BASHEVIS SINGER

✳ Isaac B. Singer was born in Poland. He came to the United States when he was thirty-one years old. He said, "My American citizenship means a lot to me. I would not trade it for all the money in the world." When he was growing up, other children had toys, but he played with his father's books. Isaac B. Singer wrote books in both Yiddish and English. He won many outstanding awards and honors, including the Newbery Honor and numerous American Library Association Notable Book awards. The greatest honor he received was the Nobel Prize in literature. *(1904–1991)*

ROBERT LOUIS STEVENSON

■ Robert Louis Stevenson was born in Scotland. When he was growing up, he was often sick and had to stay in bed. When he grew up, he wrote many poems about his childhood. He also wrote adventure stories. One of these is called *Treasure Island.* Robert Louis Stevenson said that the idea for that book came after he drew a make-believe island. He said that when he looked at the map, the "characters of the book began to appear there visually among imaginary woods." *(1850–1894)*

537

YOSHIKO UCHIDA

▲ Yoshiko Uchida's last name is pronounced ō chē´də. She once said about her writing, "All my books have been about Japan and its children or about Japanese-Americans because I felt I could make the best contribution in this area. I wanted American children to become familiar with the marvelous Japanese folk tales I had heard in my childhood. I wanted them to read about Japanese children, learning to understand and respect differences in customs and culture, but realizing also that basically human beings are alike the world over, with similar joys and hopes." Some of Yoshiko Uchida's books have been selected as American Library Association Notable Books. She also illustrated some of her own books of Japanese folk tales. *(1921–1992)*

BETTY WATERTON

✳ Betty Waterton was born in Canada, where she still lives. She says her father wrote short stories, but they were never published. She began writing poetry when she was young, and tells about the time she "once earned a dollar for a poem in the *Vancouver Sun*." After she earned the dollar, she says she didn't write anything else until "somewhere in mid-life, when I began to write for children." Betty Waterton has won several Canadian literary awards for her writing. *(Born 1923)*

E. B. WHITE

■ E. B. White's full name was Elwyn Brooks White. He is the author of *Charlotte's Web*. He wrote the story when he was at his farm in Maine. He said, "I like animals and my barn is a very pleasant place to be, at all hours. One day when I was on my way to feed the pig, I began feeling sorry for the pig, because, like most pigs, he was doomed to die. This made me sad. So I started thinking of ways to save a pig's life. I had been watching a big, grey spider at her work and was impressed by how clever she was at weaving. Gradually I worked the spider into the story . . . a story of friendship and salvation on a farm. Three years after I started writing it, it was published." *(1899–1985)*

GARTH WILLIAMS

▲ Garth Williams was born in New York City and grew up in England where he attended art schools in London, studying oil painting, poster design, and sculpture. He won the Prix de Rome award for sculpture. In 1944, E. B. White asked him to try a few sample illustrations for *Stuart Little*. "I finally did them all," Garth says, "and that was my first children's book. I have been illustrating children's books ever since." He also illustrated E. B. White's famous *Charlotte's Web* and spent ten years making the pictures for a new edition of Laura Ingalls Wilder's *Little House* books. *(Born 1912)*

AUTHOR INDEX

543